AMISAN 33

Harry Edwards

MINISTRY OF HEALTH

Joan has battled on to a Sunday stroll

AFTER 28 YEARS—SHE WINS

By PETER VANE

MONDAY MORNING

A tale of courage to begin the week

THE LONDON HOSPITAL

Push

My Father, Polio, and Me

Sarah Passingham

Gatehouse Press

First published November 1st 2019 by Gatehouse Press.

Gatehouse Press
71 Rosary Road
Norwich
NR1 1SZ
United Kingdom

www.gatehousepress.com

Set in Sabon; used under licence.

Printed and bound in the UK by 4Edge

'...the past is so hard to shift. It comes with us like a chaperone, standing between us and the newness of the present—the new chance.'
Jeanette Winterson: Why Be Happy When You Could Be Normal

Dedicated to my mother, Diana and to the memory of my father, Push 1926 - 2003

Chapter One

Burnage, Iver: October, 1952

Push was on his stomach, one hand bunching the pillow under his head. Diana stroked his fingers, astonished, as always, at the size of his hand compared with her own.

'I've brought you some water and a couple more aspirins,' she said, and put the glass and the little white tablets on his bedside table. She kissed his forehead. The skin was dry and hotter than the evening before. She smoothed his hair back where it had fallen over his eyes. It was damp and stuck to her fingers. He responded with a small noise like an animal disturbed. 'How's your head?' she asked softly.

After a long pause, when she wondered if she should repeat the question, he spoke in a whisper. 'Terrible.'

'Poor Push.' She stroked his hair some more and knelt beside the bed. 'See if you can sit up and take these.' She picked up the tablets and held them out to him, cradled in the palm of her hand. 'You know you'll feel better if you do.'

Another pause. 'Push?'

She stroked his cheek with the back of a cool finger. Usually he would reach round and catch it against his lips. But not this time.

'It's another lovely day, darling. There's not a cloud in the sky and I'm going to do a bit more in the kitchen garden later. I might tidy up the spinach, cut off the dead leaves and things, like your Ma showed me before she left yesterday.'

Diana sat back on her heels and looked out of the window at the beech tree, its branches standing absolutely still. 'I might even try cooking some for Daddy when he comes to lunch.'

'What?' She only just caught the word.

'Spinach. I might do some for our lunch today, now I know how to cook it properly. Do you think you might try and get up later?'

Push moved his hand from under hers and heaved himself onto his elbow. His head hung down between muscular shoulders as limp and heavy as wet washing on a line. His hair fell over his face again.

'Need to get up now.' He ran his tongue over his bottom lip and Diana stood up to give him the glass of water. 'Must go to the bathroom.'

She watched as he inched his way to the edge of the bed and then slowly rested his feet on the floor. The bed was not low but still his legs bent up at his hips in an acute angle. He hadn't looked too big at Thelveton, the rambling, red-bricked Victorian grange where he was brought up, but here in this little house he seemed out of proportion.

She held the glass of water and watched as Push hauled himself to his feet. He staggered forward. Diana cried out as she tried to steady him, then she lost her footing and they both tumbled to the floor.

They lay together in a puddle of spilled water while the glass rolled away, unharmed, under the bed.

Push pressed his fingers into his chest and took a rasping breath.

'What the hell's happening to me?'

He was struggling to get to his feet but soon gave up and lay, curled on his side, on the floor. His face was deep red and his breath came in hard bursts. Diana kneeled against him and tried to take his arm around her neck and shoulder. 'Come on, Push. You slipped, that's all.'

'Didie... I'm so sorry. You're all covered in water.'

'It doesn't matter. It's only water, after all.' She pulled him up so he was sitting on the floor, leaning against the bed, then she sat back on her heels and stroked his shoulder through the blue and white cotton of his pyjama jacket. She could feel heat radiating through the fabric but underneath his muscles were trembling.

'You're shivering.'

'Am I?' He closed his eyes and leaned his head back on the bed. 'How odd. I feel as if I'm on fire.'

'Come on, let's get you back under the covers.'

He shook his head, still with his eyes closed, and lifted a slow hand in protest.

Diana sat for a long moment looking at Push. Only the ticking of the clock interrupted the Sunday morning peace. Then, far down the hill, someone began ringing the church bells.

Push opened his eyes slowly, raised his head and drew a knee up to his chest with the help of his hands. He looked confused and strangely fragile. Diana, leaning forward, pressed her face against his collarbone. She slipped her arms under his and lifted with all her strength. Push drove his elbows into the top of the mattress and, with legs sliding out like punt poles, they arrived back on the bed.

Eventually, Push said, 'It's like it was on Friday when I tried to start the bike.'

They lay curled together looking at the ceiling. 'What is?'

'The weakness. In my legs. No strength, no strength at all. Like it was on Friday, only worse.'

Diana sat up and looked at him. He was breathing strangely: shallow and fast.

'How much worse?'

'Worse. Well, you saw, Didie. I didn't slip. I couldn't stand.' He turned his head and looked into her eyes. 'I can't move my legs.'

Diana got off the bed and straightened the sheet and blankets. She pulled them right up to Push's chin and added another cover. When frightened, she always resorted to efficiency. Her heart banged about in her chest and she found it hard to think. She looked around: the dusty pink silk eiderdowns, the botanical rose prints on the wall, a Chinese knick-knack dish on a chest of drawers; all wedding presents from just six weeks before. Her reflection, the only truly familiar thing in the room, stared back at her from the looking glass, and she felt her eyes pricking in the sunlight.

'In that case,' she said carefully, 'I should call the doctor.'

'It's Sunday.'

But she was already on her way down the stairs to look for her new green address book. Thank God they had registered with the Iver surgery. Push's father had insisted they do that before they left for their honeymoon. There it was on the hall table next to the telephone. She gave the number to the woman at the exchange in a firm voice: no tremble there, her training in the House of Commons Library taking over.

She waited to be connected.

At last somebody answered. She explained the situation. The voice said the doctor would be on his way and checked the address. 'You've just moved in, haven't you?'

'Yes. Please be quick.'

'He'll be there as quick as he can.'

She ran back up the stairs two at a time. 'He'll be here in a minute.'

Push turned his head to look at her, nodded and closed his eyes again. She stared at him for a moment, his shoulders erupting from the covers and his feet hanging over the end of the bed. Then she turned and ran down the stairs again, wrenched the front door open and stood, blinking in the sunshine, to wait for the doctor.

Suffolk: Present, September

My mother pulled herself to the front of the chair, her body upright but inclined towards me slightly, arms straight with her hands held in a prayer position and trapped between her knees as though they might give away more than she meant to.

She was the first to break the silence. 'Aren't you going to write anything down?'

'Yes, of course.' I opened the cover sheet of my pad and stared at the empty page. 'Could you go back a bit?'

'Before our wedding?'

'Yes, if you wouldn't mind.' There's a certain comfort in facts and figures and I realised that after a lifetime of being kept at arms' length from the truth, I wasn't quite ready for close focus yet.

She considered for a moment or two then looked towards a space slightly to my right, where my father would have been sitting if he were still with us.

'It was a rather wonderful year, really—1952. Push was rowing in the pairs with Mike O'Brien. They did the Olympic trials at Easter. Then there was a bit of a disaster. Some mix up with a special new boat which didn't arrive in time for them to practice in, so Chris Davidge and his sidekick were selected instead.

'We'd booked our wedding for September to allow for the Olympics, but in the end it didn't matter. We were married in St. Paul's, Knightsbridge with the reception at the Hyde Park Hotel, and Lavender, Mummie's dressmaker, made my wedding dress and my trousseau. We went on our honeymoon...' I'd seen the tasselled photograph album with pictures of my mother amongst the New Forest ponies many times. '...and then, six weeks later, Push got polio.'

This much I knew. Have always known. Six-weeks-after-the-wedding was one of those phrases. There's a gap in the photographic record between the honeymoon and my birth six years later. It's there, and yet, not. It exists but was never noted, never remarked on, never untangled. Six years that simply vanished. A number six that rings in my head, faint but clear, as polio.

'How did it actually start?'

'How do you mean?' Lines furrowed her brow.

'The polio. You said he'd already been feeling ill. Before then...' I found I was clenching my pen until my hand hurt. This was untamed territory. 'It starts like flu, doesn't it?'

She caught my gaze again and held it. 'Push was working at Alan Muntz's. He came home on the Thursday and said he didn't feel well. But he was busy, and he didn't want to make a poor impression because he'd only just started his new job. So he struggled to go in on the Friday morning.' She smiled at me and paused to be sure that I understood how committed to his work Push was. He was committed to everything he did.

'He used to ride a motorbike in those days and he said that the kick-start was stiff that morning. But it wasn't really. It must have been his leg.' She stroked her soft blue needlecord trousers, still fixing me with her gaze, remembering. 'That was the start.'

'Did you have anyone you could talk to?'

'You have to remember that we didn't really know anybody. We'd only been living at Burnage a few weeks. Three or four, maybe. Ma P had been staying. She was helping me with the garden. There wasn't much in it except a little veggie garden at the bottom.'

'Ah! The spinach.' I was relieved to move onto

lighter things and a familiar family story.

'We were so innocent, so inexperienced. We were given a pressure cooker for a wedding present and we cooked spinach in it. It completely disappeared below the trivet.'

'To a green slime. I know.' I returned her smile. 'I'd love to have seen your faces.'

We sat in silence thinking of those very few weeks they had had together as newlyweds. 'So, what happened then?'

'Ma P said to give him some aspirin, that he'd often been a bit headachy as a child, and she left to go back to Thelveton on Saturday morning. I thought he'd be up in an hour or two so I did as she said and didn't worry.'

'But then you thought it might be more serious.'

'To be honest, I began to feel a bit out of my depth. At first, Push didn't want me to do anything. It was Sunday and it was a bit difficult. But after we crashed down together, I insisted on getting the doctor.'

Burnage, Iver: October, 1952

The doctor took two hours to arrive. He was short and dark and dressed for golf. Diana saw him from the bedroom window. She met him at the front door.

'Up here, is he?' He didn't wait to be shown, but strode past her and up the stairs, carrying a large brown leather bag with brass edgings. The door to their bedroom was open.

'So, we're feeling a bit poorly today, are we?'

Push nodded.

Diana had already explained on the telephone, and at the door, but she said again: 'He's got no strength. He fell down when he tried to get out of bed.'

'Did he?' It was as if he was hearing it for the first time. He stood still at the end of the bed, rubbing his chin and staring down at Push.

'I can't move my legs.'

Diana thought it was extraordinary how calm Push sounded. 'He's running a temperature. And had a terrible headache. He came home early from work on Friday with it.'

'Did he?' The doctor didn't make a move to get any closer. 'Since Friday. And he's no better?'

'Feel worse,' said Push quietly.

The doctor rubbed his chin slowly, round and round, and looked at the place where Push's legs lay under the bed-clothes. He put his bag down on the bed, opened it and took out a small hammer with a black rubber head. He rolled back the eiderdown, reached under the sheet and blankets and took out Push's left leg.

'So, no movement at all.' He put his elbow under Push's knee and lifted it high so that his foot was left dangling, and tapped the hammer smartly under the kneecap. Nothing happened. He repeated it. Again, nothing. He dropped the leg as if it were unattached, leaving it outside the covers, and walked back to the door. He turned to look at Diana.

'He's got polio. He must go to hospital.' Then the

doctor walked quickly across the landing, down the stairs, and out of the house.

They sat together in the bedroom waiting for the ambulance to arrive. Of course they knew about polio, but it wasn't something you thought about. Not like measles if you got a nasty rash or tetanus if you stood on a rusty nail or got a rose thorn in your hand. One or two girls at Diana's school had caught polio, had gone home and hadn't returned the next term. There were cases reported in the newspapers but it mostly affected children. Diana was twenty-three, Push was twenty-six: starting a life together as adults. And they were physically fit. Diana played tennis. Push had spent the summer training for the Olympic selections. People like Push didn't get polio.

But maybe they were young and fit and ignorant. You trusted doctors, even ones you didn't like.

He might never row again. Diana couldn't get the thought out of her head. All the time she'd been finding the number for the hospital and calling for an ambulance she kept thinking about Push being pipped at the post for Helsinki in the summer and how they'd assumed that because Push and Mike were still young, they could wait out their disappointment to try for the pairs at the '56 Olympics. Now all that was to be swept away like marks in the sand when the tide comes in.

'I can feel it creeping up my legs. I can feel my nerves jumping,' Push said suddenly. 'They jump, then stop. Then it starts again further up.'

They hardly spoke after that: there was nothing to

be said, no comforting to be done. When Diana heard the gravel crunch under tyres again, she ran down the stairs, opened the door and was bewildered for a moment to see her father standing on the step. She'd forgotten that he was coming to lunch. He was smiling and scratching his bald patch.

'Such a beautiful morning.' He folded his gauntlets up with his cap. 'I came on the Tailwind. Thought I'd give it a good run.' He faltered, seeing Diana's face. 'Whatever's the matter?'

'It's Push. The doctor says it's polio. We're waiting for an ambulance to take him to Uxbridge.'

'Uxbridge?'

'There's an isolation hospital there.' She looked over her father's shoulder as if, miraculously, he had the ambulance there in the driveway instead of the little hand-built putt-putt that he had ridden over from Berkhamsted. She met his eyes again. 'I thought it was them.' She folded her arms around her body and shivered despite the sunshine.

Her father looked down at her and gently shook his head. 'Oh, Diana. What ghastly luck.' He drew her in against his chest and hugged her to him just as he had when she was a little girl. He smelled of pipe tobacco, oil and leather, as familiar as a pair of slippers. She didn't have to stay stiff and strong anymore, she could bend like grass in a hurricane and Daddy was here to take over. 'Where's Push now?'

She gestured with her hand, unable to speak, tears on the brink.

Fifteen minutes later, they were in the kitchen,

Diana's father making her drink tea: the first thing to eat or drink that she'd had all day. She couldn't eat the toast. Push had refused everything. Said that he didn't want to risk doing the wrong thing. They might not want him to have eaten or drunk anything when he got to the hospital.

Diana was so anxious for the ambulance to arrive that when the door bell sounded, her hand shook violently and she nearly spilled her tea.

'Where's the other one?' Diana asked as the man opened the back doors of the ambulance and took a stretcher from the inside.

'Other what?'

'Man. Ambulance man. You'll need two of you.'

'Only me. It's Sunday, you know.' He held the stretcher on its side as he walked into the house. He stank of alcohol. 'Where're we going, then?'

'Upstairs. It's my husband.'

He looked at the narrow staircase as if eyeing it up.

'What's wrong with him?'

'He's got polio,' said Diana's father. 'So he can't possibly walk down the stairs.'

The ambulance man put the stretcher down very deliberately and folded his arms. 'I'm not going to touch him. He's infectious.' He looked from Diana to her father and back again.

There was a surge of noise in her ears as Diana felt her heart race again. She touched her father's arm. 'We're going to have to get Push down the stairs ourselves.'

They sat Push up on the side of the bed. He was

burning, had no balance and was barely lucid. They sat down beside him and pulled his arms around their shoulders. They tried to stand. Push was six feet, four inches tall, heavy and with a body of solid muscle. Diana's father was almost six feet, but Diana was slight and nearly a foot shorter. Painfully mismatched, they staggered and grunted and rearranged Push's weight until he stood supported, somehow, between them.

They started to lurch towards the landing. Push's feet dragged, snagged and flopped on the edges of the rug. They scraped his shoulders on the door frame and banged his elbows against the banisters. There was nothing comfortable or reassuring about any of the journey from top to bottom stair. Push jerked and flapped his legs, trying to take some weight at each step. He clung like a man drowning, grasped their arms, gripped like a vice with his hands.

Slowly, step by step, they descended to the hall. Diana was grimly pleased to see that the ambulance man looked ashamed.

They arranged Push on the stretcher. It was too small for him. Diana's father and the ambulance man carried him across the gravel to the waiting vehicle. Diana kissed him before they lifted him in and closed the doors. Then the man stinking of beer drove Push away.

Diana and her father followed in her little beige Ford. It had a history of false starts but today it fired first time.

They stopped outside the redbrick building. The ambulance driver walked around to the back of his vehicle and threw open the doors. People ran from the front door and gathered around but no one came to speak to them or even looked in their direction. When Diana and her father went towards the ambulance they were told to stand to one side. The stretcher was drawn out and carried swiftly to the front door. It was clear that neither Diana nor her father would be welcome inside. They watched the doors close behind Push and everyone else, then there was nothing to be done except climb into the car and return to Burnage.

'We mustn't expect much,' said Ma P when they arrived outside the hospital the next day. Diana had kissed her mother-in-law good-bye on Saturday, yet here she was back again barely forty-eight hours later. It was hardly possible that so much had changed in the meantime.

Ma P stared ahead. 'I've been warned that the nurses in these places haven't had much training,' she said steadily. 'They have to pay them danger money, you know.'

'Danger money?'

'For the risk of infection.'

'I didn't know'. Diana's voice was hardly above a whisper.

Ma P looked at Diana and gave a small, kind smile. 'You ready, Didie?'

Diana nodded, hardly noticing that Ma P had called her by the pet name that Push always used. Together they got out of the car and walked to the double doors of the hospital. Diana tried the handle but it didn't open. Ma P rang the bell.

After a very long time, they heard footsteps before the door was opened to a narrow slit. A powerful smell of

Jeyes fluid greeted them. The woman standing in the door-way was dressed in a navy blue uniform and had hands scrubbed raw and red. It was impossible not to notice that she was quite unexpectedly and extraordinarily pretty. She asked them what they wanted.

'My son was brought here yesterday,' Ma P explained. 'We've come to see him.'

'You can't. This is an isolation hospital; that means all patients are kept separate due to infectious disease and there is no access for the general public.' She spoke as if she was reading from a handbook.

'But I've been with him all the time until yesterday lunchtime.' Diana found herself speaking too loudly. 'It makes no sense to say I can't see him.' She paused, then lowered her voice. 'Please let us see him.'

She heard a pigeon on the roof coo four or five times before the woman spoke again.

'Name?' She turned to Ma P.

'Pulman. Prockter Pulman.' Ma P gave his proper Christian name.

The woman looked at Diana. 'And you are?'

'Diana Pulman. I'm his wife.'

'You'd better come in.' She opened the door a lit-tle. Diana stood aside for Ma P to go ahead of her but the woman put out an arm to prevent her.

'Not you. Next-of-kin only.'

Diana turned in astonishment. 'She's his mother.'

'Only you.'

Diana made to take a step forward then stopped, overwhelmed by the injustice of the situation. 'But she's his mother,' she protested again. 'We've only been married six weeks, I'm hardly next-of-kin. She needs to see her son.'

'I shouldn't be doing this at all. Next-of-kin only. That's you.'

Diana stood in horror as Push's mother snatched a handkerchief from her sleeve. 'I'll see you in the car.' Ma P's voice was high and thin and, clamping the little white square to her mouth, she practically ran back down the drive.

Diana watched her go, feelings of guilt and abandonment rising in her chest, before turning to walk into the hospital. Ahead of her there was no hall to speak of, no reception desk and no waiting room, only a small lobby from which stretched an empty corridor down which the nurse was walking swiftly, heavy black shoes clumping dully on the bare boards.

Push was in a room on his own, lying on a white metal bed, flat and narrow as an operating trolley. A monkey pole dangled above his head and a structure like a small Wendy House lifted a brown blanket high above his legs. His feet emerged from underneath strapped to wooden splints, keeping the toes at right angles to his legs: bare toes that looked grey and cold. A small cabinet beside him held a jug of water, a blue mug with a spout and a glass with a thermometer standing in it. There was a window overlooking a tightly maintained flower garden ablaze with dahlias in a dozen different colours, but no curtains, only a blind made of wooden slats, pulled high enough to give her a clear view. A shelf like a shop counter ran along one wall. A single central light with a glass lampshade and dark linoleum completed the furnishings.

Diana stood in the open doorway. Push looked pale and still and sort of polished. For a split second she wondered if he were dead, then he turned his head and looked at her. The relief at seeing her flooded his face, tugging her towards him as forcefully as any rope.

'Didie.' His voice was low and strained. Small flecks of white gathered at the corners of his mouth and cracks had formed in his lips. Diana stroked his hair back from his forehead and kissed his brow; his skin, even his hair, smelled of Jeyes fluid.

Present: September

My mother had stuttered to a halt. I'd been staring at her without moving during the whole story, my eyes burned as if I'd been standing before a bonfire. I blinked quickly, once, twice, took a deep breath and released it. I opened my mouth to speak—I couldn't let her stop—but what emerged was no more than a whisper.

'What happened that first night in Uxbridge?'

She spread her fingers in front of her with an unconscious glance at the gold wedding and signet rings on her hands, then clasped her knees. 'I don't blame the girls.' She shook her head. 'They were terribly young and desperately poor when they were brought over from Ireland to work in those horrible hospitals. They were rough and completely uneducated and were virtually untrained.'

My mother's blunt statements of apparent fact have

often left me feeling uncomfortable, and I flinched inwardly. 'They must have been brave. Brave to work where they knew they might get polio, I mean.'

She gave a characteristic shrug. 'Maybe. They came for the money and sent their wages home.'

I didn't like what I was hearing, but I thought back to my own mother-in-law who died six months after my father. She'd been one of nine siblings and came from Ireland to England when she was just nineteen because work was almost impossible to come by back home. It occurred to me that maybe the Irish nurses didn't get polio because they'd been exposed to it when they were children. I'd recently read Tony Gould's examination of polio, *A Summer Plague,* and he'd touched on Irish herd immunity. Since 1956 the goal had been to achieve nationwide immunity through sufficient uptake of vaccinations, but his theory was that in the first half of the last century, when polio was endemic in Ireland, most children would have developed a natural resistance due to an earlier, mild and uncomplicated infection, resulting in a natural social immunity, or the clinically termed herd immunity. However, in mid-twentieth century England, that protection had all but vanished with a fashion for smaller families and the rise in living standards, giving an opportunity for polio cases to swiftly reach epidemic proportions after the war when the troops came home. Older victims were often attacked with the more severe, paralytic, form.

It seemed incomprehensible to me that anyone would deliberately choose to put themselves at risk of living the life my father had been forced to live for fifty years, so I wondered if the girls from Ireland had been victims themselves, victims of a recruitment drive that had been economical with the truth.

'What was unforgivable...' My mother wagged her finger, insistent that I heard what she had to say. 'Was the drinking that went on. I suppose they had nothing else to do. But it nearly did for Push.'

Uxbridge: October, 1952

Diana got into the car, sat beside Ma P and stared ahead through the windscreen.

'We have to get him out of there,' she said at last. 'I know you said that the nursing wasn't very good, but that's the least of it.' She turned towards Ma P. 'I'm so sorry that you weren't allowed in. I really did try. After I saw him, I had quite a fight about it but that Matron would not be moved.'

'Perhaps I can see him tomorrow.'

Diana put her hand over her mouth. 'That's the thing. This is it.'

'What do you mean?'

'We can't visit anymore. It's a one-off.'

Ma P uttered a single wordless sound and took her hankie out of her sleeve again.

'Nobody can visit until he's no longer a risk to others.'

'How long is that?'

Diana shook her head. 'Three, four weeks? She

wouldn't say exactly.'

'My God!' Ma P fumbled for Diana's hand. Icy-fingered, they soothed each other, their rings clicking together as they sat, silent and dry-eyed, staring at the blank brick facade of the hospital. Eventually, Ma P spoke again. 'I know it's impossible, but I want to swoop in there, grab him up and take him back with me to Thelveton.'

Di thought of her in-laws' Norfolk home; the comfortable drawing room with its yellow and sage-green chintz, the creamy jasmine flowers and scent that filled her senses in the cave-like cool of the porch, and the great brass ship's bell that hung by the front door. She remembered a lively dinner party to introduce her to Sir Jack Mann from the Hall and other family friends. She thought of the Thelveton cook, Lily, in the kitchen and the warm chatter between Marjy and Mrs B. Pa P's pipe tobacco smell—so like that of her own father—and his constant, unconscious humming. But above all, when she thought of Thelveton, she saw Ma P, ever present at its centre, instinctively understanding everyone's needs, keeping the peace between the menagerie of animals and a houseful of visitors, seeing the potential in a pile of broken crockery for a mosaic covered plant pot, gathering armfuls of flowers to decorate the large, airy rooms: nurturing, joyful, something vaguely Bohemian in amongst Victorian values.

She slowly withdrew her hand. 'Might as well go home. Back to Iver,' Diana corrected herself, not wanting to think even for a second how long it might be before Push could come back and make it their home. Ma P nodded. 'Did you get to speak to him?' she asked as Diana started the engine.

'Oh, yes. That's why we have to get him out of there.'

On the way back to Burnage, Diana told her mother-in-law all that she and Push had talked about.

On admission, it had been discovered that the hospital was ill-equipped for anyone over six feet tall. It was important that Push's legs didn't hang over the edge of the bed in their wooden splints so instead an arrangement was rigged up with stools to support the pillows under his head. He wasn't quite certain what had happened during the night, only that as the fever increased he was suddenly awake, lying on his back with his head hanging over the end of the bed completely unsupported, an agonising pain radiating out of his neck, and his windpipe severely restricted. He was totally unable to move himself to a better position or shout for help.

The nerve damage from the polio had by now travelled up from his legs, practically as far as his shoulders, and his hands were almost paralysed, but there was still some residual movement in his right arm and fingers. After a long while he managed to inch his hand out of the bed and ring the bell on his locker, but nobody came. Eventually, after many attempts, he knocked the little hand bell onto the floor with a great clatter.

He heard footsteps in the corridor, and with enormous relief he saw the night-nurse look through a small window in the door. She must have decided that all was well because she turned around and went away again.

Push lay with his head tipped back over the end of the bed, on the verge of suffocation, for many hours. At around six o'clock in the morning the night-nurse came again to do the rounds before she went off duty. Push could smell alcohol as soon as she walked into the room but, mercifully, she wasn't so drunk that she couldn't see what had happened during the long hours of darkness. She grabbed his head and propped it up again on the pillows. By this time, his neck was so stiff and painful that this thoughtless action was almost as agonising as the hours that had gone before.

Present: September

I'd never heard this story before; not even a hint, and I was appalled at the careless brutality of the world my father had found himself in, and his profound helplessness and suffering.

'Did you feel part of the Pulmans?'

'Apart?' she said, mishearing me.

'No. Part of... A member of... You'd only been family for such a short time and you were suddenly having all this...' I didn't really know what I was trying to say. As a child growing up in East Anglia it seemed we were always Pulman grandchildren; that I had another grandmother, along with an aunt and uncle and cousins from my mother's side, often came as a surprise. But it may have been an accident of geography.

'Always. Push's parents were so kind. I felt part of

the family from the moment Push asked me to marry him.'

'And then you went to live with them at Thelveton.'

'Yes, and of course, you and Will were born there, but that wasn't until much later. My Daddy, your Grandpa Latta, said I must come back home and live with them in Berkhamsted after we got Push moved from Uxbridge to the London Hospital.' She paused for a moment. 'I think if we hadn't, he might never have come out.'

That was another shock, in all my life, I'd never heard anyone talk of the possibility that my father might have died. Polio didn't often kill its victims. I'd looked up the WHO statistics for 1952: total reported cases 3,910; deaths 295; paralytic form 2,747, of which my father was just one. If a polio patient died, it was usually due to respiratory failure, but I hadn't expected to hear that there might have been deaths due to inadequate care.

'It was Ma P's efforts, really, that got him moved. ' She sighed and I saw the hint of shadows beneath her eyes.

I suggested we talk some more another day and stood up.

'Here you are. I found these for you.' She pushed a bundle of letters into my arms. 'I haven't read them through, so I've no idea what you might find.' She raised her eyebrows slightly and gave a short embarrassed laugh.

I clutched the pile to my body, trying to stop them slipping to the floor. I noticed my mother's handwriting and the red twopence-ha'penny King George stamps and started to thank her, but she walked away to the swing door beside the stairs. I followed her to the back of the house and into the kitchen. My father's enormous silver tabby cat wound around her legs and threatened to trip her up. I slid the letters onto a work top. There seemed to be dozens.

'Typical Push, keeping my letters all these years.'

I looked more closely at the envelopes. A small number in thick cream laid were from before their marriage, which I put to one side. The next block were more modest with the first dated December, 1952. I arranged ten or twelve into a fan, careful to keep them in order. 'These are all addressed to The London Hospital. Do you think the Uxbridge letters are missing?'

'I shouldn't think I'd have written any.' The kitchen table was unusually tall, designed by my father so that he could fit the armrests of his wheelchair comfortably beneath it; although he no longer needed his high table, it still stood between us as my mother paused, thinking back over the years. 'I think I stayed living in Iver for the first weeks so I could visit every day.'

'You went to visit? I thought...'

'I went to the hospital and I looked at Push through the window.'

Chapter Two

Home, Suffolk: 1969

What you must understand, Sarie...

These words sting.

What you must remember, Sarie, is that Daddie can't sit for that length of time. That we can't stay until the end because Poor Dad will sit through his poor backside.

You have to remember, Sarie, that sometimes Daddie is on a short fuse because his legs ache all the time and he doesn't sleep properly. He doesn't really mean it.

You must understand that it's very disappointing for Daddie when you don't want to... go for a walk, play tennis, join friends swimming in the sea; he would give his eye-teeth to be able to do what you can do.

And I do remember.

And I understand. Up to a point. But only up to a point. Because all we know is that he hurts; he aches; he doesn't sleep.

But I don't understand—not really—what he must be feeling, what he's gone through, what happened in that lost time of no photographs in the years before I was born. I want to understand, I really do, but Will and I are supposed to just know by virtue of being the children of... and at this point I always stumble because I don't know what to call him except Daddie.

He is not an invalid—far from in-valid—and not a victim. He is no longer sick, certainly not a cripple—well, he is, strictly speaking—but even seeing the word, let alone saying it aloud, makes me cringe with embarrassment for him. Paraplegic is technical and unsayable. Disabled sounds as if he should be drawing a pension. Impaired or incapacitated denies that he is cleverer and can get more done than nearly everyone else we know. His great muscular arms mean that he can't be weak. He is absolutely not useless—he is the most use-full person I know. I don't even say that he can't walk. When describing him to my friends I sometimes add, more as an afterthought than anything else, that he uses a chair. If they look blank, I might explain that it's a wheelchair. I don't know what Will says to his friends; we've never discussed it.

We see Daddie come in from work, grey with tiredness, and head for the drawing room. He bumps himself off the chair and onto the sofa with a heartfelt sigh of relief. Sweeping a lick of hair back from his forehead with one hand, he pushes the chair to the side of the sofa with the other so that it's out of the way. Often, a cat will jump up, curl onto the still-warm, ring cushion and my father looks fondly at its comfortable purring. Cats can be forgiven almost anything, even getting cosy on his wheelchair.

'Get us a whisky, would you, Didie?' he says, and my mother walks briskly to the back of the house to find an old cut glass decanter kept on a slate shelf at the back of the larder.

He doesn't toss the whisky down in one, and rarely

has it neat: he likes it with ginger ale or water. But he often has a second, until one day, he doesn't.

'Shall I get you another, Daddie?' I ask.

My father says nothing but looks at his glass, seems to hold it up to the light and scrutinise it, then puts it down deliberately in the very centre of the mat with the hunting scene on the squat, round table in front of him. He straightens the mat to align it with the Radio Times beside it, then brings a pen and an ashtray to heel too, so that there's a strict one-inch gap between everything on the polished mahogany surface.

I wait to be given the glass so I can take it back to my mother who is cooking supper in the kitchen. My father leans on the coffee table, using it as a support, hands outstretched, fingers wide.

'Do you know, Sarie? I don't think I will.' He remains looking down at his glass. 'In fact.' He narrows his eyes. 'I don't think I shall have a whisky in the evenings any more.' He picks up the empty tumbler and sets it down again on the far side of the table. It is short and stubby with a heavy base that distorts the flames in the fireplace. 'I look forward to this from the moment I turn into the drive but now it takes two before it deadens the pain.' He gazes blankly into the fire. 'The next thing is, that it'll take three.' He looks up at me. 'And then where will we be?'

I'm reading in bed again. I am always reading. I used to spend my half-a-crown pocket money each week on a new Enid Blyton from the whirligig stand down the town or from the same stand, miraculously transported to

Cornwall, at the Poldu Beach shop every summer. Then it was the Narnia Chronicles and all the books by Malcolm Saville or histories by R J Unstead. Last year I raced back in time through Sherlock Holmes, then everything ever written by Agatha Christie, and recently I moved to Africa with Flamingo Feather by Laurens van de Post.

But today I'm reading something different.

I've read this book all the way through just once since finding it in the bookcase on the landing, tucked innocently within a row of Argosy magazines, Readers Digest and old editions of Stephen Leacock that once belonged to Grandpa Latta. I can't leave it alone. I've been compulsively reading and re-reading certain sections for the past few days and scaring myself witless.

I have a feeling that my parents might consider it 'inappropriate' if they found it in my room. They'll say that eleven years old is too young, and I can't risk it being taken away, so I've made it into my bed—tucking it between the sheets each day—getting it out in the evening only when I can be sure of not being disturbed.

As I reach under the covers and touch the book, my heart starts to thump and my palms feel damp. With eyes half closed, I draw it out and turn the pages.

You think too much, that's the only trouble with you, one of the characters tells Deborah, the girl at the centre of the story, who tells me more than I can ever imagine. My mother is always saying the same to me. 'The trouble with you, Sarie, is that you think too much.' Maybe I do, but I also talk too much because that's the only way I've found to switch the thinking off. They call it showing off,

and that's frowned upon as well. In any case, I like thinking. Perhaps she means that I imagine too much.

I flick through the pages till I come to one where the
corner is turned down. My focus dances across the para-
graph hardly daring to read it.

*Metal coffin. Hospital. Stretcher. Pushing on your
chest, pressing till you wanted to faint; then relaxing, then
pulling instead, pulling till your mouth opened and air went
in; relaxing, then pressing again, pressing till the air came
out... You wanted to scream and daren't because if you did
a sort of bubble might form in your throat and make you
cough and then you'd suffocate... It was torture because
you were really dead and it was keeping you artificially
alive... If you whimpered loud enough the nurse would
come...*

Then on another page.

*...this terrible sound of a great animal breathing: I
couldn't see it but it was somewhere near; and all the time
the men were watching the dials... And the pain wasn't yet
there, but I knew, I knew it was going to start.*

My heart is beating almost more than I can stand; my breath
coming in gasps to keep up with the words on the page and
still I can't close the book. I have to know. I have to know
how my father had felt in hospital. I need to understand
what happened when he first got ill, why his legs ache so
much, why he can't sleep, why he needs the whisky each

evening. And Deborah, in Winston Graham's *The Walking Stick*, is telling me.

Deborah was ten when she caught polio. Even her parents, who were both doctors, hadn't realised that she had polio; they thought she had a cold. She was paralysed and put in an iron lung. Had Daddie been put in an iron lung? With the snot running over his face? Had they taken him out one day, watched him start to die, like Deborah, and had to put him back? Is he terrified of suffocating now? Is that why he snores so gigantically that, sometimes, I think the wall separating our bedrooms might actually shake with the force of it?

Deborah recovered but had grown up with a 'thin' leg. Both my father's legs are thin as straws. I try to imagine a pretty young woman wearing a mini skirt and tights with one leg looking normal and the other thin and white as my father's.

Then there's the pain. Deborah remembered terrible pain. *'You didn't really lose any feeling in your body when you had polio; it was all there, but helpless.'* I read the passages that I have marked over and over and over again until my heartbeat is back to normal and tears are running down the side of my face. I snatch at the light cord above my head to plunge the room into blackness, let the book fall shut on the counterpane and lie still as Deborah and Daddie.

I feel as if I'm becoming paralysed. As if I'm struggling to breathe. I lurch out of my bed, tearing the sheet and blankets away from my throat. I gasp in gulpfulls of cool air and grope for the door. I can see the light around the frame but I'm crashing around the room looking for a way out and keep hitting pieces of furniture: my chair, the tallboy, the wardrobe.

All at once the room fills with light and my mother comes through the door.

'Whatever's happening, luvvie?' She reaches out for me before I bash the wall again and I lean against her. I realise that I'm shouting and crying. She smells of Ô de Lancôme and Mummie, but even in the height of this panic I realise that it's not wise to tell the truth. Or at least, not the whole truth.

'I had a dream. A nightmare.' I wipe my eyes and sit on my bed. On the book. 'I'm sorry.' I'm still sniffling and gasping. 'I couldn't breathe.' I realise that this is exactly what Deborah told her parents before they took her away in the ambulance and put her in the iron lung. I force myself to breath naturally, to calm down, to relax. My mother sits beside me, puts her arm around me and strokes my shoulder.

'We couldn't think what was happening,' she says. 'It sounded as if you had an army up here.'

'I'm all right now.'

'Really?'

'Really.' I nod and try to smile. 'I'm sorry. I'll be fine. I'll go back to sleep now.'

'Just think nice thoughts.' My mother gets up and leans over to kiss me. 'Goodnight, Sarie.'

'Leave the door open,' I say quickly, as she begins to pull it to.

When my mother leaves the room, I resolve to read *The Walking Stick* only in the day time. Now, I think, I shall have something real to tell my friends at school and already I imagine describing my father—poor Daddie, how could he have borne it?—in the iron lung, waiting to have the gunk wiped from his face. I think about Deborah, her boyfriend and her responsible job at the auction house. I think about my father, the engineer, and inventor of a unique and miraculous valve, which he has named after the rainbow that God threw into the air as a vow that He would never again flood the earth. I smile when I think of his excitement now that the Rainbow Valve Company, his own manufacturing firm, is truly taking off and all his hard work is being rewarded. Grimly, I think of the physical details that I'll be able to give the girl who told me that my father was a nut-case.

Present: September

My mother had entrusted me with her letters: the letters that she discovered after my father's death and couldn't throw away but chose not to read again. The letters between whose pages, I imagined clues to the past lay waiting to be uncovered.

I sorted everything into date order, found a shoe box that fitted their width nicely and stood them in the middle of our sitting room table.

Each was slit with almost surgical precision, presumably with my father's jack knife or a letter opener. There were several from after my parents' engagement in 1951; ten from Strasbourg, which came as a complete surprise (I had no idea that my mother had been working there), and ninety letters covering dates from 14 December, 1951 to 23 June, 1955. There wasn't a single letter from my father, although I imagined that he couldn't move his hands enough to write at the beginning. Or perhaps they'd been destroyed; certainly the authorities were aware of the risk of infection, however it might be carried.

For all my life I'd made my own stories about my father's illness. I had no choice. The boundary between fact and fantasy had been uncomfortably blurred since the time I was old enough to start gathering clues and fill the holes in my own narrative. Now was the time for me to swap fiction for fact.

Uxbridge: 1952

Diana went to visit Push every day. She was never allowed inside to see him again but she would walk around the building until she found his window and stand looking into the room. Mostly, she stood under an umbrella wearing her cream trousseau coat: it seemed always to be raining.

After the first day, she noticed that another item of equipment had been moved in with him. It was the biggest thing in the room by far, dull green and covered in steel knobs and dials. Push was still in his bed and the machine was tight up against one wall, looming over the tiny space so that Diana couldn't take her eyes off it. At the front door, where she occasionally rang the bell for information, she was told that it was an iron lung.

Each day when she peered in through the window she expected to see Push's head emerging from the black hole at one end of the lung. But he stayed lying on the white bed and one day, maybe a week or so later, the machine had been removed and Push's bed pushed under the window. She felt they had turned a corner.

Slowly, slowly the acute stage of polio began to reach its end. The extent of the paralysis would be assessed over the next weeks and weakened muscles, often in great pain from spasms, would have to be stretched and worked. An occupational therapist came in to help encourage dexterity. Push was given materials to make a small wicker basket. His back, once powerful from rowing, was now so weak that sitting up was almost impossible but, like so many polio patients, isolated from family and friends and at the mercy of strangers, he became totally compliant and outwardly tolerant, so whatever banal a task he was asked to do, he applied himself with determination.

One day Diana saw him bent almost double over his work, desperately trying to make his unwilling fingers perform an impossibly intricate task. Another day, he looked up to see her standing at her place by the window and angrily waved her away. She stood still, distressed, and his fury increased as he gestured violently for her to move away. In tears, she rushed back to the car and sat shaking in bewildered confusion before slowly driving home. At her next visit, clearly full of trepidation that he might not want to see her again, he was remorseful and they managed a short conversation through the thin glass and ill-fitting window frame. He explained that his semi-paralytic bowel had just begun to work again and he had been left to take control over his own bodily functions. The thought that his new wife was observing him through the window was unbearable.

A few weeks later he complained of a continuous pain in his heels. His feet had been strapped into two ninety-degree wooden splints from the moment he had been admitted to prevent the achilles tendons from contracting, so that the angle of his feet could be maintained for when he started his rehabilitation. If he'd been shorter, he would have had his feet pressed onto a footboard, which would have allowed a little movement, but the unrelenting pressure on the splints was becoming intolerable.

The next day, with the wind threatening to blow her umbrella out of her hand, Diana tried to hear what had happened when he told the pretty matron about the pain in his feet.

'Don't know what you're complaining of,' she had told him. 'There's a woman next door with a sore on her back the size of a dinner plate.'

That evening, Diana telephoned Thelveton. She wanted advice.

'Honestly, it was as if Matron was proud of it. I can't believe that anyone could take that attitude.'

'Yes, Didie.' Ma P's voice was quiet and the line was crackling, but there was no doubting that she agreed with everything Diana had decided for herself. 'We've got to find a way to get him out of there and into somewhere more compassionate.'

Present: September

I'd never needed a run as I did on the day after I received the letters from my mother. I couldn't find my running shoes although I always put them away in the same place. Anxiety had made me impatient. I pulled out everyone's shoes and left them littered about the hall, then I saw my trainers through the glass door, neon blue and yellow, leaning against the outside wall and glistening with dew.

They were clean, but soaking wet. I put them on, laced them up and felt the cold seep into my toes. I didn't care. After ten minutes running, wet socks turn warm, keeping your feet toasty until you slow down. I left the house and set off running faster than was comfortable, my breath coming in sharp puffs in the cool air. After a lifetime of conjecture, I'd discovered the truth about Uxbridge and it was terrible. Yet it was also better than anything I had imagined. For decades I'd been bowed by what I thought to be real. In the absence of any corroborated facts, I'd used the only information available to me.

I realised with sudden clarity that Graham's book had become an obsession. Of course! Why hadn't I seen it before? It'd become a short cut to the emotions I needed to feel on behalf of my father, so I could answer questions with authenticity. On returning home from learning the truth, I'd dug out the book and re-read it in a day. At the iron-lung passage, those self-same feelings of suffocation and terror had welled up, recognisable from when I was a child but totally unexpected, and all at once I could appreciate the significance any detail, however tiny or misrepresented, had been to my ability to say, OK, that's another black hole I've filled.

I left the road and started up the hill-track towards a spinney of overgrown cricket bat willow. What I'd found out wasn't great, but I resolved to go over and over it in my head until it no longer hurt.

I'd been running for barely half-an-hour but already I could feel the soothing effects of the countryside, just as my grandfather had taught me. Much improves with a dose of the clear, country air that was denied my father for so long. I ran down another short length of road, nodded to the egg man, then turned into a lane where there had been peacocks when our girls were small. I clambered up a steep path past the round summerhouse that stood like a look-out on the edge of the Court's garden, and into a footpath that stretched across a newly ploughed field. My feet grew heavy as the mud stuck and compacted. I hesitated at the junction of two newly fenced and signed footpaths and rubbed a complaining calf muscle while I made a decision.

I doubted there would be many water fowl on the broad, but half-an-hour in the bird hide would be enough to fill my field of vision with light on the water, of reeds that were turning brittle and the colour of sand and, who knows, I thought I might get lucky and see a late-to-migrate reed warbler. I would allow myself to become small, part of a bigger plan, absorbed in the present. I wiped my feet clean on a patch of weedy grass and set off, away from the route that would lead me home.

Chapter Three

Present: October

My grandparent's Norfolk home, Thelveton Grange, was the heart of the family. Until the mid-eighties, when my grandmother died, it represented security, love, warmth and, above all, continuity. My grandfather had been a hoarder and custodian of inanimate things; my father was the guardian and editor of family stories, and his many tellings and re-tellings ensured that we received them with as much respect as he had accepted the physical heirlooms bestowed upon him as the eldest son.

My grandmother, however, was a collector of quite a different category altogether; Grannie (or Ma P as she was known to my mother) gathered in living creatures and people. She never turned away any person or animal that came to her for help, and Thelveton expanded accordingly.

When it came to her own son's needs, my grandmother was desperate to relocate him as soon as possible. If it couldn't be within the nurturing walls of her own home then, at the very least, she must have him moved out of Uxbridge to somewhere more humane, and where she could bring what she could of Thelveton's sanctuary to him.

When he was well enough, my grandmother determined that her son and his new wife would return to Thelveton to be cared for. They would be healed and restored with clean Norfolk air, and eat plentiful, fresh, familiar food that, at a time when rationing was still in place, was almost certainly unavailable in London.

The house was large and already home to several people who were not family. They had come to stay for whatever reason and, somehow, the right moment had never arrived for them to leave. Another couple wouldn't make much difference to the smooth running of the house, and a copious staff, many of whom had been let go for war work a decade or so before, were on standby to return.

Lily, my grandparent's cook produced a continuous variety of plain food with calm efficiency. There was Mrs G. who did the rough work, whose hands and arms were puce from buckets of scalding water. Florence, the table maid, came a couple of times a week to clean the silver; the pantry was her private domain. Miss Philpott, known to everyone as Aunty, was so bent and deeply wrinkled it was as though she had been left outdoors to weather. My grandmother had encouraged her to retire, but she wouldn't leave, so she remained responsible for cleaning what she could reach, making the beds and emptying any chamber pots. Astonishing, that in a house with plenty of bathrooms, they still used chamber pots!

Mrs Briscoe was more of a family friend, although she helped wherever she was needed, and spent most of her 'down-time' at the front of the house with my grandparents. She'd been gathered into the fold after her army husband disappeared—perhaps he had been killed, or died after the war—but whatever it was, she needed help and a home. She made her way to Thelveton and my grandmother took her in.

As a small child, wherever I wandered in this huge playground of a house, it seemed as if there was always a pair of doughy arms to sweep me up for a cuddle, allow me to 'help' with the cooking, to show me how to flick cobwebs with a feather duster or join the whole crowd as they spent hours in the kitchen chatting and drinking Camp coffee. Everyone mucked in, as my grandmother would say, from the youngest to the oldest, and everything got done eventually, so time wasting was looked upon with indulgence, rather than exasperation.

The person I loved the most was Marjy; she taught me to love books. Marjery Khan had been one of the Eton Dames, she looked after the welfare of the boys in her house and my father had been under her care from the day he'd arrived at the school aged eleven. At the end of the summer term, and unconsciously echoing his mother's hospitality after he learned that she had no other home to go to and would be spending the holidays in a house empty of boys, he asked her to stay. She returned to Thelveton from July to September every year and, on her retirement, it became her permanent home.

Visitors must have thought Thelveton very eccentric but when we were small, my brother Will and I knew no different. We slotted into this household of family, staff and strays, as easily and unremarkably as slipping a bookmark between the pages of a much loved book.

Thelveton: 1963

Here, in the back kitchen, I'm under the table sitting in a cardboard box, Kilner seals adorning wrists and ankles. I'm straining to match voices to the legs around me.

I'm eating Lily-biscuits; picking the cherry off the top, and playing with the Fire Engine, Grannie's mangy cat. I'm squirming around in the box in an effort not to rub up against his scabby body. His purrs are so loud, it's hard for me to hear what's being said. The smell of vinegar has kept the other cats outside. Gert and Daisy are sleeping in front of the fire in the smoking room. Only the Fire Engine's desperate need to be loved has kept him indoors: that, or the disgusting ointment he has to endure has ruined his sense of smell.

All this to a background music of Kilner Jar-clinks, as the household collects to pickle onions for a second day.

A corner of a Field magazine—one of many protecting the table—twitches and my grandmother's face appears, upside down.

'This one's full,' she says. 'We're ready for another band, Sarie.'

I slip the flat, rubber band, red as rust, from my fist and silently pass it up.

The Fire Engine takes advantage of my divided attention, climbs into my lap and turns the volume up another notch. Grannie smiles and winks before disappearing again.

There are eight people around this table. Lily, Florence, Aunty Philpott ('Miss Philpott to you, Sarah'),

Mrs Gardener, Marjy, Mrs B, Grannie and Mummie. Mummie's shoes and stockings are easy to pick out: her legs are slim and smooth, tipped in fuchsia pink, pointed sling-backs, like Swan Vesta matches. I like stroking them but she's spoken firmly to me and I've had to stop. I know Grannie's shoes too by the bunion lumps, but I'm having trouble identifying the others. All except for Marjy, whose legs are so thin and knobbly, they're like birch branches in Lisle stockings.

Eight women pickling onions, nine if you count me under the table, and one man to oversee operations.

Grandpa bumps open the green baize door separating the front of the house from its engine rooms; he pokes his head into the kitchen like a tortoise popping out of its shell to test the weather and the buzz around the table falls silent. He points to a space where another onion can be pressed into the vinegar.

'Rather fun, really,' he says.

It isn't. Pickling onions is a mucky and painful job. Yesterday, I wanted to join in the chatter and be on pickling duty like everyone else, until I dropped a jar and it shattered on the floor with a noise like gunfire. Which is why I'm in a box under the table playing, silent and ashamed.

Only Grandpa and Daddie like eating pickled onions, but every year the harvest from the kitchen garden is preserved for presents, village fêtes and the Harvest Festival, and nobody complains. Satisfied that everything is filled and sealed to his specification, Grandpa carries off two more jars into the larder.

This time, I push the Fire Engine off my lap, tip the

cardboard box over onto its side and trot after him.

In this larder, Grandpa is harvesting Kilner Jars. In the gentle cave-like light they glow and glint like jewels: amber of Seville marmalade, jade of green tomato chutney, emerald salted runner beans, ruby red strawberry jam and pearly onions. And last year's walnuts, black as the blackest-black.

The larder is big, almost as big as my bedroom. Opposite the door is a window covered in a zinc grill. In the garden outside, shrubs and climbers sway gently which adds to an underwater, other-worldliness. It is cool, cold even, and I'm reminded of the same damp coldness in an icehouse that we once explored with my mother.

A blue-black slate shelf runs the full length of the walls. It's as wide and deep as my bed and covered with piles of vegetables: marrow, carrots, the last of the runner beans, some of them as long as my arm, a red cabbage, and mounds of shallots. In one corner it reaches over the edge of a shallow stone sink. Here cream and butter are kept protected from the heat by a wet muslin. A Stilton as big as a pram wheel keeps company at Christmas but today its pedestalled plate stands clean and empty on the side.

Grandpa lifts a corner of the muslin. 'Nearly out of butter. Ready for a trot, Susanna?' I nod, although I wish he would call me by my proper name, and he hands me a polished clam shell as big as a table tennis bat, and a corner of waxed paper to protect the slab on my return journey. Obediently, I follow him down the passage: past the women murmuring in the kitchen, past the glass cupboards next to the back staircase and the lines of bells, through the panelled doors, frosted with stars, past the back kitchen where I know Grannie prepares owl's food, even though I can't bring myself to watch, and then two storerooms filled with everything if only Grannie can find it, until we reach the back door. Grandpa lifts the latch and we let ourselves out into the early autumn air to walk slowly down the back drive towards the farm and the dairy. Here, if the team is in, I can stand leaning the back of my head against the thick warm leg of one of the plough horses while we wait to have a wooden paddleful of butter, fresh as grass, splatted onto the silvery surface of my shell.

Present: October

The two Thelveton butter shells migrated to my own family kitchen. We lived a less formal life but I used them every year at Christmas and sometimes for parties, just as I used the Thelveton summer service, which was so extensive that Will and I divided it between us and each still had settings enough for twelve. Occasionally, I liked to take the shells from my cupboard and stroke the smooth, pearly interior. Nobody knew where they came from or how old they were.

My grandparents had rented Thelveton Grange from my grandfather's friend, Sir Jack Mann, just before the outbreak of war in 1939 in a temporary arrangement until such time as the family home, Drakes Place at Wellington in Somerset, should pass into Grandpa's guardianship. During the war, Drakes had been requisitioned for use as a home for orphaned boys, and my grandfather's mother (by this time a widow) had come to live at Thelveton for her last years, dying before the end of the war. It was due to Grandpa's patriotic generosity (or was it xenophobia?) that an initial request from the Americans had been turned down; had he accepted, Drakes may well be in the family today, as all properties used by US personnel were fully restored before being handed back to the owners. On return to the family by the British government, however, Drakes was so profoundly damaged that, in the absence of the necessary wealth to repair it and with no money from an almost bankrupt nation, they did the only thing possible, which was to sell up. The great unwieldy house went for a pittance, Grandpa lost his *raison d'être,* the temporary arrangement at the Grange became permanent and my grandfather spent the rest of his life grieving for a house that had been his to sell, but which he had never owned long enough to live in.

Jack lived 'up the drive' about half a mile away in bachelor isolation at Thelveton Hall, a splendid Elizabethan palace of Tudor brick and leaded windows set in extensive grounds, where the rooms were as big as tennis courts and as cold as death, and there was not a wireless to be found except, perhaps, in the butler's pantry.

During the long years of the war Jack could be found every evening, plodding his way towards the Grange in order to listen to the nine o'clock news sputtering from my grandmother's round Bakelite Ekco and drink a glass of my grandfather's whisky.

Jack had two loves: shooting and horses, and the

estate was designed for both. He kept his horses well into the nineteen-sixties, long after other, more money-conscious, farmers had switched to tractor power. It was good for the land and the pheasants, but he was also an altruist and farming with horses was labour-intensive, providing a good number of local men with a job for life. My grandfather approved, and his friend Jack's benign eccentricity ensured that my nineteen-thirties style childhood continued beyond the gates of my grandparents' house.

There was a certain serendipity for my father in having Jack as a neighbour in Norfolk. Prior to the start of the National Health Service in 1948 and the abolition of the House Committee of the London Hospital in the Mile End Road to make way for the new Group Hospital Management Committee, Jack Mann had been chairman. By 1952, when the NHS was four years old and my father became ill, Jack was still heavily involved.

My mother and grandmother decided that The London Hospital (today The Royal London) was the perfect alternative to Uxbridge when isolation was no longer imperative. My mother told me that the journey from Iver was manageable for frequent visiting by train or even by car—un-metered parking was available directly outside the hospital on the road—and there was a fairly straightforward route from Thelveton, catching the train at Diss, to Liverpool Street via the LNER line. Together they worked on Jack until, finally, he announced that he had arranged to make a place available at The London on the men's orthopaedic ward.

Uxbridge: December, 1952

'You must take them something.'

'What sort of something?' Diana asked her mother the day before Push was due to be moved. She'd gone to Berkhamsted to tell her parents the good news in person.

'Something to show your appreciation and to say Thank you.'

'Thank you for nothing.'

'Nevertheless. It will be expected.'

'I'll make a cake. Susie will help me, I'm sure.'

'That'll be perfect.'

Diana baked a large Victoria sponge under the watchful eye of Susie, their housekeeper who had come with them when they moved south from Ayr in Scotland. It had four eggs in it: the whole week's ration and most of their sugar ration, too. Jam was no longer rationed so Susie gave Diana a full jar of strawberry jam from the summer crop and she filled the cake generously. It was a beautiful cake and they both admired the finished result.

'I always knew you'd be a guid little cook if you tried,' said Susie in her tight Perth accent. 'Though why you're taking it to those graceless good-for-nothings I'll never know. It's your Mr. Push who should be eating a cake as grand as that.'

'I don't like to leave things on a sour note and they have got him this far.'

'Aye, but you'll no be sad to see the back of them, I'll be bound.' Susie busied herself with finding a tin into which to put the cake. Still with her back to Diana, she suddenly said, 'You'll be moving back here to Larchmoor, I'll be guessing. You'll not be wanting to stay in your wee house at Iver all by yourself over Christmas.' She found a tin that she approved of and brought it to the table. 'Just temporary, of course, until you can be together again.'

The next day, Ma P arrived. She and Diana went over to Uxbridge together and took the cake and an empty leather grip to collect Push's belongings. At the entrance, locked as always, they rang the bell. The pretty matron opened the door and told them that Push had already been taken by ambulance to The London that morning. Nobody had contacted Diana to say he was on his way.

She recovered from her surprise and disappointment, grateful only that Jack's promise had been acted upon so quickly. She held out the cake in its floral tin. 'I just wanted to give you this,' she said with a smile.

The matron looked at the tin and then at Diana. She didn't make any move to take it or to return Diana's smile. 'What's this?' she said. 'A bribe?'

Diana felt her smile slip from her face. She couldn't quite believe what she'd heard. 'No,' she floundered. 'A bribe? What for? It's just a cake to say thank you for looking after my husband.'

The next time Diana would see Push, she consoled herself as they left the Uxbridge Isolation Hospital, they would be able to speak to each other for the first time in eight weeks without a glass window between them. Since getting married, they had been separated by that glass longer than they had been together.

Present: October

It was mid-morning. A pale sun had struggled through to light droplets hanging from a thousand cobwebs on the grass that I ran through that morning, and finally the early mist had rolled off the water meadows at the edge of the garden. The *liquidambar styraciflua*, grown in the twenty-odd years since we'd moved here from a small whip to a perfectly conical tree of over forty feet, had begun its autumnal transformation. Its maple-shaped leaves taking on burgundy hues, vibrant reds and translucent lemon yellows. The previous owners planted this American sweet gum shortly before they left and every year I blessed their garden wisdom, foresight and generosity. Here was something to value that my new family had inherited from outside my past, and it was almost impossible not to feel uplifted and restored while a tree of such extravagance stood near.

With all this beauty to ground me, I reflected upon the facts: my father caught polio, he was kept apart from his family for eight weeks, he was paralysed, he was never put in the iron-lung. His family had got him out of isolation. This is the truth that I would pass on to my children about their grandfather. And I resolved to enfold this truth in something else I'd learned, a gift to be taken out and used at times when a gift is far from thought. Do not hold back the truth; veracity can be agony, but uncertainty is worse.

Burnage, Iver: 1952

On the twelfth of December, Diana sat down to write the first of what would turn out to be well over a hundred letters.

I'm so happy, she wrote, *that the London has turned out to be so nice—I feel absolutely confident in... the atmosphere of efficiency and friendliness and humanity hits you like a bomb after St Johns at Uxbridge.* She felt as if they just had to *get over this one last hurdle,* and all would be fine and, crucially, back to normal.

After spending so many weeks communicating by shouting or trying to lipread through the window, the first time that Diana visited Push and was able to stand in the same room or sit by his bed, she found herself tongue-tied. All she could do was hold Push's hand and say how wonderful Jack Mann had been.

She resolved to write Push a short letter every day and visit him twice a week. Despite all they'd been through over the past few weeks, she realised that they still didn't know each other very well and she found it easier to gather her thoughts quietly at home. She looked forward to the time when she could receive the odd letter between visiting days, but Push wouldn't be able to start writing for many weeks.

He had begun a little occupational therapy in Uxbridge, but it had been little more than the basket she'd observed him making when his back had been so weak, his nose almost in his work. At the London, the regime was very different and he was encouraged to begin a programme of serious physiotherapy as soon as possible. Seeing Push begin to sit upright was a tremendous morale boost to them both.

Alone at Burnage in Iver, Diana had started an ambitious knitting project for Push's Christmas present, working on the garden, and travelling to Uxbridge every day. But Susie's predictions had been spot on and life in her married home became increasingly irksome. She had no job, having had to give up her work as secretary in the House of Commons Library a few weeks before their wedding; married women not being allowed to work there. She had shared a flat with two other girls in Notting Hill from where they had enjoyed a lively London social life, and she'd found her job stimulating and exciting. Exactly a year before she'd been part of a delegation sent to Strasbourg where she'd worked at the Council of Europe. After a hectic twelve months of Strasbourg then London, watching Push racing for the Olympic trials and planning their wedding, the quiet village of Iver couldn't offer very much in the way of distraction for a young bride of twenty-three thrown into bewildering circumstances. She stuck it out for the two months that Push was in the isolation hospital because it made a base that was convenient for travelling, but the house they had chosen together was hardly a cosy home. They'd only lived in it a few weeks. What's more, a few days after Push was taken to Uxbridge, she had been turned out of her own bedroom when a man from the Sanitation Department had taken all the bedclothes away to be sterilised, and taped up their room so that it couldn't be used.

Christmas that year was very different from the one that Diana had imagined. The day that Push went to the London, Diana moved back into her family home with Push's blessing. In doing so, she could cast herself solely as Push's motivator and rock. She had lived away from home for several years, so was perfectly able to make decisions and care for herself, however she had expected, if not to be dominated by her husband, at least to be directed and guided. She had always taken her lead from Push and reflected it back unaltered. What made it easy for her was her implicit belief that Push was an exceptional person. Determination was a trait she recognised in herself.

On December twenty-third, Diana went to Hanbury Ward, to find Push talking to the ward sister. Even from the doorway, Diana could see that Push looked excited. She walked down the long ward and was greeted by several of the men, who had come to recognise her.

'Good afternoon, Mrs. Pulman.' Mr. Barnes was a consultant dentist in the neighbouring bed to Push. 'Good news, I think, for you today.'

Push looked up and smiled. 'Didie! I've something to show you.'

Sis gently took off the thick sock keeping Push's left foot warm, lifted his leg and rested the knee over her arm so that the foot was hanging loose. 'He's been practising this for the last couple of days. We're very pleased with him.'

Diana watched as Push looked at his foot with great concentration. All at once his big toe flickered, his ankle twitched and then his whole foot made a small but distinct movement.

'It moved! Push, your foot moved! I knew you could do it.' Sis, Push and Mr. Barnes were all grinning fit to bust at her; she felt her own mouth widen with delight.

'Well, Pete, that's a good Christmas present for you both.' Mr. Barnes called him Pete as a variation on PT, Push's initials, and the name stuck.

'It most certainly is,' said Push as Sis eased his sock back on, then slipped away to see another visitor so that Diana and Push could hold each other in their excitement.

'I felt that this Christmas was going to be a rather sad one a few days ago,' Diana said into Push's shoulder. 'But now it isn't after all.'

'No, you're right. Now I can make little movements, I don't mind nearly so much because I can keep practising them and I really feel I'm getting somewhere.'

'You will be soon. Getting somewhere, I mean. Getting all the way down the ward and out.' It was a silly joke but they couldn't stop laughing, and suddenly the day didn't seem so bad after all.

Chapter Four

Present: October

'I'm sure you'll want to chuck them away but Mum didn't want to go through them all, and we thought you just might find something useful.'

Will had arrived at my house, bringing with him two oil-starved leather stationery cases and three cardboard boxes of increasing size, each releasing a fusty fragrance not unlike some of the lesser-used spaces at Thelveton. I doubted that they'd been opened in twenty years.

We hauled them into the middle of my sitting room and Will sprawled on the sofa while I sat on the floor. It had been several years since my father had died and now our mother wanted a clear out. She'd asked Will to travel up from the West Country to help her with sorting the study and his workshop. All the tools and machines that were no use to Will were going to my father's friends Angus and Susan (who, for years, were notable for having a stuffed mechanical elephant in their barn). Both were as skilled engineers as they were unconventional and my father had loved them dearly. The rest would have to be assessed, piece by piece.

Will suggested that we open the first case together.

It was small, brown and dry as an old conker. Our father's initials, PTP (Prockter Thomas Pulman) were stamped in black on the centre of the lid but across the bottom left-hand corner, curiously, was stamped in the same black, serif typeface, 23 April, 1931. He would have been just over five-and-a-half years old.

As we went through the photographs inside, I was struck by how like our father Will now looked. He wasn't as tall as our father's six feet, and four inches, but he had the same strikingly healthy appearance: sun-blonde hair—although it'd become darker over the years—wide mouth and powerful shoulders and forearms. My father gave me his grey eyes and his sensitivity to sun; Will had inherited our mother's freckle-free brown skin and eyes of a deep marine blue. His hands, despite being very large, were delicately picking over the pictures. Encircling the little finger on his left hand was a heavy, gold signet ring. They could have been the hands of my father.

Mostly we dug out formal photographs of rowing crews from time spent in the RAF, at Cambridge, as a member of the London Rowing Club or competing at Henley Rowing Regatta. And then something altogether different emerged.

'Here's the Snowdon picture,' Will said, unwrapping thick brown paper from a ten-by-eight black and white print.

It was smaller than I remembered, and the faces of our parents so very young. Anthony Armstrong-Jones (later Lord Snowdon), four years our father's junior, had just overlapped at Eton but was a contemporary at

Cambridge during our father's post graduate time and was, according to our parents, never to be seen without a camera slung around his neck. Early one morning, the dawn following the 1952 May Ball at Clare College, our parents were strolling over Clare Bridge when, so the story goes, Tony called out, 'Hey, Push!' and the image was captured. Will turned the picture over. Pencilled mark-up lines showed how the picture was to be cropped, *The Tatler and Bystander* was rubber-stamped in purple ink on the back and the caption to be used written in fountain pen: 'Mr P.T. Pulman, who used to be up at Clare College looks over the bridge with Miss DIANA LATTA.'

But history must have been confused, because the couple in the picture weren't looking sideways towards the bank and the photographer, they were looking down at the river, presumably at someone in a punt beneath them. My father, resting an arm on one of the stone spheres that adorn the bridge, was leaning over the parapet. My mother was a little ahead of him and had turned back to see who he was talking to. They were resplendent in evening dress, a couple in the background were chatting and smoking and the sky had just begun to lighten with early dawn streaks of sunlight. It must have been about half past three on a midsummer morning and they were smiling. Such smiles! So wide and carefree and untouched. And on our mother's finger we could see quite clearly, her diamond engagement ring, a ring that had belonged in the Pulman family for generations before it was stolen in a burglary when I was ten.

Will slipped the protective paper off another picture. We'd seen this one before, but only in the magazine for which it was taken; I couldn't remember the original. It was a portrait in profile of our mother taken by the American society photographer Pearl Freeman for *Mayfair* magazine, at the time of her engagement on October 20th, 1951. She was twenty-two, with dark hair waved in the style of the time and wearing a dress in blue silk chiffon with a pink pleated in-fill to cover her décolletage. Wound around her neck was the same string of pearls she still wore today. The picture was black and white, but I knew the dress was blue with pink because I'd once seen it hanging in my mother's wardrobe. She'd told me of her panic to finish making it and how she'd had to stay up half the night sewing, so that she'd have something suitable to wear for a grand party to which she'd been invited at the last minute. Even then, when under pressure, our mother proved that she could rise to the occasion spectacularly.

We laid the photographs aside and delved into the cardboard boxes: cheque stubs, piles and piles of letters, contracts for letting the house in Iver (a maximum of six months at a time; ever hopeful that they would return). An unopened advent calendar for 1955 attached to a story by Dorothy L. Sayers, boxes in boxes, manilla envelopes, more newspaper cuttings. What was all this stuff, why was it never thrown away, and what were we supposed to do with it?

Then, two things that I never expected.

'What do you think this says?' I pushed a torn and folded sheet of cream pale blue Basildon Bond across the table towards my brother. He leaned forward, picked it up and relaxed into the cushions of the sofa again as he opened the notepaper and tilted it to catch the last of the afternoon light through the window behind him.

'I think it's his name, P. T. Pulman,' he decided, finally. 'He leaned forward again to examine it more closely. 'But it's quite hard to tell. It's very wobbly. I wonder why he kept it.'

'I think so, too.' I reached my hand out for another look. At first glance it had seemed like nothing more than random marks made by mistake, but something had made me look closer. 'I think maybe he wrote it when he was learning to write again. Perhaps he couldn't for a while and then this was the first time that he managed to write his own name.'

I couldn't help it, but I kept staring at the little signature written in the faintest, scratchy ball-point pen ink. I imagined the relief and pride when he had managed to uncurl those great hands of his and grasp a pen with enough control to move it across the paper so that it began to spell out his name.

All at once, I was certain that my reluctance to give a description of my father's condition stemmed from his own difficulties with identity. I'd never felt like the daughter of a disabled person, but I'd always been happy to be recognised as Push's daughter. My father worked with his brain and with his hands, so recovering the use of his hands was paramount. He was proud to be a research and development engineer, he would wish to be remembered as an engineer, and I had always been an engineer's daughter. I raised the scrap of paper closer to my eyes and examined the feathery marks.

Will drank his tea, one arm stretched along the back of the sofa, and looked calmly into the garden. He didn't attempt to break the silence. I laid the paper to one side, got up to switch on some lamps and we resumed opening cigarette boxes. Then I had the second shock. I discovered a picture so private and surprising that to look at it at all felt like I'd crossed a line. Silently I passed the tiny portrait-style, black and white and slightly curling-at-the-edges photograph to Will.

'I don't think I've ever seen a picture of him actually in hospital,' he said, at last.

'Or alone.'

I'd never thought of it before, but I'd rarely seen our father pictured unless he was part of a group—with me and Will, our mother, or friends—or in the carefree times before he was ill. Photographs of our father at the time of illness and recovery were conspicuous by their absence; as though it simply wasn't the done thing to make a record when he was not as he wished to be.

I got up off the floor and sat down beside my brother. Although we'd often discussed memories of our father, this is the nearest we'd ever come to sharing how we felt about him. Together we studied the picture anxious to take in every detail, from the striped pyjamas that exposed his fragile ankle bones to the depressing, home knitted bed-jacket with its uneven hemline.

Will pointed to the bottom of the picture. 'Look at his feet. He's wearing heavy leather business shoes?'

'With no socks.'

We looked at each other in disbelief.

Standing at an open French door, the man who was to become our father faced the photographer who must have been on a balcony or perhaps in the garden. His arms were locked straight with his hands holding the ends of a pair of parallel bars that disappeared behind him into the dark ward beyond. At Thelveton there were long lengths of metal exercise bars, like scaffolding, screwed to the floor on an upstairs landing outside the laundry cupboards. I don't suppose we gave a passing thought to them at the time; they were part of Thelveton's fixtures and fittings and were as familiar to us as the brass door handles, the baize-covered swing doors or pots of cacti and rose-scented geraniums that adorned every windowsill. Parallel bars, standing upright from a landing floor were simply some-thing we grew up with. But we never, ever saw them being used. And here he was, not with others or at Thelveton but unmistakably in hospital, and some unknown photogra-pher had captured my father, alone with the bars.

And, more surprising than even the existence of the picture was the expression on his face, which was one of wild, abandoned joy.

The London Hospital: 1952

It was Boxing Day; the hospital was short-staffed over the holiday and on Christmas Day had been closed to visitors. As soon as the bell rang, Diana streamed into the hospi-tal with dozens of other visitors; they clacked down the polished corridors marking the start of visiting time—two hours, from two until four—not one minute early and not one minute late.

Hanbury ward was as spotless and bare as always—no tree, no decorations, nothing specific to indicate that Christmas was here—but there was a buzz of excitement and something different that made the large room welcoming and warm.

Most of the men had family arriving at the same time as Diana. Those without greeted her as usual and wished her a Merry Christmas.

'You'd have thought they might extend the visiting hours a little over Christmas, especially since we couldn't see you on the big day itself.' Diana felt slightly aggrieved that she would inevitably have to share Push with several other visitors. 'It goes so quickly.'

'I'll sort out a rota and David can tell everyone else,' said Push. 'Now, come here.' He reached for her with his long arms. 'We need a Christmas kiss,' and he caught her in a bear hug.

Mr Barnes smiled at her from the next bed; he was alone. 'The best of Christmas wishes to you, Diana. He's been getting on well with his exercises, haven't you, Pete? Not one for giving yourself a holiday.'

'What's so good about this place is that they give you techniques to practice on your own, Didie. And I got my knee to bend a little today.'

'You won't wear yourself out, will you, Push?'

'No fear. They say the more I can do, the better.' He squeezed her waist and she laid her head on his shoulder, reassured. 'Now, you'll have to sit up because I've got a

Christmas present for you.' He directed her to his bedside locker and she saw a small package done up in pale green tissue paper and a gold ribbon.

'How pretty. Whatever is it?'

'Well, open it and then you'll find out.'

She undid the ribbon and gently folded back the paper. A pair of deep-red gloves lay on the tissue. She picked them up and held the butter-soft kid against her cheek. 'They're beautiful. And look! Three perfect little buttons on each wrist. These are just beautiful, Push. Thank you so much.' She turned his face towards her and kissed him.

'It was Mother, really. The gloves were my idea because you have to travel so often to see me, and I remembered that you said you'd bought your bag in Marshall and Snellgrove so Mother went to see if she could get gloves to match.'

'What a clever family I've married into,' said Diana. 'And speaking of presents, I've got something in here for you.' She pulled a soft parcel from her bag and placed it in Push's lap.

'For me?'

Diana watched how Push shifted his weight on the bed to support his back then jammed an elbow into the side of his pillows for balance in order to use both hands to open the wrapping. She didn't try to intervene, but to her alarm his face suddenly screwed up in pain.

'Oh, Push!'

The parcel slipped to the floor as he lurched forward, scrabbling with his hands to find a place to grip the side of the bed. He locked his elbows and held himself supported in the air for a moment or two. All too soon, his arms started shaking, his breath came in short gasps and then he very gently, returned to a sitting position.

'Shall I get Sis?' Diana was always frightened to see her strong Push in such obvious pain.

'No, I'll be fine. Just give me a moment or two.'

Diana watched as Push closed his eyes and concentrated on getting his breathing back to normal. Beads of sweat appeared at his temples and his hair hang damply over his face but she knew better than to argue or distract him. When he opened his eyes and gave her a small smile, she said, 'It's your poor pom again, isn't it?'

'It's fine.'

'It's not fine. Can't they find anything to help? And what about your heels?'

Push made a face.

'Uxbridge. That place...' Diana shook her head. 'I thank God every day that Jack Mann was able to get you out of there.'

'Come on, Didie. Let's not think about that today. It's Christmas and you were about to give me a present, which I have just ungratefully dropped on the floor. I only hope it wasn't a glass vase.'

Diana retrieved the parcel and put it back on the bed with a grin. It didn't matter what the circumstances were; Push was always able to make her smile. But she was worried about this extra pain. Ever since a fistula had developed as a result of the exhaustive training in the summer, it had remained horribly resistant to treatment, even defying a once and for all operation the week they'd returned from their honeymoon. It seemed so unfair that, just as he was getting well enough to sit up a bit, he should suffer so much, particularly as this had nothing to do with the polio.

'If you don't mind, Didie, I think you'd better help me. I don't want to frighten everyone by falling out of bed.'

Diana undid the parcel that she had wrapped that morning. She had made the finishing touches to her present only the night before and she hoped it would fit. Push pulled the last of the paper away and smoothed out the sleeveless jumper that she'd knitted from creamy-brown lamb's wool with a Fair Isle pattern in greens, yellows and browns decorating the top third. It was complicated and intricate and it was a labour of love.

'I made it.' She was unable to hide her pride or wait for him to ask.

'You made it? You mean you knitted all this Fair Isle?' Push turned the jumper over. 'Front and back. You are clever, Didie.'

Diana loved how Push always showed genuine admiration for anything creative and skilled. 'I did it from a pattern. I didn't make it up.'

'It's far harder to follow a pattern.' He kissed her. 'Thank you, Didie. It's absolutely what I need in here. I can be warm without having to fuss with getting in and out of sleeves.' He looked over Diana's shoulder. 'Here's David coming now. Quickly, I need to ask you if you've spoken to Mother about Burnage.'

'Not yet. I thought I'd wait until I got to Thelveton after New Year.'

'Fine. But you won't forget, will you? We can't go

70

on paying the mortgage with no money coming in and you not even living there. And I'm worried about keeping it secure with no one there to look after it.'

Present: October

Casting a fresh eye over the first few letters from 1953, I saw my family's word for backside crop up again and again. For as long as I'd been aware, my father's comfort, or most likely discomfort, was rarely about his legs, instead it centred on the part of his body that took his weight. He seldom complained but would reply, when asked if he was hurting, 'my pom's giving me a bit of gyp' or 'problems with my pom'.

My father's backside was a cause for great concern and, in what was to become a long list of obstructions to his recovery, a particularly frustrating one. Put simply, an anal fistula born of the abscess he had sustained while training for the Olympic selections—a not uncommon complaint for oarsmen in those days—kept breaking down and was exacerbated by exercise. The cure was to lie still but the pressure sores on his heels inflicted in the early weeks could not sustain further stress. As always, the balance between rest and movement became a source of debate between the doctors and their nursing staff.

These were the first shoots of a conflict that was to dog the rest of my father's life: the search for a balance between what he needed to maintain health—both physically and mentally—and what his body could endure. We once had a conversation about mind over matter. It was a tiny vignette of first-hand description to support the fragile jigsaw puzzle that I was beginning to piece together and I was certain that it belonged in early January 1953.

He explained that in the physical therapy room, he could take the pressure off his back and heels by lying on his stomach on a couch set up with a mirror beneath, angled in such a way that he could see his own feet. Away from the other men on the ward, my father would drive himself for hours staring at the mirror, in the effort to extend the small movements of vandalised muscles in his toes and visualise the new pathways that his stimulated motor nerves must take to form and grow.

'You can achieve a lot through visualisation,' he'd insisted. I think we might have been talking about tennis matches or possibly exams, and he believed in applying this technique to many areas of life.

It's true that in many cases the paralysis could be reversed: polio survivors from the 1930s had fellow sufferer, Franklin D Roosevelt, the former president of the United States, to thank for that. Although today it's thought that Roosevelt's paralysis was not due to polio, but the equally debilitating condition known as Guillain–Barré syndrome, FDR's foundation at Warm Springs nevertheless developed mobility techniques used all around the world for treating polio; previously the treatment had been complete rest, with frequently disastrous results.

My father made himself into a polio expert in a very short space of time, badgering the doctors to explain the exact mechanics of recovery, frequently asking them to draw diagrams and working himself to exhaustion with a whole phalanx of therapists whom he quizzed at length about the methods used by Sister Kenny, an Australian nurse using revolutionary new polio treatments in the United States.

I wondered when the tipping point had occurred. The point at which my father felt he might have a future worth fighting for. Clearly sometime after that first Christmas and early summer of 1953, he could see real improvements. The body may have been damaged, but the engineer's mind was fit and well and making it its business to explore, analyse and look for a solution.

Chapter Five

Present: October

I cleared my diary so I could lose myself in my mother's letters. Her writing had barely changed in fifty years and her personality seemed to materialise off the page as if her twenty-three year old self were standing right beside me. There she was in my mind's eye, dressed in a floral shirtwaister, small velvet hat like a fist of red petals on the crown of her head with a woollen coat tucked tidily over one arm. Desperate and optimistic, chatty and innocent, and so, so young to be dealing with all this agony. This wasn't a sterile family history as we'd been fed before, this was very much my history, his-story, her-story and the story of what would become my future. I was taking two steps backwards—back into my parents' past, and back into my own childhood—to finally move forwards.

What I had was a one-sided conversation but despite this, I was aware of my father's state of mind, as well as the day-to-day developments and improvements in his physical health. My mother's words concealed nothing and opening each letter was akin to peeling back layer-after-layer of protective tissue to reveal the true natures of both my parents. These were the characters, then, from whom I was made;

this couple full of indefatigable spirit and buoyant trust in their future, before the burden of endless false hopes introduced to my father a level of wary pessimism.

I had thought that my mother's tendency to square her shoulders, stick a determined chin forward and face what was coming head on, must have been born of these times, but it was clear from the first letter that this has always been her character.

Together, my parents saw what they thought lay ahead, they made decisions, and in just a few days, my mother had, efficiently and without any self-pity, made arrangements for Burnage, the home they had barely lived in together, to be rented out for the princely sum of £25 a month.

That last night she lay trying to sleep in her marital home surrounded by packing cases, alone and ill. It was typical of my mother that she dismissed it in a sentence, writing that she was horribly sick all night and 'must have eaten something my tum didn't like!' A great wave of sympathy welled up when I read her brave words but it was all too obvious that the emotional turmoil of packing her home away in crates, and by implication her marriage, had finally found a chink in her armour. And her own mother was also in hospital, not for the first time—she had her own continuing mental health difficulties—which must have added to the stress of those past few months.

In the morning, help arrived to transport the last of the boxes and their personal belongings back to Larchmoor and by the end of the day, just four months after the start of their marriage, my mother was once more living with her parents.

In almost every letter there was a reference to Thelveton. On her wedding day she changed her surname from Latta to Pulman in a moment, but clearly it wasn't only her name that had changed. In her heart she shucked off her own family and embraced the Pulman mantle, accepting without question that the new aim was, not to get her husband well and back to Burnage—or even to Larchmoor—but to get him well enough to return to Thelveton.

In the New Year, she visited her in-laws in Norfolk and continued to write letters. Her optimism was impressive, bouncing words off the page like fizz in the cocktails at the many parties she enjoyed, dancing from one subject to another, people, friends and family pets all making an appearance, and liberally scattering dashes and exclamation marks impulsively.

Thelveton: 4th January, 1953

My darling Push,

Here I am at Thelveton having a lovely lazy time— eating an enormous amount! In fact I feel rather guilty. However I really am enjoying it.

Willie [Push's younger brother] came up by train yesterday afternoon and we went and had dinner with the Michells in the evening. A sumptuous dinner, with all the men in dinner jackets. After dinner the "young" were left to their own devices. We played charades—something I haven't done for years—but great fun—& finally left after 1.30—in a blizzardy snow-storm. Willie goes back this afternoon in his car, which I must say looks lovely—he has had it painted black all over now.

Marjy is here—the same as ever—. We are busy choosing 'Charm Models' in order of merit in the "Sunday Graphic" the same idea as our Motor Competition. I hope I may win £400 on this one!! Some hope!

A Squadron Leader Marland has rung us up here & is interested in letting 'Burnage"—I'm not doing anything until we have seen Hobhouse [their solicitor] *on Wednesday & then if all is in order Ma P will come down to Burnage on Thursday & will help me show him round—but that will just be a preliminary of course. He hasn't any children—but has a cocker spaniel—which sounds as though he might be quite nice—!*

I hope I haven't given you my sore throat that I had on Friday—Ma P dosed me up when I arrived here in the evening & it is only rather a faint cold now, instead of being a real big sniffle!

It seems very queer being here without you as I associate Thelveton with you so much—but in a way it's rather nice to know it's all just the same as ever, waiting for you when you come back.

Foxy Dog for one is the same—he disgraced himself in the hall yesterday! & so Pa P is raging about & quite furious with him!!

Willie told me you gave him a demonstration of the left foot on Friday evening! Let me know when there are any more "private viewings" on show!!

Please give my very best regards to your partner in crime "Monsieur Barnes" & don't forget I love you very, very much— "Didie"

Present: November

There are times when my mother's words brought me close to tears but often, and especially when her references moved from London to Norfolk, I couldn't help smile in recognition. Even as a child, Thelveton felt like an island marooned in its past, an island on which I was desperate to remain. To my friends at school I must have appeared an alien from another planet. They went to fashionable continental holiday destinations every summer and conversation was littered with Mary Quant, the Monkees, and Melody Maker. They knew precisely how short to wear their skirts, listened to the weekly pop charts without fail, and understood exactly when to use 'cool', 'groovy' and 'hip'. I'd never been abroad, wasn't bothered about clothes despite my mother's interest in fashion, and the only unusual words I cared about were those we made up ourselves. It wasn't that I couldn't find a way to fit in, I simply wasn't interested and the things that absorbed other children seemed hardly worth the time it took to have the conversation. I read books about Arthurian legends and heraldry. I'd never been skiing, but wore hideous corduroy ski pants with hand-knitted jumpers without a care, and buttoned my shirts up to the chin. I was good at craft and sold my creations in a local gallery. I could build a fire and light it from a spark. I knew the folk names of common plants and birds, how to splint a bird's wing and that you could raise an orphaned rabbit kitten but rarely a leveret.

In time, of course, I learned to integrate and in later life I chose to shed much of Thelveton's private and anachronistic world. But reading it off the page, I realised what fond memories I still carried with me, and how quickly the tinder-glow of those lost times might flare up if we could have brought them back.

A love of language was in my genes. As a family we plunged into words with abandon, like a terrier after a rabbit down a hole. Changes, adjustments and improvements cascaded around us like dirt. We pulled and stretched our native tongue, added extra letters, wantonly changed spellings and names or exacted new pronunciations to our liking and delighted amusement.

The tobacconist became the toe-beh-coe-nist. Mrs Mullinger dusted the wireless and 'played haddock' with the dials. We ate with nap-tables on our laps, counted telephone-graph poles alongside the roads and drove to church, not in my grandparents' Austin 10, but in Little Old. Family lore has it that my Uncle Willie insisted on playing the sello and, upon polite correction from my mother, at a time then unversed in the ways of Pulmanaria, he replied teasingly po-faced, 'You may chose to call it the cello, but I prefer the sello'.

Preferring something was what it was all about.

While most of these were peculiar to the family, and we were not unique in having family words, the Alfalfa language was in an altogether different league. Devised and perfected by my father with his University friends and comprising an extra L and F after each vowel, as soon as my brother and I were old enough to twist our tongues around its tangled consonants, we adopted Alfalfa with enthusiasm.

Will and I practised diligently and soon we could speak it as proficiently as my father and uncle. For a time, we did just that, all four of us speaking Alfalfa whenever we were in public, to the irritation of my grandmother and mother, who steadfastly refused to join in. We were already different by dint of my father's all too obvious wheelchair, so my family made being different something exclusive and important. Unlike most children, we weren't afraid to plough our own furrow, and we loved Alfalfa especially because it was something of my father's past that he shared with us.

My grandfather had a fear of being thought ordinary. My grandmother was the daughter of a Welsh parson; the Italian in her ancestry, her grandmother, was studiously ignored. Grandpa considered himself Gentry and although he despised the label, nevertheless felt, if not a cut above, at least a cut apart. We aped Nancy Mitford's U and non-U without knowing that it existed; we knew all that was "jolly utter" instinctively and wouldn't dream of saying servi-ette, lounge, toilet or going-to-the-coast, but became more exclusive still with our own impenetrable family idiolect.

Grandpa had a gigantically inflated sense of family, more suited to Sicily than an old Devon family uprooted via Somerset into East Anglia. He accepted only a few select first names as genuine Pulman, names that went back cen-turies, repeating themselves like a loop: William, Prockter (another unusual spelling), Thomas and Walker. When I unrolled the vast family tree that he had meticulously made his life work, I could see that the surnames of the women they married were appropriated as Christian names, perhaps to keep the family name alive when there were only daughters. Grandpa was baptised William Prockter but, as a young man was known as Push and later suffered the indignity of being known as Prock, his own father also being a William. He inflicted this ghastly nomenclature on his elder son, my father, Prockter Thomas, who immediately became Push, which was curiously prescient for someone who would spend two thirds of his life in a wheelchair. He was PT or Push to friends and family but, from the letters in the boxes that Will had brought to my house, it seemed that in hospital he was known almost universally as Pete, or even Peter. It saved intrusive enquiries about the initials PT.

Primogeniture featured large in Grandpa's list of priorities, but family names were not reserved for male children. When I was born his will descended on my mother's new-birth excitement with the force of falling masonry.

She will be called Susanna, he decreed.

She won't, insisted my mother, with the first of many small rebellions. Fierce, Scottish Presbyterian stock was more than a match for him and Grandpa retired into his smoking room. However, he called me Susanna until his dying day.

Home, Suffolk: 1971

'Come into the workshop, Sarah. I want to talk to you,' Daddie says after breakfast one morning and my heart drops like a lead weight. It's that use of my proper name that does it. To be called in just by myself always means that it'll be serious, but calling me Sarah instead of Sarie means that I've done something dreadful.

As I wait for him to collect letters, reading glasses and notes into a pile and balance them on his lap, I cast about desperately for the terrible thing I may have done, but I can't come up with anything that couldn't be said in front of the rest of the family.

We bobble across the cobbles to the workshop and Daddie delves into the pocket of his tweed jacket for the key. Once in, he asks me to get the folding garden chair that he keeps for visitors in the corner. I put it up beside his desk amongst the dust and dirt and crumpled dried leaves that have blown in through the open door. The green marbled lino is dry and cracked and has become so brittle that parts of it have broken away.

Daddie's desk is wide and solid like everything he designs and makes. Its lines are pure and functional and I remember, when I was six or seven, helping to hold parts of the drawers together while he glued and screwed them. Now these drawers are full of paper and it has become so difficult to open and close them that he leaves the top one permanently open, on which to balance more paper like a shelf.

'Sit down.'

I sit in the garden chair on the blue seaside-striped nylon material slung between aluminium tubes and immediately static electricity grabs my hair sticking it in a fan behind my head. A wheelchair is higher than a dining chair—one of the reasons Daddie had to make his own desk—and the garden chair is lower. I'm about level with the sludge-coloured knot of his knitted tie. I sit in an enforced relaxed position because to lean forward and look as if I'm concentrating might cause the chair to suddenly fold itself up and tip me onto the floor. This has happened before and I'm in no hurry to make myself look a fool before he's even started to tell me how I am one.

Daddie makes a small three-point turn, then rolls his chair to face me.

'Now that you're thirteen,' he begins gravely, 'I've decided that it's time to talk to you about some family things.'

I feel the blood seep back into my veins and my heart rate reduce, just a little.

'You know about Wellington and West Monkton, of course.'

I nod, then think for a moment and shake my head too. 'Well,' I say, 'I know about Wellington.' Grandpa had been brought up at Drakes Place, Wellington. Great-grandpa had been one of the few university students to claim a blue for both cricket and rowing and I remember being told that in 1875 he'd played for Oxford against W G Grace. So, the family connection to Wellington town is well known. I might have heard the odd reference to Longforth and even West Monkton, but I can't really remember anything specific.

'The Pulmans come from the West Country,' he says, as if that were news to me.

'I know.' I have known for ever. Daddy wears a signet ring showing an otter holding a bulrush, which we've often been told with pride, shows the place of the family's origins, Ottery St. Mary in Devon.

'Somerset and Devon.' Daddy continues as though I haven't spoken. 'And although Drakes is no longer in the family, there are still farms and farmhouses in the West Country that are.'

I nod again.

'How do you think properties like that stay in families?'

I look into Daddie's pale eyes and wonder what I'm supposed to say. It seems too obvious. 'They're passed down the generations?' I try.

'That's right. They're passed down the family line.' He stops and looks at me closely. There's a large pink rose outside the dusty window behind him bobbing in the wind, and it looks as if it's tapping him on the head. 'How do you think you might pass things on fairly?'

I can feel my heart speed up a little and, regardless of the insecurity of the chair, I lean forward to show that I'm taking this conversation seriously. But I'm uncomfortable. It seems to me that we might be talking about wills, and I wish it would stop.

'Would you make sure that everyone had a bit of something?'

'I suppose so', I say slowly.

'And how would you do that?'

'I'd divide it up and give everyone the same amount.'

Daddie leans back in his chair and slips an elbow behind him under one of the white plastic handles at the back. 'That seems very reasonable.'

We look at each other for a long moment. Outside, I can hear the rose grazing the window and the distant sound of a lawn mower. I'm the first to slide my eyes away. Both windowsills are so encrusted with dust, cobwebs and dead flies that I wonder if the office has ever been cleaned. A Pirelli calendar on the wall is stuck at June 1969, showing a girl in a bikini walking out of the sea, but I can only see part of her because he's hung another calendar over the top with the picture of a magnificent silver tabby lying on its back.

'What happens if you have things you want to pass on?'

'Things?'

Daddie looks up at the ceiling, then back to me. 'Things. Items, objects, like jewellery, for instance.'

I feel myself frowning and look at my knees. 'I'm not sure. I suppose you give one thing to one person and one to the other. Another,' I add quickly, not wanting it to sound as if we are talking about Will and me.

'Land?'

I take a deep breath. 'Give one bit to one person, and another bit to...'

The outer corners of his eyebrows suddenly twitch and he looks at me as if I've fallen off the chair.

'And what happens to the house? Or the land when it gets to the second or third generation?'

'I don't know.' I screw my eyes shut for a second. 'It might all get rather small.'

'Quite.'

We share another silence and, all at once, I

deliberately refuse to think around the problem. I make my mind go blank and hold his gaze. Daddie knows where he wants this conversation to go and I'm not going to let him lead me by the nose any more.

'So what do you think has happened over the years to avoid that?'

I say nothing.

'How does a family hold on to things that are important?'

I still say nothing, but now it's his turn to stay silent and my resolve is short-lived.

'They're passed to the eldest son,' I say, eventually. There is no other answer.

'Good. You're a clever girl. I knew you'd understand.'

I carry on looking at him.

'But,' he says. 'That doesn't seem very fair on you. So, where I can, I want you to understand that I will make it up to you. You'll marry so you won't be a Pulman any-more and won't have Pulman children to pass down to. In fact you'll be part of your husband's family and he will have his own inheritance.'

Daddie has seen light at the end of the tunnel and is running with his subject, but I've stopped listening. I don't care that Will is younger than me. I understand why it has to be that he inherits the Devon stuff that I don't even know anything about. But something far more horri-fying has suddenly hit me; how can I have got to thirteen and not realised that my membership of this family isn't forever? That being a Pulman, for me, is temporary. That even if I never marry, like Great Aunt Sue and Great Aunt

Harry, and keep my name, I can never produce an official son and heir, so I'm not considered to be a true Pulman. I'm even less a true Pulman in the family's eyes than my mother, who started off a Latta and is only a Pulman by marriage. Mummie even wears a Pulman signet ring.

'We'll talk about this some more, Sarie, when you're older.' Daddie is smiling at me. 'You have my word that I'll make things right for you.'

I'm not sure if I'm supposed to say thank you, so I do, just in case. Then I scramble out of the garden chair, fold it up and put it away against the wall before leaving.

Outside, everything seems normal. I walk away from the workshop and wonder what to do. I find my mother emptying the Ransomes' grass-box into a barrow in the shade of a copper beech tree. Her skin is brown and she's wearing a pair of navy shorts, a sleeveless checked shirt and an old pair of Green Flash tennis shoes; she never wears jewellery at home except for her pearl studs and two gold rings. Both her wedding ring and the signet ring are stained green with grass-juice.

I walk up to her.

'Mummie,' I say. 'Do you think I could have a signet ring?'

'I expect so.' She rattles the grass-box onto the front of the mower. 'When you're older. Maybe when you're twenty-one.' She opens the throttle, lets in the clutch and swings the heavy mower around to start the final stretch. She follows at a brisk walk, the muscles in her arms rippling with the effort of keeping the beast under control. She glances my way as she passes me. 'Stick the kettle on, will you, Sarie? It'll be coffee time soon.'

Chapter Six

The London Hospital: New Year, 1953

To have spent their first Christmas Day apart was unthinkable, but Diana believed in fresh starts. It was a new year. What had happened was in the past, they had done it and they were through it. With Push out of danger, Diana felt a determination to tackle the bigger issues, such as work and home. The truth had hit them hard, but reality was that it frequently took twelve months or more from the first onset of illness to get polio patients rehabilitated and living at home full-time. And this was before a return to work might even be considered.

'I have good news, Didie!'

'Oh, how lovely, Push.' Diana thought he looked a little less tired than when she had last seen him nearly a week ago. She kissed him and stowed her handbag down by his locker. 'Luckily I got a parking space directly outside the main doors today. I think people must still be away because of the snow.' She shrugged out of her coat and tucked it in beside the bag. 'Now, what's this great news? Is it the new sorbo cushion that I see you're using?'

Push shook his head, took her hand and held it in his. It was warm after the freezing weather and Diana realised just how much she'd missed him over Christmas.

'It's about my heels,' he said. 'They've agreed to let them get better in their own time and so, God willing, they've promised no operations for the time being.'

'What a relief!'

'But what it really means, Didie, is that I won't have my exercises interrupted any more. If I was all bandaged up, I wouldn't be able to carry on with the physio for a while. This way, I can keep working on the progress I'm making. Look!'

Push pulled the blanket away from his feet and concentrated hard. After a moment his left foot began to move and the big toe lifted.

'Well done! That's marvellous. Soon it'll be your whole foot and then your entire leg.'

'But you do know, Didie, don't you, that it won't all happen in a trice?'

'Yes, but you couldn't be in a better place. It's got all the right staff and up-to-date knowledge and equipment to help you.' Diana looked around at the nurses handing out tea, the hoists and wheelchairs lined up against the wall and the bar dangling above Push's bed. She sat down suddenly. 'To think we'd have had to pay for all this a few years ago. We're so lucky.' She lifted Push's hand and stroked it. 'And these seem to be getting much better too. It was awfully sweet of you to write to me and such a lovely surprise. I know it's still a real effort for you, but I did so appreciate it.'

The physical therapists came several times a day and worked tirelessly to encourage mobility; any twitch or tremble was a sign that new pathways for the motor nerves were regenerating and could be developed. Movement was excruciating and exhausting but Push told Diana that he didn't mind the exhaustion and that he found the muscle charts they used to assess damage and improvements an endless source of fascination. Diana didn't doubt it, but for all his brave words, she knew that his days were frustrating and repetitive. They would both have to learn to wait.

If time passed very slowly for Push, outside Diana had hardly enough hours in the day to achieve all that she wanted to do. She'd had a tiny taste of married life—an amuse bouche—and patience had never come easily, but now she had to learn forbearance. She continued to distract herself with parties, the theatre and all the fun that London had to offer but she was also caring for Push and all his changing needs with dutiful attention. Push had said he loved her loyalty and, despite her apparent giddiness, she was not about to let him down. She loved him.

Home, Suffolk: 1968

We've been told to get ready as we're going to the sea. Daddie has a yen to see the sea about once a month. We always go to the sea; never the coast which is for swarmies, a Pulman word for tourists, nor the beach which should be all silver sand and palm trees. Our sea is usually Minsmere: cold, wind-swept and brownish-grey.

We're here in the baccus with wind cheaters and gummies on, knitted hats and red metal spades in hand,

90

waiting for Daddie to get the shooting brake out, as he calls it. We have to be ready first, never the other way round. Daddie has to pace himself because of his pain, and can never be left waiting.

He checked with us that we have the proper clothes on, that we've thought of all that we'll need, that we're warm enough. We know it'll be windy but he's told us again anyway. Then, balancing his cap, camera and newspaper on his lap, he pulled the door wide, bumped himself over the threshold and bobbled across the cobbled courtyard to the garage.

We're used to watching through the open doorway as he goes through the same sequence every time he takes us out. We might jiggle about, sigh and roll our eyes theatrically, but only to amuse ourselves. We don't really mind and we never move from our spot.

He wheels between the cars which are parked quite close together. Daddie's is the one on the right. He opens the passenger door of his car, pulls the chair as close as he can, reaches down to lift his feet on to the floor and flick up the foot plates, then he wriggles to the edge of the cushion. The chair tips alarmingly but we stay on the doorstep. This is his routine, he has to concentrate and we don't come near. We can't see from here, but we know that he is taking his weight on his shaky right arm, his huge, calloused hand spread wide on the sticky plastic of the car seat. His left arm is bent behind him, keeping his chair steady against the car. He slides with short, sharp jerks from the edge of the cushion on the wheelchair to the edge of the seat of the car. At the last minute, just as you think he must tip everything forwards, he's in. He pauses for a moment and everyone catches their breath. Then he grabs the thick sorbo cushions off the chair and sweeps them in one big swooping movement from the chair, over the back of the driver's seat and into the back. This makes a perch for Will to sit on, cushions in constant use and never a chance to cool down between backsides.

He slides across, avoiding the gear stick, onto the driver's side, dragging his legs after him. He reaches down to grab his trousers, swings his right leg up in the air and over the lump in the middle of the car to tuck it in tight by the sawn-off accelerator pedal. Repeat with the left leg and stow his foot against the clutch. Then he wriggles and reaches into his trousers to arrange and rearrange his shirt, underpants and trousers so that he's not sitting on any creases. Creases cause pressure sores, or make the ones he already has worse.

With his clothes organised to his satisfaction, he finds his special hand brake, fumbling for its socket so it sticks up between the seats like a curved black walking stick with a white snooker ball at its tip. Now he's ready to start the car and, using the hand controls next to the right side of the steering wheel, he heaves around to look out of the back window as he backs the Morris Minor estate out of the garage and into the courtyard.

Only when he's completely stationary do we make a move. Will sits on the cushions behind Daddie's seat, I sit behind Mummie. Daddie puts on his cap, running a finger under the greasy edge at the back to make his hair lie straight, and we're ready to go. The car smells of tobacco, engine oil and warm sorbo rubber.

We wait for our mother to appear at the door.

Five minutes later she's there with a red scarf tied around her hair, a pair of old tennis shoes on her feet and James on a lead. She's been checking all the windows and outside doors to the house and now she locks the backdoor.

James gets into the front passenger foot well. He can't sit in the back like other dogs because the whole space is taken up with a spare wheelchair. It's kept there so Daddie can be independent and arrive anywhere complete with out-of-car transport.

'Have you locked the back door?' Daddie asks this even though he must have seen her do it a moment ago.

'Yes. All safe.' Mummie gets the key out of her purse again and shows it to him before climbing in and slamming the door. Daddie winces. James thumps his tail on the floor; he knows exactly where we're going and is excited.

When we arrive at the edge of the heath, we'll let James out of the car to gallop alongside as far as the coast-guard cottages and Daddie will park as close to the edge of the cliff as he can. From our place on the back seat and unable to see through the windscreen, it feels more risky than it is but we know Daddie will keep us safe, and Will and I are never nervous about the crumbling sandstone, orange and flaking as ancient sunburn. Daddie faces the car towards an imaginary place he calls the Hook of Holland, then winds down the window to sniff the air like a pointer.

He always says the same thing. 'Out you all get, but stay where I can see you once in a while.' We tumble out of the car, running, jumping, sliding and shouting down the sandy cliff path towards the bird reserve and the sea. James bounds along the surfy sea-edge, ears flapping, paws splashing, tongue lolling. Will and I dig dozens of holes, collect shells, crab claws and stones, dropping them into our pockets to show Daddie later. We touch the sea, let the water lap over the top of our boots and run to catch up with our mother who strides towards the grey cube ahead of us, which is Sizewell nuclear power station. We stretch our arms and legs, hair whipping into our eyes, tasting salt on our tongues and pretend to jump from one tank-trap to another. After the war they were left to edge the shore in a higgledy-piggledy line and we leap off into the stones and marram grass before clambering up onto the next. At the end of the line and, dancing to keep our balance in the gusty wind, eyes watering, arms around each other and laughing until we hurt, we each raise an arm to wave at the car, the size of my thumbnail, balanced high on the cliff top.

Left in the quiet of the Morris, Daddie will take his Uncle Jack's telescope from the glove box, lean an arm on the ledge of the open window and train his eye on fishing trawlers from Lowestoft and the occasional gas tanker, pale as a thought, on the skyline while he waits for us to return.

Present: November

My garden and the countryside in which I lived was in stasis. It had been shutting down in stages over the last few weeks. First to go were the wild fruits. We'd gathered blackberries, wild cherry-plums and sloes and my neighbours had left me windfall apples outside my back door. We gorged ourselves on blackberry fools and apple-and-everything crumbles and cooked plums for the freezer. The last leaves dropped, exposing a mass of brilliant red spheres on a new crab apple tree by the house, like early Christmas baubles left to tantalise the birds. Our girls were stuck behind closed doors hoping for days of relentless rain to stop. My husband watched his sloe gin, turning it carefully every Sunday, and I continued to read my mother's letters.

Members of the medical team were constantly changing their minds about the treatment needed for my father's fistula or his heels. Sleep became an obsession and he started a regime of sleeping tablets, but they left him feeling dopey and irritable in the mornings. He started to sink into depression and, although he didn't give up his exercises, he seemed to do them more for my mother's sake than his own. He stopped valuing any vital little improvements. Exercise had been his routine and he had an athlete's expectation of progression. Being sick was a new experience; he began to see the whole recovery process as hopeless.

The London Hospital: February, 1953

Diana had always looked forward to seeing Push whatever the circumstances, but anticipation had begun to be tempered with apprehension. One long night, lying in her childhood bedroom at Larchmoor, she felt a creeping despondency clutch at her own heart and she feared for their future. But by the morning she'd managed to talk herself out of it.

It was obvious as soon as she walked into Hanbury Ward that Push was exhausted and anxious but she wanted to share her new conviction. After greeting him with her widest smile, she launched right in.

'I've been thinking about things, Push darling.'

Push lifted his head and she detected alarm in his eyes.

'You know you said last time that you didn't know how I coped with all this?' She looked around the busy ward and waved the red gloves she was still clutching in her left hand to encompass the whole room. 'I've realised that it's all for a reason.'

'Didie, I don't think there's any reason. I mean there'll be a cause. Polio is a virus that's carried in water and I spent an awful lot of time on the river, but so have dozens, hundreds probably, of other people. I was just terribly unlucky.'

Diana shook her head. 'No, not that. I mean how I've coped.' She accepted two cups of tea from a nurse pushing a trolley and handed one to Push. 'The thing is, I think it's kind of a lesson we have to learn to prove ourselves, and in a funny way, I think I, for one, now feel much stronger and more sure of myself than before all this happened.' Push started to say something, but Diana wanted to finish her little speech. 'And Push, darling, my love for you has grown as you've shown yourself even more wonderfully strong, brave and courageous than I could have believed possible.'

She searched Push's face for a response but he said nothing and concentrated on finding his balance with one hand so he wouldn't spill his tea. Finally he put the cup on his locker.

'They've decided that they will have to operate on my heels after all. They've detected gangrene.'

The gangrenous plugs were cut out the very next day. There was immediate improvement; the sores dried up and the infection was no longer at risk of spreading. Diana began to wish that the decision had been taken earlier, even though she knew that Push had resisted it fiercely.

'It's all very good news, isn't it?' David caught up with Diana as the usual crowd made their way down the polished corridors to the various wards one Saturday afternoon.

'*I* think so.' Diana felt tears sting her eyes, but she squeezed them away. 'Actually David, it's all a bit of a strain.'

David put an arm out and slowed their pace. 'You're not saying that Push is unhappy with the decision?'

David was one of Push's best friends and his rowing partner, but he'd been Diana's boyfriend before she met Push. He was also a doctor. She needed to talk to someone, David understood her and she could trust him to be discreet. They paused in a doorway.

'There's no question, it had to be done,' David said.

'I know that, and so does he. It's just that... It's all because he can't get on with his exercises again. He thinks if he doesn't that he'll never get well.' She looked at her watch. 'Push will be wondering if I'm stuck in a blizzard.' They started walking again. 'Do you know? He actually said to me that I was shackled to him and that I deserved better than this.' Diana stopped at the ward doors. She took a deep breath and wiped her eyes. 'It's not true. I love him and I'll stick by him. And it's not because I should, it's because I want to.'

'Shall I have a word with him?'

She turned to face him. David had always been so kind. His round face and broad, easy smile raised her spirits. If anyone could make Push see sense, he would. 'Oh, could you, David? It doesn't matter how often I reassure him, it doesn't seem to make any difference. He's got it into his head that he'll never be any good. He'll have to believe you.'

There were two round windows in the doors beside them and Diana risked a quick look. There was no risk of Push seeing them; he was lying on his stomach with his head turned to one side, resting his forehead on one arm. 'He's got to stay like that for most of the time until the new skin on his heels is strong enough to be stretched without tearing.' She looked at Push for a little longer. 'Thank heavens for the wireless.'

It snowed almost continuously for the next few days and Diana's father urged her to stay at home. The depth of the drifts as she walked into Berkhamsted to catch the post frightened her and she had no difficulty taking his advice. David had convinced Push that a week or ten days convalescing from this entirely necessary procedure would be a good investment. So, secure in the knowledge that Push could do nothing but rest in her absence, she used her time to write long reassuring letters.

Even if you won't be able to row in your competitions again. Even if you feel that you're not as you want to be, it doesn't matter at all really, nobody will care. After all people's opinions of a person have nothing to do with whether they are big and tough; it's what they are in themselves that makes them respect you. Especially the people who work for you. And love you, like me. There is so much more to you than being a hunk of beef, Push darling, and you mustn't forget it. And you are very lucky that there is. There are so many things you could get to the top of without having to do the 100 yards sprint!

Chapter Seven

The London Hospital: February, 1953

When the roads became passable again, albeit with a great deal of care, Diana made the journey from Berkhamsted to the East End and found Push in a much better frame of mind. He was sitting up with his knees raised by a mountain of pillows and his feet flat on the bed. She was thrilled to hear that his heels were nearly better and a week later she was euphoric at having witnessed him standing for the first time since he became ill. All the way home, she thought about the possibility of getting him out of hospital for a weekend visit. She could hardly wait to get out of her coat and boots before running up to her room to scribble a quick note telling him of her thoughts and give him something tangible to look forward to.

When she went to visit again at the weekend, Push's response wasn't at all what she expected.

'I honestly don't think you should be making plans like that. You can't think we'll be able to cope at Burnage. The truth is...'

'What's the truth?' Diana bent over Push as he turned his face away again. She waited and when he spoke again, it was so quiet she could barely hear the words over the chatter in the ward.

'The thing is you mustn't get too excited.' Push closed his eyes for a moment. 'You mustn't believe everything you see.'

Diana shook her head. She had no idea what he was talking about, but she was beginning to think that she could never say the right thing.

Push heaved himself up to roll over and took Diana's hand in his own. He covered the base of her thumb with his, stroked it back and forth and slowly her thumping heart calmed a little. 'The truth is, Didie. I didn't stand; not really.'

She could see his eyes searching her face to check that she understood, but she still couldn't make sense of his words. 'But I saw you. Last time I was here, I saw you and so did Willie.'

'Yes, I know. But, Didie, you have to understand. It was a trick. I know what I did and you were all so pleased, but it wasn't true. You saw what you wanted to see, but it was a deception, a useless piece of magicians' tomfoolery. I deceived us all.'

Home, Suffolk: 1969

I'm standing in front of Daddie, not allowed to sit down or even talk, while he makes this pointless chart. It's very quiet: only the hum of the fridge and the sound of the ruler moving around on the table and the scratch of Daddie's yellow Bic pen moving in that jerky way of his across the paper. The ceiling is so high that sounds have a faintly hollow quality as though we've only just moved in. The cats have all disappeared and James has taken to lying flat on the stone floor next door in the baccus because of the heat, his Labrador tongue hanging pink and wet with hardly the energy to pant.

It's been a horrible morning. There was a thunderstorm last night and nobody's slept very well. It rained and rained and, although it's stopped now, the long grass was very wet and my trousers got soaked when I went down the back. And it all started again this morning even when I'd found the stupid purse. It was lying deep in the long grass where it must have fallen out of my pocket as I'd jumped over that fallen branch, pretending to be a pony when I was walking back up the Rose Walk yesterday afternoon.

Daddie taps the table to get my attention.' Do you think we should divide each day into two? Morning and afternoon?'

I look down at the surface of the table with its sticky blue Fablon cover pinned with coloured drawing pins around the edge. Daddie is almost exactly at my eye level and he is looking at me with that steady, reasonable stare which I find so paralysing.

'I don't know.'

'You don't know.'

An unbearable silence drops on us. The sun is shining through the window but the atmosphere is thick as fog. I know my face is bright red, and it's not just the dampness of the morning or the heat from the Aga which is never allowed to go out. I can't meet Daddie's eyes. It's unfair but I'm also angry with myself because I know I could've prevented this.

'I found it,' I find myself saying all at once. 'I knew I'd find it eventually. I wasn't going to just leave it.'

'We've been through all this.' Daddie leans towards me resting on his elbow. 'I know what you said. But I still don't understand why you couldn't have just told Mummie that you'd lost her purse as soon as you came back with the shopping. Then she'd have been saved from all the worry when she found it was missing in the evening.' He shrugs his shoulders under the heavy tweed jacket he's still wearing despite the heat, and puts the pen down carefully to line up with his chart. 'But there you are. You didn't. Instead, you swore blind that you remembered putting it back in her shopping basket. And we believed you.'

More silence.

'No. It's not the fact you lost the purse. My concern, as I have said, is: All. This. Lying.' I meet his eyes, and they are grey and clear and fathomless. I swallow.

'It's habitual. Not once or twice when you think you'll be in trouble; that would be understandable. But all the time. Even when you've not been asked, you say, "Wasn't me". Don't you? And it was. You say, "I don't know", when you do know. You say, "It's not my fault", when you're standing there over the body with a smoking gun in your hand.'

I've heard this expression before so it doesn't surprise me. It only depresses me, because I know it's true. Only it's not so much lying as keeping back the truth. Not to hurt anyone else, that would be the last thing I'd want to happen; mostly it's to keep my nose clean, as Daddie would say. And, yet, even as the non-truth is spilling out of my mouth, I know I'll be found out and that it'll be much worse than if I'd told the truth from the start. But I can't. I'm always in trouble and I want to not be in trouble. More than anything it's because, although I know he loves me, I want Daddie to like me as well. To like being with me as much as he likes being with Will.

'They're only fibs,' I mumble.

'They are not fibs,' Daddie says loudly, bringing his fist down on the table so hard that it makes me jump and all the breakfast things leap into the air and rattle. 'They are not fibs, they are not porky-pies, tall tales, stories or even excuses. You're not telling the truth, so you are lying.'

My cheeks are burning and my eyes sting.

'This family does not lie. You're a Pulman and we have to be able to trust you. Being trustworthy is the most important thing you can do.' I know without looking that his eyebrows are doing the pointy thing at the corners that I find so frightening. In a minute, tears will start to come. I squeeze the lids tight shut and clamp my teeth over the inside of my bottom lip. I taste salt and the tang of blood and my nose prickles. Dimly, somewhere at the back of my brain I'm aware of a car driving into the back yard.

'I'm worried for you.' Daddie shakes his head, but his voice is quieter again. 'I really am, Sarie.' At the sound of my nickname, I look up and meet his eyes again. 'You're eleven years old. Plenty old enough to know the value of truth.' He pauses to pick up the pen again. 'You won't be at your little prep school much longer. This has to stop.'

He draws diagonal lines from corner to corner across each of the boxes. 'This here is the morning, and this is the afternoon of each day.' He indicates the spaces with a trembling finger. 'If you get through to lunchtime without telling a lie, you get a red tick. And again, through to bedtime with no lie, a red tick. If you tell a lie you get a blue cross. And we'll know,' he says warning me against finding the flaw in his argument. He picks up the piece of paper and hands it to me across the table. The tears have come now and I can't look at it.

'Is that clear?'

I say nothing.

'We have to be able to trust you,' he repeats. 'Is that clear, Sarie?'

I nod.

'Now, get the Selly out of the drawer and stick this to the wall by the door above the light switches.

I do as I'm told and am cutting my last piece of tape as the doorbell clangs dully somewhere in the cupboard above my head. We hear the handle of the back door and in a minute one of my parents' tennis friends is standing in the kitchen. She sees me sticking the chart to the wall and asks what it is.

'I think you'd better explain, don't you, Sarie?' And I realise in a flash like electricity that my punishment is not the blue crosses or the lecture at the end when I fail, but when I have to tell people, over and over and over again, every time someone new comes into our kitchen. I burn again, this time with humiliation, as I explain the purpose of the chart for the first time, and I resolve to absent myself whenever I hear the doorbell ring or a car sweep over the cobbles.

Present: December

God, how my father hated deceit and lies. I recalled the events around his creation of the lie-chart with toe-curling clarity. It was a tough lesson and one that cut both ways.

'We have to be able to trust you. Being trustworthy is the most important thing you can do.' I realised that the words I'd spoken to my own children over the years weren't my own but my father's. If my father had prioritised our family's moral standards, honesty might well have stood at number one, with patience not far behind.

I trusted my children not to tell me lies but I imagined they might be selective with the truth. I defy the most trustworthy of us to suggest that they have never held something back, often to protect others. My parents had a complex collection of reasons not to tell my brother and me about the early years of their marriage, but protecting us would have been high on their list.

I never knowingly heard my father tell a lie, but in the letters my mother continually comes across truths that he's held back to protect her. And to protect himself. When, inevitably, they were exposed, my mother was always hurt and disappointed. For her part, I could see that she was blind to the hints my father was giving her about his lack of progress, or perhaps her optimism caused her to ignore them. Both made assumptions about the other. My mother concluded that her new husband couldn't trust her internal strength. In turn, my father clearly felt it was his duty to appear fearless and in control, even when that was far from the truth. They had different agendas and neither was being completely honest or really hearing the other. I could see how their tender, fledgling relationship suffered.

I kept looking at the words in my mother's letter, her seventeenth. *'I know you say it was a trick...'* she wrote in her cursive hand, but then shrugged it off and on to the next boost of encouragement. I admired her tenacity and her resolve but she didn't know my father then as we did in later years. She could never have convinced him that it really didn't matter that he'd deceived them. Or even that there were mitigating circumstances.

But there was photographic evidence of my father standing at the parallel bars, wearing his hand-knitted bed jacket and leather business shoes.

How could my father with his almost pathological hatred of untruths have allowed that photograph, steeped in humiliation, to be taken? How dare he make that lie-chart with shame as its core. A child-like fury flared in my chest, but I couldn't be certain if it was my own anger, or if I was enraged on my father's behalf that he'd been caught out at a time that he was vulnerable and weakened.

I studied the photograph. Why had he kept it?

Beyond the scruffy bed jacket and the mismatched pyjamas, I recognised the pigskin-strapped Omega watch that he'd worn every day of his life. The wrists were large and bony and he was very thin. But his arms looked rock solid, elbow-locked and tight with sinew, knuckles white with effort on the smooth, wooden bars. Dozens, maybe hundreds, of men may have taken their first recovering steps along those bars. Pushing, driving, faces made ancient with the effort of hope.

But my father wasn't walking. He was hanging.

Hanging from his locked shoulders, square and powerful against his neck. Suspended over the bars. Shoes barely brushing the ground.

Not walking. Not standing. It was a trick and he had smiled, wild for joy, for the photographer, whom I was certain was his brother, my Uncle Willie. And, to make my mother happy, he had lied.

The London Hospital: March 1953

Push watched his mother-in-law make her way down the length of the ward, a sealskin coat swinging from her shoulders and diamond-cut Bakelite buttons winking in the glare from the lamps that were hanging from the ceiling on their long flexes. He sighed and wished that it were John coming to visit. From the moment he'd met Diana's father, they had got on famously. Engineering was a shared language, and John Latta had the same inquisitive nature and love of innovation. He'd not warmed to Diana's mother in the same way.

She arrived at the foot of his bed and launched into her mission without preamble. 'Diana has influenza. She's not well at all so I thought I'd take the opportunity to come and talk about something.'

'I thought she looked a bit peaky a couple of days ago. Is she alright?'

'Susan's looking after her. She's in very capable hands.'

'Good. I'm glad.'

'You probably think I should come more often but between your friends and Diana, you seem to have the visiting hours pretty well divided up.'

And thank heavens for that, Push thought, but he smiled and said, 'Wednesday's always a quiet day.'

She looked around vaguely before reaching into a capacious leather handbag and pulling out a long black, jewelled cigarette holder and a packet of Rothmans Kingsize. She offered the pack to Push, who took one. They lit up and smoked in silence for a minute or two.

'There's something I need to know.'

Push took the smoke deep into his lungs and drew an ashtray towards the edge of his bedside locker before letting it out again.

'Go ahead,' he said.

'Diana tells me that you'll soon be allowed out for a weekend.'

So that's what this was all about. Push took another drag and balanced the cigarette on the edge of the ashtray. 'It's tough luck, Di getting flu the first week into her new job.'

Ma Latta rested a manicured hand on the clasp of her bag and half-a-dozen heavy gold bracelets slid down her arm with an irritating jangle. Her left hand held her cigarette vertical in its holder.

'Is it true about your having a home visit?'

Push sat perfectly still and sucked his lips together into a thin line. 'That's what we've been told,' he said at last.

'Well, that's wonderful.'

Push didn't reply. He wasn't about to tell his mother-in-law of all people what was really troubling him. He could hardly admit it to himself.

'Isn't it?' Ma Latta puffed expertly on her Rothmans then held out her other hand for the ashtray. Push shoved it down the bed towards her and she lay an inch and-a-half of ash column in the base. He felt her blue eyes boring into his, and feared what might come next. Her expensive clothes, harsh red lips and heavy cloud of scent added to a faint air of threat.

'Yes, of course.'

Ma Latta raised her eyebrows. 'Now, listen, Push. Diana's very excited.'

'I know.' He smoothed his bedclothes; he didn't like the tone his mother-in-law was taking.

'She's been making plans.'

He paused with his hands an inch above the sheet. 'She wants to hurry things that won't be hurried.'

'Diana always was an impatient child.' Ma Latta looked down the ward and wrinkled her nose. 'How does one get a drink in here?'

'They'll bring a tea trolley soon, I expect,' Push said, although he had the distinct impression that she'd be happier with a gin and It.

She was obviously here to stay despite her earlier protestations, and Push hated visitors looming over him. It highlighted that they had the freedom to walk about while he was stuck in bed. 'Please, won't you sit?' He held onto the frame of his bed and indicated where a chair might be found with his other hand. He thought she might refuse, but she dragged a chair forward and sat down, her bag still held firmly on her lap.

'I'll not beat about the bush. How will you cope?'

He let his breath out with a long sigh. 'We won't.' He'd thought he was about to be reproached for something, but for all his mother-in-law's forbidding brusqueness, she seemed to have seen straight to the heart of what was bothering him. It was almost a relief. 'The trouble is, Didie thinks that the main difficulty will be getting me from the car to the house. But that's not the half of it.' He shook his head. 'Actually, that's not even five percent of it. She has no idea what I need; what the nurses have to do for me every day.' He looked up and forced a smile. 'How can she?'

'But you are improving.'

'I must be or they wouldn't have put such a damn-fool idea in her head.' He stopped and looked at his mother-in-law again, biting his lips and clicking his thumb against the nail on his middle finger.

'The nurses say you're doing terrifically well, now you can exercise again.'

'I'm certainly not going to give up, but I know I still have an awfully long way to go.' He rubbed his forehead while Ma Latta waited in silence. 'In here, they're used to people like me. Everything's geared up to people who can't... Who can't do what they did before. Didie's been wonderful. She's stuck with me through all these months, but she's not a trained nurse.'

Ma Latta sniffed. 'She'd do better to think a little more carefully.' She toyed with the packet of cigarettes for a moment. 'A whole weekend will rather put the spotlight on what you can and can't do, I imagine. Much better to come to us just for the day as your first home-leave. And, of course, John can help.'

'He could,' said Push slowly. 'But honestly, when you think about all the arrangements and inconvenience, what's the point for only a few hours?'

'It's no inconvenience.' She paused, then got up and buttoned her coat to the chin again.

Push felt his colour rise and his heart start banging about in his chest. He should have kept quiet, and all of a sudden he wished he had a smarter bed jacket. He couldn't begin to imagine how he would cope, cast like a sheep on its back in his parents-in-laws' house, amongst the perfectly polished, reproduction mahogany furniture, matching African violets in every room and acres of immaculately vacuumed Axminster. He would rather make his first stab at independence amongst his own family at Thelveton, if he could stick the journey. But of course that was a ridiculous idea, it was far too far away. He reached for the monkey bar above his head and pulled himself up straighter against his pillows. 'It'll take time,' he said, and he heard his voice take on a formal note. '...but I will be all right again. I'm making quite sure of that. I'm learning all about various treatments and I'm working as hard as I can.

I will get better.' He smiled to reassure her.

Ma Latta fixed him with a deep blue gaze and pursed her lips together. 'Now, look. I'll speak to Diana. She must wait until you say you're ready.' She looked at the locker as though appraising the items there. 'What are you doing with your time?'

'Like I said, I'm doing my exercises and working on getting upright.'

'You can't do that all day. You'll go potty.'

Push smiled. His mother-in-law had a lot to learn about him. Exercising was what he was used to before he was ill. He was good at it and if he couldn't get better through exercise, nobody could.

Ma Latta turned to him. 'Do you like reading?'

'I love reading.'

'I knit, listen to the wireless and read, all at the same time. I read crime mostly. I can usually work out who's dun it before half way.' She paused and took a loud breath in through her long nose. '...sometimes they surprise me.'

'I've got a wireless. I like The Archers.'

'That's not going to occupy you for long.' She glanced about her. 'Does this place have a library?'

'I've read most of what they have.' There was a clatter at the far end of the ward. 'Here's the tea coming now.'

But Ma Latta pulled on her gloves and tamped the leather down between each digit. 'It's time I went.' She pointed a finger at him. 'Now, listen, I'll get you a membership for the Harrods Library. They'll sort you out. Just tell them how many and the sort of books you're interested in, and they'll do the rest.' She gave a sudden snort of laughter.

'I'll give Diana your love and I promise to keep her well away until she's stopped coughing her bugs over everyone. All right?' She leaned forward and pressed her cheek for an instant against Push's. It was ice-cold as though she had just walked in off the street, not spent the last half-an-hour in an overheated hospital wearing a fur coat.

'Thank you. For the chat as well as the membership, I mean.'

Ma Latta waved his thanks away. 'Here, you'd better have these,' and she tossed the opened packet of Rothmans onto his bed.

Chapter Eight

Present: February

In the beginning, I was reading my mother's letters to fill the blanks. She'd been advising my father not to rush things and I was struck by a quote she used, "the inevitability of gradualness" (often attributed to Sidney Webb but actually from a much older source). She counselled my father well, given his character, but she wasn't following the advice herself.

Improvement had plateaued after his initial recovery from the surgery on his heels and there appeared to be no consensus for future treatment. Impatient to fulfil her own belief that he would feel better if she could only get him out of the confines of the hospital, my mother did the very thing that my father hated; she began to force the issue. She suggested that he complain.

I longed to have the other half of the conversation, but from my mother's stumbling apologies in the next letter, it was clear that my father's response must have been unequivocal. I knew what he would fear most of all, and words that he might have said floated into my head.

'For God's sake, Didie! Why? So, that I can irritate the socks off them? So, I can compromise my care? No, it's better if I do as I'm told, don't make a fuss.' I shook his voice out of my head. Oh, the vulnerability of the sick!

She promised not to interfere.

But my mother has never liked being told what to do. She'd already told me how quickly my father became institutionalised and how low his moods would sink.

I imagined how much she must have resented the advice from my father and also from her own mother that she should stop planning for an overnight visit. Did she feel that they were ganging up against her? Did her opinions have no value?

'They were a bit,' she'd said when I asked for some behind the scenes clarification. 'But Ma P agreed with me. We felt it was wrong that Push should stay in hospital until he felt ready to be moved.' She sighed. 'It was all so uncertain, but we knew we had to do something or he would only get more dependent.'

'Shouldn't you have waited until his doctor said it would be OK to have trips out?'

'Oh he was encouraging him all the time, but Push thought he needed to make more progress first. I think he was determined to stay put so he could do his exercises.'

And he was afraid. Afraid of the world outside. Afraid of revealing how reliant he would be on his new wife.

I was astonished that my mother was prepared to go against my father's express wishes. It was absolutely unthinkable that she might have believed that she knew better. But I was also rather proud of her. I liked that my mother was her own woman even in the nineteen fifties. I wished I'd felt able to take a stand against my father occasionally.

With my Grannie Pulman's blessing, my mother went to work searching for somewhere suitable to rent short-term with, crucially, a hospital near-by specialising in rehabilitation for polio patients. The Orthopaedic Hospital, formally the Cripples Training College, at Stanmore was identified as their hospital of choice.

I'd been slowed in my reading with sadness for the marriage my parents might have had. Now I found myself reluctant to learn of the unbearable decline of their united front, of their disagreements and their quarrels. It was another shock.

Gradually I began to understand why I was doing this. When my father died, all other emotions were swept aside. There is nothing like death to distil love from its complications. But time goes by and regrets start to appear. The briars of long-gone hostilities. They had threatened to choke me in the past, and now they had to be cut back to allow me to grow. I was intent on exposing, cutting, plucking and raking out.

I couldn't be sure that any of it mattered, except to help me understand where my own childhood experiences were rooted. The last thing I wanted was to lay blame for my confusion—there was none to be laid—but I began to get a sense of the ambiguity of my upbringing. I felt the need to justify, explain and even defend. I wanted to get to the purity of my father's character; to rip out all that might have been contaminated, polluted, overridden and obscured by the polio, fear and hospitalisation. I wanted to learn about the man I never met so that I could understand the father I'd loved for forty-six years.

The London Hospital: Easter, 1953

'You've been going behind my back,' Push said before Diana had even got to his bedside, one afternoon in early April.

'What do you mean?'

'You promised that you wouldn't interfere.' Push was so furious that his skin—already pale from lack of sleep and months without the sun—had turned almost grey. 'You promised that you wouldn't do anything until I said I was ready and then I find out that you've practically had me packed up and bundled out of here.'

'Bundled? I only…'

'You've been telling all the doctors and nurses that I should leave hospital, that I should be at home.'

'Not leave. I only wanted…'

'You had no right! You have no right to tell them what I need. What I want. What makes you the expert in all things medical?'

'I'm not. I only wanted what…'

'What? What did you want? Didn't you remember what I said? Didn't you think for a single moment that this might not have been what I wanted? You've betrayed me.'

Diana had no idea that Push could be so angry. 'Stop, Push. Stop,' she whispered, there were curious visitors at the side of almost every bed, and she wanted to cover her ears with her hands. 'I'm so sorry you think I went behind your back, but how can I stand by and see you stagnate day by day? I only did it because I can't bear it when you withhold information from me. Your Ma told me that you were trying to protect me but, Push, you have to understand that it has the opposite affect. I have to ask Sis and the others what's happening to you, otherwise I can only think the worst.'

Push narrowed his eyes.

'You do understand, don't you? Push?'

Push remained silent.

Diana took a small step closer. 'As your wife, I should be allowed to take the rough with the smooth. And I'm absolutely convinced that you need some time away from this place.'

'Oh, are you?'

'It's not just me. Ma P thinks so too.'

'You've been talking to her too? I asked you not to meddle.'

'But by not telling me anything, you're suggesting in some way that I can't cope. And I can, Push. I'm strong and I can cope. You have to trust me.'

Push sat in his bed perfectly still, gripping onto the sides with both hands. Diana stopped talking and they both retreated into silence. Eventually, Push released his hands and leaned back into his pillows.

'All right, then. I'll tell you.' Push looked at Diana as if she were a stranger and she felt a momentary rush of fear. 'I don't want to come home.' He spoke quietly and deliberately. 'So, I don't want you to think about it any more, and any arrangements you've made had better be unmade.'

Diana felt herself sway slightly. She reached for the back of the wooden chair beside her and held on to it.

'Not come home?' Her lips could barely make the words. 'But why?'

Finally Push broke his gaze and she felt a physical release. Diana slumped into the chair and wiped her face. She saw him chew his bottom lip and take several deep breaths before finally, it seemed, he had taken control of his anger.

He reached for her hand and gripped it tightly.

'I'm not...' It was Push's turn to struggle for words. He looked up at the ceiling, scrumpled the bedclothes in his fingers and pressed his lips into a line. After what seemed an eternity, he looked back at her and she saw his eyes soften slightly.

'I don't want to come home because I don't think you should see what I've become.'

'What do you mean?' Diana searched Push's face for an answer. 'I know what you've become.'

'I'm so tired,' Push said, dully. He looked away again, over her head and out of the window. He did look exhausted.

'I don't want you to have to look after me,' he said at last. 'I know you're strong. I know you say you can cope. But you have no idea what I need. We won't manage, and I don't want you to see my legs.'

The last words seemed to escape his lips before he could catch them and bite them back. He looked away again but didn't give her time to reply. 'They're so thin, they've wasted and it doesn't matter how many exercises I seem to do, they're not looking like my legs yet. Nowhere near, and until they do, I don't want my wife to see what I look like.' He released her hand gently and turned away.

Diana sat speechless with astonishment. Of all the reasons that Push might have put forward to explain why he didn't want to leave the hospital, she could not have imagined this one.

'But, Push…' She tried to persuade him that this was the least of her worries but he would not be moved from the hospital or his conviction. Fear or stubbornness or vanity: she couldn't decide which had motivated this devastating news.

Over the next few days, Diana tried out different approaches in her head to get Push to change his mind. On Saturday afternoon, when her visiting time was a luxurious hour-and-a-half, Push gave Diana no opportunity to encourage him. They did little more than exchange formal greetings and sort out the housekeeping; she gave him his clean pyjama top and went home.

For nearly two weeks over Easter, Push refused to discuss his situation. Diana responded by keeping her emotions on a short rein. She was hurt, confused and wondered how it would all end. She continued to write every few days but she no longer tried to explain her actions. Having been accused of going behind his back, she felt unable to ask advice from Push's mother, and could only pray that time would grant a rapprochement. In a weak moment, she broke the emotional dam, ending one letter with the heartbreaking entreaty, *Please don't hate me*. However, she never stopped telling Push how much she loved him.

On Monday 13 April, Diana went to the hospital for an out-of-routine visit, and could contain her distress no longer.

'All this meddling, as you call it. Please forgive me. It's only because I felt so frustrated.'

Push sat and looked at her, as cool and undemonstrative as he had been for the last fortnight.

'Oh, Push! Don't be like this, I can't bear it!' Tears blurred everything before her. Why would her husband not want to be at home with her? Wasn't this what they'd longed for all these months? She let the tears overflow unheeded, then spoke in the lowest whisper. 'Don't you love me any more?'

Diana dragged a chair closer to his bed and sat down. She reached up to put her arms about Push's neck and buried her face against his shoulder. 'I feel so engulfed by doctors, nurses and all the rest. I can't just sit on the side-lines doing nothing, but how on earth am I supposed to know what's best for you if no one tells me?'

As she rambled and wept, she felt his hands begin to stroke her arms then wrap themselves around her and finally hold her tight in the bear-hug that she needed so much.

'Oh, Didie! Is that what you thought? That I didn't love you? I'm so very sorry,' he said, his voice choking, too. 'I think it must be the pills they give me to sleep. They make me so groggy and sometimes I'm so low.' He drew her even closer. 'You have no idea how much I love you. It's been an agony, but I just couldn't see a future for myself. And that meant no life together for us. It's too cruel. You're so young and we've been married such a short time. You need better than this.'

Diana pulled away just enough so that she could look into Push's eyes; she thought she'd never seen him look so tired.

'I thought...' He was holding her hand so tightly it almost hurt. 'I thought you'd be better off without me.'

'Without you?' She shook her head. Push might be the great Cambridge academic, but he really didn't understand her at all. 'Oh Push! Did you really think you could stop me loving you? I thought you couldn't forgive me.' She blinked away a second threat of tears. 'It's because you were taken away from me so early on, before we had a chance to get started, that we both feel like this. You mustn't hide things from me anymore. And, whatever it is you have to tell me, now I know that you do really love me, I'm never going to leave you.'

They fell together again, not caring who might be looking at them.

'I've been assuming that I have to take sole responsibility, Didie. That's my problem. And I will learn to share things more with you.'

'Well, we'll both resolve never to make assumptions for whatever reason and, if the past few months have taught us anything, it's to always count ourselves lucky that we still have each other.'

'I am lucky, Didie,' said Push, drawing her close again. 'So lucky that I have you with me.' He paused to cough, then doubled over in a sudden attack of choking and catching his breath. 'Even if I have to thank you for giving me your horrible cough,' he added with a wry smile which made Diana laugh with relief.

Present: February

Unless our mother prompted us, we were unaware of how much physical pain my father had to contend with. He rarely complained in our hearing or allowed it to cloud his judgement. But an especially bad night could reveal another side. Sleep was never taken for granted and was to be coaxed and planned for. His life-long quest for an undisturbed night must have had its origins in the never-silent, pain-filled and anxious world of the men's orthopaedic ward of the London Hospital.

I never knew a time when my father hadn't found it difficult to sleep. His semi-paralysed digestive system meant he often suffered from indigestion, his legs rarely stopped aching and he had to wake himself up every couple of hours to change position to prevent pressure sores. Perhaps it was the hours of waiting to slip gently and soundly into a painless unconscious that made him so insistent that Will and I should go to bed early and get our full eight hours or more. My brother fell asleep as soon as his head touched the pillow but he awoke early and would sit on the floor of his bedroom building great edifices with his Lego, oblivious to the fact that he might be blue with cold. Later, when he was old enough to use the fan heater, on winter mornings he sat pressed against it with his pile of plastic bricks slowly warping and stinking in the heat. Will's quiet early morning creativity went unremarked, but my late night wakefulness and fear of the dark did not. From an early age I'd frequently read myself to sleep at night, allowing the book to fall over my nose, the light still glowing under the door, only to be discovered when my parents came to bed.

Home, Suffolk: 1965

I don't know which came first, being afraid of the dark or not sleeping. One seems to bring on the other. I turn my reading light off and lie watching the few precious inches of landing light around the door.

It's a few weeks since I was punished for leaving the light on and wasting electricity. Daddie had me stand on a chair in their bedroom while they slept. In the morning they found me curled up asleep on the tapestry pad like a cat. It did some good, because Mummie has allowed me to have the landing light left on and I have a small pink 'glimmie' left shining at the far end of my room.

Tonight this is not enough.

Outside there's a terrifying noise of hail and wind and thunder. My window's rattling and the curtains are billowing into the room. my glimmie is swinging on its flex and dark green shadows get big, then small, to menace me from behind the wardrobe.

I'm awake and I can't stop sobbing.

Then, beneath the wind, I can hear the whine of

Daddie's lift followed by a comforting wheeze when it comes to the top. The door rattles open and Daddie's chair squeaks out backwards, past my brother's room and onto the landing. He puffs and grunts with the effort of hauling it around so he can wheel forwards. He pauses outside my room, the handle turns and then the door lurches open and gently bumps my bed.

'Sarie?' Daddy squeaks his chair into the room and peers around the door in the dark.

'Mmm.'

'Are you all right?'

'Mmm,' I say again. Then another roll of thunder makes me to bury my face in the pillow. 'No! I don't like the dark.'

He reaches for my hand and I put my clammy fingers into his great warm bear paw. He folds his hand around mine and strokes me jerkily with the thumb that doesn't work properly. Lightning jabs the room and we can hear the hail hurling itself at the window and I grip his hand really tightly. I don't want him to leave me and shut the door again.

'Come out of bed. I want to show you something.'

I didn't expect this and I raise my head to look at him in the half-light. I can make out his eyes and teeth. He's smiling. 'Come on, Sarie. Sit on my lap.'

I slide out of bed and he grips me around the tummy to swing me up and over his knees, my feet dangling either side of his shins in their flappy trouser legs. He fumbles on the bed for my dressing gown and together we pull it round my shoulders. I lean back into his chest as we roll across the room towards the window.

'Open the curtains.'

I look at him over my shoulder to see if he means it, and he nods. One after the other I shove the curtains aside and away from us, while Daddie grips me round my middle so I can't fall off his lap. He gets as close to the glass as he can.

'Look out and tell me what you see.'

Outside it's just inky blackness.

'Nothing,' I say.

'Keep looking.' Daddie's voice is soft and low but I hear excitement behind the gentleness.

'But I can't see anything.'

'Be patient.' And together we stare into the darkness while the hail dies away and the wind begins to calm. One minute, two minutes, three…

Suddenly, the whole sky shatters with a light as fast as Daddie's camera shutter. I have a picture as bright as the brightest thing burned onto my eye as the dark folds in again and thunder explodes around our heads. I jerk back in fright and Daddie hugs me tightly.

'Did you see that?'

'Yes!'

'Tell me what you saw.'

I put my hands over my face, squeeze my eyelids shut and see everything all over again in my mind's eye. 'Lightning. Lightning all over the sky. I could see the branches of the trees, black against the green light.'

'Did you look at the ground?'

I search my memory. 'Oh!' I say in wonder. 'Green

snow, like icing sugar. Long, long shadows and the roofs of the houses in the valley all sparkly, like diamonds.'

'You see?' says Daddie. 'You wouldn't have seen all that without the darkness.' We sit together for a moment or two longer and the sky lights up again, blasting its way into every corner of the window. This time the thunder is duller and a little quieter.

'The storm's moving away,' he says, and our faces are so close to the glass that our breath makes foggy marks. 'The thunder is the sound of the lightening. Light waves are faster than sound waves and we see the lightning before we hear the thunder—but it's all one and the same event.'

I nod, not really understanding.

'This is a special evening, Sarie, because you hardly ever have thunderstorms when it's freezing outside. They're usually triggered by hot weather. This was caused by freak conditions.'

Freak conditions. I like the words and repeat them to myself.

Daddie reaches around me and we close the curtains again. When we've rolled back to my bed, I slip off his lap and climb in under the covers.

'Next time you turn off your light, I want you to think about turning on the dark. You have to have the dark so you can see the light.' Lightning floods the room again and the thunder, when it comes, grumbles away towards Walpole. 'Now, Sarie, I'm not going to switch off the landing light, I'm going to...' and together we say, 'switch on the dark.'

'Good night, Sarie.'

'Good night,' I say and think about Freak Conditions until I fall asleep.

Chapter Nine

Present: April

After the insecurity of many years in hospital with my father unable to work, my parents chose to save rather than spend. We saw the benefits of simple pleasures and luxury was frowned upon. Our annual family holiday was taken at a modest B&B in Cornwall, occasional days out were to the seaside and treats were chosen at Fox's sweetie shop in the Thoroughfare. This magnificent building lay on a corner near the Jubilee lamp and opposite the Angel Hotel. Double-fronted, dark-panelled, gold-curlicued and covered with confectionary advertising plates; Fry's, Cadbury Bournville, Trebor and Caley's. Inside, temptations were piled high on glass cake stands, jostling for places on two antique mahogany dining room tables, everything glittering and winking in the lamplight. It was an emporium for bad teeth and indulgence, and was our favourite place to spend our pocket money. We dithered over red shoelaces, aniseed balls, gobstoppers, Batman bubblegum with collectable cards, sherbet space ships, four-for-a-penny chews, and boxes of sweet cigarettes which would warm up in your coat, bend in the middle before bleeding the red-dipped glow onto your hands and sticking to the fluff in your pockets.

Then, when we'd filled our heads with the scents of chocolate and beeswax furniture polish, made our decisions and stuffed our mouths before shutting the door, we'd walk out of the shop and past the little boy wearing leg irons without a second glance. It never once occurred to us that the Crippled Boy holding onto his collection box had anything at all to do with our family; that *Action Research for the Crippled Child* might mean action for affected adults also. That people might describe our Daddie as a cripple too.

At aged six or seven, when I was a pupil at the PNEU school in the centre of the town, we walked crocodile-fashion to Mr Baxter's cafe for a hot lunch of fish pie or mince in gravy, mashed potatoes and carrots or electric-green tinned peas. We danced along the pavements, skipped up the riverside walk by the curving crinkle-crankle wall that my father had only ever heard about. (He teased us that it had been built by a drunkard and we believed him utterly, imagining the scene before our eyes.) Emerging from the main square, we balanced along the stone wall that encircled the churchyard and still showed signs of metal pegs left from when the iron railings were requisitioned by the war effort twenty years before. There wasn't a single member of the school who couldn't join in the walking, dancing and balancing; who couldn't take part in the French cricket games held in the neighbouring field, or play hopscotch in the sandy playground. Every single one of us was protected from becoming a crippled child by the vaccines we'd received as small children, which were developed in America and had been universally available in Britain for just a few years. We all went swimming and paddled in the rivers in the summer without fear of the summer plague that had haunted parents of young children less than a decade before. Headaches and fevers were looked at with concern, but not panic. Leg irons and crutches that had once been, if not a common, certainly not an unusual, sight were virtually unknown to us. In the developed world, infantile paralysis was all but consigned to the history books, along with the war. I never heard polio mentioned outside the family and only very rarely within our home. We had no idea how privileged we were: how could we? We were only children. And those who did know were doing their best to forget.

One Sunday at boarding school while listening to the Bible reading in church, I made the connection between someone with a withered leg or arm and the disease that had changed my father's life. I mentioned it to a teacher and she confirmed my thoughts, then she talked a little about a childhood friend who had worn a brace and about the pain she'd gone through. It was the first time I'd ever had any proper conversation or compassion shown to me about my father's plight, and it was the first time that I discovered that not everyone who had polio ended up pushing a chair. We found some pictures of school children from before the war and many showed at least one child in leg-irons, sometimes known as braces or, more commonly today, callipers. I began to feel very lucky.

If you didn't have to use a wheelchair, callipers were crucial to give a leg weakened by polio enough support on which to stand. Indeed, the innovative designers of the

Indian Jaipur Foot have developed modern plastic callipers that are both strong and light enough to enable polio patients to run, ride a bicycle or even kick a football.

This works well if you are small and light, but even using the successful Jaipur callipers, an adult of over six feet in height with both legs affected, like my father, would have a hard time kicking a football. It's one thing to be supported enough to remain upright, quite another to have mobility. For this, a paraplegic needs crutches, but crutches occupy both hands and arms, making it impossible to do anything other than attend to the effort of walking; no carrying, touching, linking arms or moving things other than the walking aid.

In the 1950s, leg-irons were crude things, very heavy and, as their name suggests, made of metal. My sympathetic teacher explained, from some experience, that a kick from an irate child wearing irons was not to be risked a second time.

One of the more joyful pictures I came across when polio was on my radar in later years was of an allotment of French beans, each plant supported by a single leg-iron; braces made redundant by the widespread use of an effective polio vaccine.

My father's combination of leg-irons and crutches were custom-made for him. As far back as I can remember, they sat propped against a small, black fireplace in one of the box rooms at the top of the back stairs, but we never saw him use them. In the moves from hospital to Thelveton and from Thelveton to our own family home in Suffolk, they stayed with him as a symbol of hope. Or faith, perhaps. One day, he must have thought, I will get upright once more, walk even, maybe dance and lark about, and be on my feet again.

In the days leading up to my eighth birthday, however, he must have undergone a sea-change in his thinking.

Home, Suffolk: 1966

This is the last birthday I shall have at home with my family for a long time and Mummie says she's arranged a special party. In September I'll be going away to boarding school but today, in early May, that's as far away as Antarctica.

Today I am eight. I've been praying for a camera. For the last few days, Mummie has been praying for a fine day. Every morning she comes into my bedroom, walks to the window and opens the curtains. Before she speaks I can tell from the way her shoulders look that she's disappointed again. 'Oh, Sarie,' she says with a great sigh. 'I do hope it will be sunny for your party.'

And, like a miracle, it is. In the time it's taken us to eat our breakfast, blue sky has been peeping through the clouds, and now the sun is shining steadily.

In its blossoming heat I'm chewing the last of my toast and gulping the final dregs of milk so that I can make a start on the parcels piled up on a spare chair set beside my place.

At Christmas, or when it's our birthdays, Daddie tends to arrive late to breakfast after 'rootling' in the study. When he's found what he's looking for, he bumps over the step to the kitchen, very wobbly and one-handed, trying to prevent whatever it is on his lap from sliding off onto the floor. This morning he isn't late. He doesn't have to rootle anywhere and only adds a little white envelope to my presents.

'Many happy returns,' he says.

'Thank you, Daddie,' I reply.

And now, having swallowed my last mouthful, I push my chair back with a screech that makes Daddie wince, but I don't care.

'Can I open my presents?'

If you've finished your breakfast.'

'I have.'

'No more toast?' asks Sue, our lovely mother's-help.

I shake my head, impatient to explore the pile.

'What about Daddie's half?' Will points to the curved end of the top of the toast that Daddie always cuts off and puts back in the toast rack in the hope that he'll get thinner.

'No,' I say.

'Can I have it?' Will asks the table at large.

'No.' I'm anxious to get on with the matter in hand.

'Of course.' Daddie reaches for the rack. 'Would you like me to butter it for you?' Sue passes him the butter and Daddie starts to spread it back and forth across the tiny sliver of toast, making sure that there is no area left unbuttered. He then pushes the end of the knife into the cut edge until it comes out without so much as a smear. He spreads everything in this tiresome way and it drives him up the wall to be given a piece of buttered bread or toast that has any part of the surface un-covered.

This delay is driving me crazy.

I wriggle on my chair. I've lost their attention and I want to get on with the main event.

'I'm going to open my presents,' I announce, rather loudly so I can be heard over all this silly chit-chat.

Mummie has sat down at last and is eating one of her yucky Ski yoghurts. 'What about your cards?' she says waving the spoon about in their direction.

I've forgotten this part of the ritual. We're meant to open the cards first; Daddie says it shows restraint.

At long last we've finished breakfast and everyone's attention is on me, so I get up to open my presents.

I pick up each parcel, turn it over, feel how heavy it is and read the label before putting it to one side. I have one or two book-shaped parcels which I'm very pleased about. There's also a long, slim, box, so light it could almost be empty, at the bottom of the pile which gives me no clues at all, except that it's from Mummie. There is nothing with a tag from my father alone, although there is a square present with a label that says, 'With all our love from Mummie and Daddie'. It's written in Mummie's handwriting and I wonder if perhaps Daddie has forgotten to get something for me. He doesn't go to the shops so he has to rely on other people. Or else he scans the pages of the newspaper or the colour supplements and sends away for something special.

The long present turns out to be a marionette. Daddie shows me how I can pull the strings to walk it across the room, make it crumple to the floor, or even pull its arms into the air to show surprise. It's better than ever I could have imagined and it isn't long before I'm quite good at making my American Indian girl come to life.

I've only the square box left. I kneel on the floor so I can gently fold the paper back. I squeeze my eyelids shut and pray that inside is what I've really, really hoped for all the time since Christmas. Under my fingers, I feel it slip into two parts. I open my eyes and I'm holding a smaller box in one hand and a photograph album in the other. It's dark red and tied with a silky black tassel. My heart skips a beat and I feel my prayers are about to be answered. The box is blue and white, and has Ilford Sprite printed on the side in fat italics. It is a camera! It's small and light and seems to be made of the same grey plastic used for our Airfix kits, but it is a camera and it is mine. I fling my arms around Daddie's neck and kiss his smoothly-shaved cheek, then I kiss Mummie and hold in a sigh and wait as I'm shown how to load the film into its little chamber, how to focus, point and press and how to wind on the film. Finally I'm allowed take it back and hold it up to my eye.

Daddie stays until all the paper has been folded away to use another time, and we've cleared away the breakfast things.

'I have something else for you, Sarie, if you'd like to come with me,' he says mysteriously. I look up from reading my instruction booklet and put the camera back in its box.

'Can I come, too?'

'If you like, Will.' We follow Daddie out of the back door and across the cobbled yard to the stable block. He reaches up to flick the great hook out of its eye, allowing the catch to swing loose, and asks us to pull one of the double doors wide open.

It doesn't cross my mind to wonder why we're going to the garage where both my parents' Morris cars are kept. I don't even begin to guess what might be behind the doors. All I know is that to follow my father to look at anything will always be interesting.

Once the door is open, Daddie rattles his way over the cobbles until he is just inside the door next to his car. I can't see anything different until I follow his gaze and see what he has leaning against the wall.

Unwrapped, but tied together with a piece of wide red ribbon and topped with a multi-looped bow, is a pair of stilts.

They're a lot taller than I am, made of wood with the top planed smooth as silk, then varnished to a golden glow and shaped to feel comfortable against the back of my shoulders. The bottom bit has been left square-cornered with twelve holes for the treads to support my feet. They're also carved with pleasing swoops. On the bottom they're rubber-tipped to help stop slips and skids.

I know immediately that Daddie has designed and made these wonderful extended legs himself. His way of doing things is so individual that it lives in him like a breath. We know, because he's told us, that simplicity is his watchword and functionality is its sister. These stilts are beautiful.

I reach forward to slip the ribbon off and pull them apart. With one in each hand, held high in front of me, I lead everyone out of the garage and wonder where to try them out. I lean them against me and stroke the smooth wood.

'Oh, Daddie…' I can't even smile, I'm so overcome. 'You made me some stilts.'

'I hope you like red.'

'I love red.' The paint shines in the sunlight. 'They're perfect. Thank you so much.'

'You can adjust the footrests as you get more proficient. They're fitted with bolts and wing-nuts. Do you see?'

I look. I see. I see that the top holes reach almost to my hip. I can't imagine becoming so proficient that I'll be able to walk on stilts this tall.

'I've put them on the lowest rung to start with.'

The back door opens and James gambols into the yard, tongue lolling, followed by Sue and Mummie.

'Can I have a go?' Will stretches out a hand, but I keep my stilts just out of reach.

'No. They're mine.'

'Not today, Will,' says Sue. 'They're Sarie's birthday present. I'm sure she'll let you have a turn when you're a bit bigger.'

I'm sure I won't, but I don't say anything for the moment.

'Why don't you try them on the tennis court where it's flat?'

It's harder to walk with stilts than I imagined. The first time I fall and drop them. I'm horrified that the varnish scuffs and dents are made where the stones and grit digs in. I'm going to do better. Daddie can't show me what to do, but we've learned how to listen carefully, and at last I can manage a few steps, as stiff and slow as a long-legged wading bird, then I jump off, glowing with effort and pride. Daddie sits with a smile on his face almost as wide as mine, sharing my triumph.

'Where shall I keep them?'

'In the stables,' says Mummie.

'How about in the baccus?' Daddie doesn't invite discussion.

As I stow my stilts away behind the door in the baccus, out of the way of the party guests, Mummie appears behind me.

'You know Daddie made the stilts for you himself.'

'Yes.' I'm surprised that she needs to tell me. I didn't think for a moment that he hadn't.

'He made them from the crutches he had when he was learning to walk.'

I turn around from where I've been fitting them into the space beside the walking sticks, umbrellas and old golf clubs, and stare at her. She's looking at me from her steady blue eyes with brows slightly raised. 'So you see...'

I'm not sure that I do see, but I understand that, in my parent's private world, this is something very important. My mother leaves to start getting ready for the party and I stay looking at my red stilts, making the moment last. I recognise the rubber tips, now she's told me, but I can't see any sign of the crutches that have been leaning against the fireplace in the box room.

They've been leaning there for as long as I can remember, but I haven't really looked at them. They're sort of part of the room, as necessary as the windows, walls and floors. All at once, I race to the back stairs, take each bare tread two at a time and turn the stiff knob to the door of the box room on the right. Inside it smells of dust and rot, mouldy cardboard boxes, the tang of rusting tins, sunlight and soot. The fire grate is still dark with ancient coats of Zebra blacking, the mantelpiece is also black and rough with grime. In the corner, facing the door, the gap where the crutches stood looks empty and hollow. But at the bottom there's something I've never noticed before. Two thin cages made from thick metal loops and painted as black as the fireplace, stand side by side like plant frames, waiting for Grannie's favourite larkspurs or hollyhocks to sprout and climb through and over them. There's a bit of paper tied to them. I kneel down and take a small brown luggage label in my hand and see written in faded pencil something too faint to read and on a line underneath, P.T. Pulman.

Present: April

My mother always loved parties of every kind and even in old age continued a rich social life. In her letters, at least once a week, she mentioned where she'd been and who she'd seen. I imagined it was to help my father feel included, but I wondered if it may have had the opposite effect and made him feel left out. But my mother had always done what came naturally and perhaps this early into their marriage my father was simply grateful to know that she was still having some fun, despite their dire circumstances.

Now that the polio was progressing from the acute to the chronic stage of the disease, my father needed more specialist rehabilitation. They were both looking forward to the arrival of some supportive leg irons so that remedial walking therapy could begin as soon as a place in a new hospital was secured and my father was pronounced strong enough to leave the London.

The London Hospital: May, 1953

'How's the house hunting going?' Diana's mother was standing by the French doors in the dining room smoking a cigarette. She rarely had more than a cup of coffee for breakfast. Diana's father looked up from opening his post at the head of the table.

'It's not a house, Mummie,' Diana said. 'I'm going to get a flat so Push doesn't feel he has to move in until he's really got going with his walking. Then we'll know more what he'll need.' She took the newspaper and shook it open. 'Goodness! The whole of this edition is taken up with speculation about the Coronation.'

'I thought you said he was almost ready to go. The last time I saw him, he was walking along those bars and that must have been three weeks ago.'

Diana continued to scan the pages of the newspaper. Her father put the letter opener down on his side plate with a ding. 'I'm sure they've got it in hand, Rhona.'

Diana flashed her father a smile. 'He's rather tired. They think he might have overdone things a bit. You know how hard he trained at his rowing. It's like that all over again. And he's had a couple of boils.'

'Oh well, it's obvious. He's rundown. You'll both have to wait a bit.' Diana's mother turned away from the window and stubbed out her cigarette. 'Right, I need to get ready so I'll love you and leave you.'

'I'll give Push your love this afternoon, Mummie,' Diana called after the retreating figure.

Diana wouldn't admit it, but she was worried. Push, having made so much progress over the last month, had seemed to take a backwards slide over the last week or so. He developed a persistent cough. Then there were the boils. Not just one or two as she'd told her parents, but many all over Push's body. Then the cough turned into a chest infection—they were calling it a lung abscess—and she'd heard from Push's brother that in the last few days he'd developed a bit of a fever. Nobody could say for sure what was wrong until more tests were completed.

It was hugely disappointing news and Diana knew she should tell her parents but as no one had actually said that their plans for a transfer should be suspended, she was going to continue to assume it was a blip. She was sure it was exactly as her mother had said: Push had overwhelmed his fragile immune system with all his exercising, and now it had gone into a bit of a tail spin.

Undaunted, Diana drove to the London Hospital for her usual Saturday afternoon visit. On arrival, she was greeted by the Ward Sister—not Sis, but someone whom she didn't know well—who must have been waiting for her at the top of the stairs. The Sister, impeccably turned out in a regulation mauve dress with starched apron and frilled cap, ignored her enquiries about Push's temperature and instead guided her into a colourless office away from the ward. Once the door was closed, she told Diana with great sympathy that blood tests and X-rays had been taken, and a shadow had been found on Push's lung confirming that this latest illness was not a chest infection as had been suspected, but something far more serious.

Diana left the hospital without being able to see Push. On her way out she bumped into a young registrar.

'Diana, I've just heard about Push. I can't tell you how angry I am.'

'I can't believe it. After all he's been through.' Dazed as she was, she couldn't remember the man's name, only that she recognised him as being one of Push's old Cambridge friends.

He took her by the shoulders and his face was furrowed with anxiety. 'Have they told you where he's going?'

'Brentwood. Brentwood in Essex. He'll be even further away from me there. Although, I suppose it'll be easier for his parents to visit.'

'Push always said you were an incurable optimist.'

She gave a little smile and moved back half a step so that he would let her go but he gripped her shoulders tighter still.

'I have to tell you something. I know I shouldn't but I'm so angry.'

'Angry?'

'I'll walk you to the entrance.' He released her and they started to walk down the corridor together. He dropped his voice. 'All that talk of a chest infection. I knew it wouldn't turn out to be that. There's been a case of TB on the ward for weeks, they just didn't realise it soon enough. It's put all the patients at risk. I said something at the time but my voice doesn't carry much weight, I'm afraid. I'm so very sorry, Diana. I wish I'd done something more but they just didn't want to listen.'

'But he will get better, won't he?' Diana couldn't really take in what the registrar was saying.

They walked a little further until they could see the entrance hall ahead and stopped again. 'It's going to be a long haul. I won't pretend it isn't, but we've got some really effective drugs in the arsenal now.' He gave a reassuring smile. 'It means we don't have to rely on surgery or helio-therapy in the way they did before the war. However, he will have to be on long-term bed rest. Did he tell you that?'

'No. I wasn't allowed to see him. I didn't even see Sis.' She shrugged. 'I suppose if you're ill, you go to bed.'

'Yes, but you do understand that this means no exercise at all.'

Diana looked at the people coming in and out of the etched-glass doors. It was still mild and visitors were carrying their hats and had coats slung over their arms. The square of sky that she could see between the buildings on the other side of the street was clear and blue. The corridor smelt of polish and something antiseptic. It all seemed so normal, so exactly as it had for the last six months.

'What about the exercises he was doing to prepare him for his callipers?'

Push's friend shook his head. 'That'll all have to stop now. You see, he can't risk any exertion because it might tear the places in his lung as they start to heal.'

'What about learning to walk again?'

He shook his head again. 'I have to go now, Diana. I've been indiscreet, I know, but Push is my friend and… I'm sorry.' He reached for her hand and shook it. 'I wish you luck.'

She stood still and watched as he strode back up the long corridor. His black shoes were very shiny; she thought they must be new. She watched his heels reflect in the polished floor all the way until he became very small, turned a corner to the left and disappeared.

Diana arrived back at Larchmoor only a minute or two before her father returned from playing squash. She met him at the door.

'Push has got TB.' She knew it would be a shock but she was in no fit state to think about how to say it more sensitively.

Her father walked in, took off his hat and gloves, then placed them deliberately on the hall table. 'TB,' he repeated, then sighed deeply. 'That's a killer, Diana.' He shook his head slowly.

She was completely unable to reply.

'I'm so sorry, pet. I shouldn't have said that. But you know TB was what killed your grandmother's first husband and their son. He would have been my elder brother. Half-brother.'

She reached for his hand and wrapped his fingers

around hers, taking comfort from the gesture. 'But they have new drugs now. Very effective drugs. It's not like it was before the war. They're going to get him better.'

They stood together in the dark panelled room and Diana felt that they had both lived this before.

'Are they sure?' he said eventually. 'I mean, are they sure it's TB?'

'Quite sure. The Sister was waiting for me. There's a shadow on his lung.' She saw the look in her father's eyes and added quickly, 'They wouldn't let me see him but they're preparing to move him to Brentwood in the next couple of days. It's a place especially for people with TB.' She paused. 'So, you see, there can be no mistake.'

Chapter Ten

Present: April

Since the 1980s the hospital-borne infection to fear had been MRSA, and when my mother had her hip replaced, efforts were made to ensure that she wasn't carrying the strain before she was admitted for surgery. The medical profession was well aware of the risk that she could leave hospital with a worse condition than the one she was being treated for, and strict procedures were in place to minimise that risk. If the system broke down, she could have actioned an official complaint and appealed for compensation. But during the early days of the NHS when my father was a patient, I doubt compensation had even been talked about.

Polio was always visible in our house, but we rarely thought about TB. Despite its frequent legacy of psychological trauma brought about by extended hospitalisation, surgery or prolonged drug treatment, TB was invisible. And yet, ultimately, it was TB rather than polio that may have been the more to blame for my father's inability to walk again.

On my desk beside me was the last letter my mother wrote to my father before he left Hanbury Ward at the London Hospital on the Mile End Road. It wasn't dated but the postmark on the azure envelope clearly showed 22 May, 1953.

Push, my Darling,
I don't really know what to say about this fresh blow which has befallen you. How unlucky <u>can</u> one get? But Push, all I can say is that I <u>know</u> in my heart of hearts we are both going to beat everything & that you'll come back to me & we can start to be happy again. You mean so <u>very</u> much to me, Push Darling, and <u>nothing</u> will take you away from me for ever!! I'll just keep slogging away here until you are able to come home & will that be the day!! I think we'll have to put all the flags out—just like we are for the Coronation! Only they will mean so <u>much</u> more.

If you feel sometimes that the odds are rather heavily set against you, just remember that your Pa & Ma & I are fighting to help you too—I literally am thinking of you <u>every</u> spare moment—& just when I'm waking up in the morning I think about you & just before I fall asleep.

I find it very lonely without you—

Keep your chin up & don't give in to anyone & remember,

I love you,
"Didie"

I wondered if my father received this letter before he was loaded into the ambulance for his journey into the Essex countryside, or if it was sent after him to arrive several days later. This would have been his third ambulance trip since that Sunday morning in October, seven months earlier. No member of his family was allowed to travel with him.

I recalled how much it hurt if his chair was bumped, or if someone inadvertently tripped over his feet or banged a leg. Muscle spasms and nerve pain would have been most intense in the early months. I liked to think that some of the acute pain had diminished by this point. All the same, each journey must have been a sudden, terrifying, agonising and lonely development.

Yet, knowing my father's love of machines in general and vehicles in particular, perhaps he might have persuaded the attendant to slide open the connecting window so he could talk with the driver about the Daimler engine that was transporting him, and the famous Hooper Coachworks body with its great balloon-like front wings.

And my mother. What of her? That line. 'I find it very lonely without you,' twisted my heart. How cruel that on 22 May, ten days before the Queen's Coronation when the country was in a high state of jubilation and London was covered in flags, the news should come that he was finally on the move—not to Stanmore as they had all hoped, or even Oswestry, their second choice—but to The London Hospital Annexe in Brentwood, Essex, a specialist clinic for tuberculosis patients.

'It was very different at Brentwood,' my mother said.

I had bitten the bullet and decided to ask her about what happened after my father left the London, and she agreed to talk some more. We sat together in her kitchen with my father's last silver tabby pressed against the Aga, enjoying the heat. A hanging basket filled with velvet-faced gold and violet pansies swung gently in a spring breeze outside the window. The kitchen window looked out onto a contemporary paved area that, when I was a child, was a mess of nettles and rough grass with just enough cleared space for a sandpit.

'Brentwood was more relaxed. Although Push had made some good friends at the London and he was sorry to leave them so suddenly.'

'I guess that's the nature of hospitals.' I paused 'At least, long-stay hospitals. You make sure you get on well with people, but all the time you're hoping to leave as soon as you can.'

She turned to me. 'Mr Barnes, the dentist... He was very good to Push. A very kind man. He gave Push a brand new electric shaver.'

'That was generous.'

'He said it was a spare one he had at home but Push was sure it was new. He must have seen Push struggling every morning with his water and shaving soap and whatnot.' She mimed shaving her face. 'Push guessed that he'd asked his secretary to go out to buy one.' She thought a little more. 'There were lots of East Enders in there, too. They hadn't ever seen an electric shaver.' She smiled, remembering. ' "What 'appens to the 'air?".' She managed a passable Cockney accent while pulling a face that she'd copied from my father. ' "Not air—electric!" That was Push. "Nah, what 'appens to the 'air? The 'air on yer fyce".'

The expressions she pulled during this little story were truly appalling and we both laughed aloud. I was reminded of an ancient school report that she was often happy to quote: "Diana must not make grimaces".

'So what was Brentwood like?'

'First impressions were that it was just a line of huts in the countryside. A lot of trees and shrub beds outside, and the windows were always open. Huge wards. Twenty or thirty beds in each, I should think.'

'All TB patients?'

My mother shook her head and frowned. 'I can't remember. I shouldn't think so. They were mixed wards, I do remember that. And there were children.' She leant over to look through a small pile of correspondence at one end of the table. 'I found something...

I think you'll find this interesting.' She pushed a small envelope into my hands.

I took it and drew out a piece of glossy paper folded like a greetings card. A black and white photograph adorned the front. 'Oh my goodness! What an austere-looking place.'

'It was a bit. Like an RAF camp.'

My father must have felt at home, I thought, looking at the stark brick building, metal windows and ventilation cowlings on the roof. How many years before had he been a flight engineer in the Berlin Airlift? Only five or six. I peered more closely at the little picture. Above a square archway in a flat-roofed extension tacked on to the main block, I could make out some words, LONDON HOSPITAL and in smaller capitals beneath, ANNEXE. Three women captured as they made their way towards the entrance. All three wearing calf-length skirts, nipped-in jackets and sensible brogues. All bareheaded with identical hairstyles; smooth crowns, curly around the face and waves worn long at the back below the shoulders. Around the buildings, mature trees and tidy flower beds were much in evidence.

It was a leaflet full of instructions: how to get to the hospital by public transport or on foot; what to bring; visiting hours, information about the chaplains, the barber, the library, the almoner; what to do about valuables and correspondence.

I examined it carefully. There were several puncture marks in one corner where it had been pinned to another document.

'I love this...' I read aloud in the sort of clipped accent copied from Brief Encounter: ' *"We hope that your stay with us will be a happy one, and we would like to give you our best wishes for a speedy recovery. H. BRIERLEY, House Governor".'* I read a little more, then laughed in amazement. 'Can't imagine this happening today. It says here, there was a barber that visited the ward daily.'

My mother stood beside me, reading over my shoulder:

SMOKING
The smoking hours in the wards are :-

6-0 a.m. — 8-0 a.m.

12-30 p.m. — 1-30 p.m.

3-30 p.m. — 8-0 p.m.

And provided the doctor has not forbidden it, you may smoke between these periods.

'People didn't understand the dangers of smoking then.'

*Please note that you must bring your Ration Book, and that it must contain the following Coupons: Meat, Eggs, Fats, Cheese, Bacon and Sugar. If you have deposited any of these with your supplier, you **must** get them back before coming to the Hospital.*

'The thing about Brentwood.' My mother tapped the leaflet. '…wasn't the restrictions; we'd been used to that all during the war. It was the freedom. After the London, it didn't really feel like a hospital.'

'Even so, I don't know how you coped.'

'You know, we just got on with it. You have to really. There was no option.' It wasn't the first time that my mother had used this expression.

No, I thought. You had no option. What can that have been like? I'd had it so easy by comparison. All the choices that a couple make during early marriage—where to live and work, deciding to have children, managing a budget, the interests and friends you might share—almost all these were dictated for my parents by the situation in which living with sickness left them.

Coopers, Berkhamsted: May, 1953

Extraordinarily, Diana realised afterwards, she went in to work on Monday. She'd spent the weekend explaining this latest blow to her family and the friends who constantly called her for updates. The worst telephone call had been, undoubtedly, the one she'd had to make to Push's parents. They were as devastated as she was herself. It was the sheer unfairness of it that appalled them, but Ma P recovered herself sufficiently to convince herself and Diana that at least they knew he had been diagnosed at the first possible opportunity and already action had been taken to get him to a specialist centre where they could begin treatment immediately.

'Even before the war,' she explained to Diana, 'there was a very good prognosis if the disease was caught in the first few months. It was only if the TB was allowed to spread throughout the lung, unchecked, that it became so dangerous.' They both agreed that despite their own feelings, they needed to remain strong to give Push real encouragement to face this new turn of events.

Diana was nothing if not stoical; she truly believed that everything would turn out well in the end, it was only that they would have to wait a little longer than they had expected. However, when Captain O-B asked, as he always did every Monday morning when she went into his room to take a letter, 'How's your husband this week?' she found herself unable to answer and broke down weeping.

With the kind intervention of Mrs King, the Head of Personnel, Diana began to calm down.

'Why does the TB Annexe have to be so far away?' She was in despair. 'It's going to take all day to get to see him and I'll only have an hour or two at best. And I don't even know if I'll be able to visit at all yet.'

'It does seem horribly unfair when you were just thinking he might be coming home soon,' Mrs King agreed, then checked that the door to the office was properly closed. 'Now, Captain O-B's told me we can take as long as you like in here. It's nice and private and comfortable, so let me make us both a pot of tea. I think there might even be some cake. Then we can work out what Cooper's can do to make life a little easier for you.' She smiled. 'You're a good secretary and we don't want to lose you. That's if you still want to carry on working for us?'

'I do. I must.' Diana tucked her hankie up her sleeve. 'We've got no other money coming in, apart from the rent on our house in Iver, and that goes towards paying off the mortgage. Do you know, we only lived there for about a month together and we've been married since September last year? That's nearly eight months we've been married and for most of the time I've been living here in Berkhamsted, back in my parents' house as though I were a teenager again.'

Mrs King made a tray of tea and they sat in the Captain's office drinking from the best china cups working out that if Diana took Wednesdays off, Cooper's could manage with two two-day blocks, and Diana would be able to visit Push once in the middle of the week, on a Wednesday, and again at the weekend.

The London Hospital Annexe was a haphazard collection of low one-story buildings, connected by a string of corridors and interconnecting doors. The whole thing, Diana thought on her first approach having walked the twenty-five minutes from Brentwood station, looked so temporary that it might blow away at any minute. She was astonished to learn that it was nearly twelve years old and had been put up as part of the Emergency Medical Service arrangements during the war.

Ironically, after all the abortive efforts Ma P had put into persuading Jack Mann to get Push moved out of the London, when she got to Brentwood, Diana found that Push was in Mann Ward, named after Jack himself.

There were eighteen beds for tuberculosis patients, all occupied by people who had other conditions as well as TB. Nursing was highly individualised for each patient. What was universal, Push and Diana quickly discovered, was the attitude to nursing which was committed, humane and exemplary. Despite the very high standards, they found the atmosphere on Mann Ward to be less formal than at the London, and this happy partnership of vocation and fun was largely down to the Ward Sister, Anne Johnson, under the watchful eye of a splendid Assistant Matron who maintained discipline at Brentwood without making the patients or staff feel rule-bound.

Present: April

If my mother wrote any letters to my father when he first went to Brentwood, they hadn't survived. Or been found yet. It was perfectly possible that my father kept them and we had yet to discover the box where he'd stored them, but at that moment there was nothing other than my mother's memories to work on. And Sister Anne Johnson's own recollections.

Anne never married and considered nursing both a vocation and a privilege. She was quite simply wedded to her career. She looked after my father for a relatively short time—barely eighteen months—but such was her personality and the gratitude of the family that she'd remained a valued friend ever since and often came to Thelveton for her annual leave.

During these visits when I was very young, she noted my love of reading and made a point of bringing me books, and we read them aloud together. One day she came with the first of Dick Bruna's Miffy books. Somehow we decided that I should call her Miffy, and so she remained ever since. Sometimes I stayed with Miffy in London and she showed me the sights on her days off, and we exchanged Christmas cards every year.

I wrote to Miffy with a list of questions about her time at Brentwood, most of which she answered in a clear blue-ink script, unchanged for decades. She was long since retired but her memory and ability to recall was as strong as ever. Where she refused to answer a query, she wrote 'Really!' in the margin to leave me in no doubt as to my impertinence. She was exactly as I remembered; an engaging mix of brisk no-nonsense, scrupulous morals and limitless down-to-earth kindness.

From a combination of my mother's memories, the letters, Sister Anne's descriptions of her experience nursing TB patients along with a little independent research, I felt as if I'd formed a clear idea of The London Hospital Annexe, where before, I had none. In fact, it had never really dawned on me before that my father went through several very different hospital episodes before he was allowed home for good, and this was just the third. To Will and me, hospital was just hospital, but to my father each hospital was unique, and some better tolerated than others.

In 1953 the treatment for TB was, in the first instance, rest, rest and more rest; lesions in the lung had to be allowed to heal. The treatment for recovering polio patients was exercise, exercise, exercise. Paralysed muscles became wasted and frail from inactivity, but what had kept my father from sinking into a full-scale clinical depression after his first Easter in hospital had been the discovery that there was movement, which meant neurological development and regrowth. The understanding that he could effect any improvement through his own effort was all-important. For all the advantages of Brentwood, my parents found that the predictions of my father's medical friend were all too real. Active exercise had to stop while treatment for the TB was established. It must have been devastating news.

After bed rest, the importance of regular, nourishing food of the best quality was thought to be a crucial factor in making a full recovery. Although many things had come off rationing by June, 1953, butter, cheese, margarine and all types of meat were not yet freely available. Given the restrictions, the staff ensured that hospital food was good enough and included plenty of fresh vegetables.

The nurses walked about the wards in regulation Daniel Neal brown lace-up shoes that were almost silent. They wore made-to-measure mauve uniforms—student nurses in mauve overalls known universally as Purple Passions, until their uniforms arrived—although at night, patrolling the wards, they had permission to wear matching mauve cardigans to counteract the ubiquitous and perishing cold. Morning, noon and night, summer or winter, excepting the very worst of weather, the windows were wide open, as fresh air was thought to play an important part in their patients' treatment.

I wondered how my father had fared with the cold. One of the first things we learned as children was always to close the doors. My father had an almost pathological dislike of draughts, suffered dreadfully from a fall in temperature and developed painfully swollen chilblains every winter.

Fresh air aside, once their antibiotic treatment started, patients were surprised how soon their fever would begin to come down. After a very few weeks they began to feel better, coughing reduced and breathing became easier.

My mother found her new trek around London took time but wasn't as onerous as she had feared. With my father quickly showing signs of improvement and settling in better than they could have imagined, life for her established itself again around work at Coopers.

However, after the initial elation following such a swift improvement, patients often experienced a period of despondency when they realised that treatment would be prolonged. For my father, life went back to an exasperating waiting game. The little control he'd managed to regain drained away like water slipping through his fingers; all the work he'd done on rehabilitation from the polio seemed wasted now that he could only lie on his bed waiting for his tuberculoid lungs to become strong enough to start some passive physiotherapy.

The London Hospital Annexe: June, 1953

'Ah. It's the delectable Sister Johnson come to torture me again.' Push greeted his favourite nurse with a wide smile and tried not to think about the reason she was standing beside his bed.

'You're getting cheekier every day, so you must be feeling better.' Sister Johnson took Push's thermometer off his locker and checked it before putting it into his mouth.

She stood in silence, looking down at her watch while taking his pulse. Push concentrated on avoiding the eye of the patient opposite who was trying to make him laugh. He raised his eyes to the open window through which he could see the trees. He enjoyed being on the ground floor after months spent on an upper floor at the London, with only the roof-tops to look at and the clouds in the sky. While he waited, he calculated that he must have had his temperature checked at least five hundred times since he was first taken into hospital. Sister Johnson removed the thermometer and wrote the results down on his chart.

'All normal, I'm happy to say.'

'Do I really have to keep having these injections? You wouldn't believe how much better I feel.'

Sister Johnson looked up from writing her notes. 'I'm afraid so. And for several months yet.'

'Why couldn't those evil torturers have found a way to stick this stuff into a pill?'

'You're lucky the evil torturers found a way to stick it into you, however uncomfortable it is. A few years ago you wouldn't have been so lucky. Now give us your arm and we'll soon have this done.'

Push leaned onto his left side and tried to relax his right arm as Sister Johnson pushed up the sleeve of his pyjama jacket and found the big fleshy triceps muscle. Every day was worse. The whole upper arm was covered in red puncture wounds and an arc of bruising ran from his shoulder down to the elbow and beyond. She pushed the hypodermic needle in as gently as she could, pressed in the syringe then withdrew the needle very slowly. She held a pad of cotton wool against the site. Push screwed up his eyes but remained silent.

'I'm sorry, Pete, I am trying to avoid the bruised areas but everywhere's become very swollen now and it's vital that we get this into a muscle.'

'I never thought I'd say it, but I wish you could stab that thing into my backside.'

'Or the top of your leg. Thigh muscles are ideal, but

I'm afraid that those are no-go areas for you as yet.' Sister Johnson rolled his sleeve down so Push could lie against his pillows again. 'I know you're worried about getting ulcers, but there isn't enough depth of muscle to inject your legs as well. It's as simple as that.'

'There would be if I was allowed to exercise.'

'Bed rest only. You know that, Pete.'

Push frowned and looked towards the window again. He was trying to be patient but it was becoming more difficult every day to lie in bed doing nothing but read. Everyone felt the same and, despite the relaxed atmosphere, the ward sometimes erupted with outbreaks of bad-tempered bickering.

'You do realise that every day spent in this bed is a day wasted,' he said eventually.

Sister Johnson walked to the bottom of the bed and hung his chart on the rail, then she reached behind Push and pulled out a pillow to plump it up. 'Dr. Rusby knows what he's doing. He's a very good doctor and he understands that you need to work your legs.' She straightened his bedclothes and re-did the hospital corners at the foot of the bed. When she'd finished she leaned towards him and lowered her voice. 'They're sending a physical therapist down from the London to see you soon.'

'Really?' Push couldn't keep the surprise out of his voice. 'So I can start my exercise programme again?'

'Sort of. Not exactly, but Dr. Rusby will explain.'

Push sighed. 'So for now, you're saying, it's right arm every morning, and left arm every evening.'

'No flies on you.' Sister Johnson smiled and moved away to the next bed.

Chapter Eleven

Present: April

A few days later I wrestled from sleep with the roar of my father's Aston Martin in my ears. It took me a moment to realise that I was hearing a tractor and spray boom turning under our bedroom window.

My father's Aston Martin was now in Spain, fully restored. Will and I had seen so many pictures of it that it was almost as if this car had been part of our childhoods and, although the licence plate, AUC 798, hung forever in my father's office, the reality was that neither of us had ever seen the car for real. The great, British-racing-green, 1935 Le Mans Aston Martin sports car, that was my father's pride and joy in the years before he was married, was sold soon after he was diagnosed with TB.

Whenever the subject came up, our mother liked to tell the story of how she was allowed to drive it during the time our parents were courting.

'I'd never driven anything like it, so when I put my foot on the accelerator it just went...' She'd throw her head back and push her arms out straight to demonstrate the power of the car. 'We came to a corner and I couldn't hold it. We went up the bank, leaped a sort of ditch thing and ended up in a ploughed field.' She always paused for effect at this point. 'And do you know what Push did?'

Of course we knew. We smiled and nodded but she told us anyway.

'He turned to me and said: Are you all right, Didie? And I realised he was the man for me.'

I can't remember what our father would do at this point. Perhaps he was never in the room when our mother relayed this tale of vehicle-abuse. I don't even know if they managed to drive it out of the field or if it had to be towed.

'It was too big for the garage at Burnage,' my mother said when I called to ask what had happened to it. 'The doors wouldn't close. It was made for an ordinary runaround and the Aston was much longer than other cars at the time.'

'Wasn't there something to do with Graham Hill? I have this bizarre notion that Daddie taught him to drive.'

'Oh no. Not how to drive. They were both members of the London Rowing Club. Push took Graham for a ride in the Aston and showed him how to double declutch. After that, of course, Graham got into cars and didn't want to ride his motorbike any more.'

'What did happen to the Aston?' I asked again.

I heard her sigh. 'Push loved that car,' she said after a pause. 'It was the only time I ever saw him cry.'

The London Hospital Annexe: June, 1953

'What are you reading?'
Push picked up the book that was lying on his bedside table

and looked at it without interest. The bookmark showed that he was still near the beginning. 'Casino Royale. William brought it down for me last weekend. He says that it sold out in four weeks, but Foyles have some more now and everyone's reading it.'

'Any good?'

'Not bad. Although I can't really stick with anything at the moment.' Push fanned the pages of the book, then closed it and put it back on top of his locker again.

'I expect you're excited about meeting Miss Hillier next week.' Diana tried to bring some brightness into Push's leaden mood.

'Mmm.'

'Push?'

'What? Oh, yes. It'll be good to get moving again. Every time I try to do some exercises by myself, they tell me to stop.'

'So what's she going to do that's so different?'

Push raised his eyebrows. 'Passive exercise.' He flexed his fingers on his right hand for a moment or two. 'Bit of a contradiction in terms. Passive exercise.'

'Well, that's good. It sounds as if you can do it lying down and it won't hurt your lungs.' Diana reached for the book. She read the fly-leaf then found the opening page and scanned the first few lines. 'Perhaps you could lend this to Mummie when you've finished it.'

'I can't imagine that exercise done lying down could be any use whatsoever.'

Diana carried on reading. She turned a few more pages and stopped to read again. 'Mummie likes card games; I think she might enjoy this.'

Push looked at her. 'Take it now.'

Diana glanced up and saw Push flexing his hand again. Over and over again he spread the fingers as wide as they would go, then relaxed them onto the folded top of his sheet.

Diana closed the book with a snap. She grasped his hand and held it so he couldn't flex it any more. 'I thought we weren't going to keep secrets from each other,' she said gently. 'What aren't you telling me?'

'Nothing like that, Didie.' Push turned his palm face upwards and threaded his fingers through hers. 'You don't have to worry.' He was silent for a moment or two then shook his head and took a deep breath. 'It's ridiculous.' He reached for the pale blue tin on his locker in which he kept his letters. It had Merck & Co. written in black on the side. Diana had noticed dozens of them around the room, they had all contained the powdered streptomycin that was slowly but surely curing everyone in the ward. Push flipped back the lid and took out an envelope. 'It's gone.' He passed it over to her.

'What's gone?' She unfolded the sheet of paper within and read the few lines printed there.

'I'm being ridiculous.' Push set his mouth into a thin line and looked away.

'He's only done what you asked him to.' Diana folded the letter up again and replaced it in its envelope. She handed it back but Push didn't take it. 'You decided weeks ago that it was the right thing to do.'

'I know. It is. I just had no idea I'd mind so much

when it came to the crunch.'

She reached over to Push to comfort him and tried to think of something helpful to say, but nothing came to mind. 'He's got a very good price for it,' she said eventually.

Push turned around and buried his face in Diana's neck. It wasn't just the loss of his car, she realised with a rush. How could she console someone for whom driving, cars and engines were his very soul? He knew he might never drive again.

Thelveton: 1969

We call it a garage but it was made to be a coach house for the main house at Thelveton. It sits among trees that have grown tall so it's very shady. Now the roof is green with moss and the wooden posts holding up the bit over the door are dirty cream. There are two great doors that roll back on rusty, grating, bare, iron wheels which are painted with some red stuff that comes off on your hands and clothes if you aren't careful. Grannie takes a good grip on the handle on one side of the door with both hands. Her handbag swings on her arm as she leans in and pushes hard against the door frame with one foot. To begin with nothing happens and then, very slowly, with terrible creaks that make me put my hands over my ears, the door begins to roll sideways.

As soon as I can, I slip inside and dart past Grannie's horrible Austin Maxi (Daddie's description) and look into the gloom beyond. There is nothing in this world that makes me feel safer than a mix of engine oil and tobacco. In this garage-within-a-garage, the smell of engine oil bubbles up like the cosy fug of some sleeping animal. I take deep breath after deep breath and close my eyes with a sigh of happiness.

Grannie walks in behind me. 'Do you want to take the dust sheets off?'

I nod.

'Both cars?'

I shake my head. 'Just the Special.'

Behind Grandpa's Austin 10 lies Daddie's Special. It's covered by a mustard yellow and white checked dust sheet. It almost fills the whole space left and I wonder how it was driven in here. My heart is racing.

'You stand there, Sarie, and hold those two corners and I'll stand here. Then we'll fold towards the middle and we'll keep any mess out of the way. Are you ready?' I nod. I follow her lead and soon we have the dust sheet folded in a tidy square on the ground.

The first thing that I think is how enormous the car is. It's very near the ground and has only two doors. It is wide and very, very long, almost as long as the whole garage. Daddie told us all about it and how it's made from fibreglass which is very strong and very light and he painted it British racing green with a white circle on its huge bonnet ready for a race number. He has the steering wheel at home in his study under the painting of his prized Aston Martin. He carved the wheel himself from veneered wood and studded it with silvery nuts to stop the steering wheel from slipping through his hands when he wants to go fast. I stroke the back wing sweeping up and over the rear wheel. It's smooth and cool.

I walk around and look into the empty headlamp spaces. There are holes in the front waiting for the bumper to be fitted and there's no windscreen. That's at home too. Daddie said that it only needed about thirty more hours work for the car to be finished. That's way less than a week.

I peer inside. The seats are missing but you can see the dashboard and the gear box. A patch of oil has dripped onto the stable bricks and made a stain, but the glorious smell rises up warm and comforting from the car's workings. It's like glimpsing into my own father's head. Daddie designed this car. He made it and worked on it and spent hours in this garage putting it together. And the really wonderful thing is—I have to remind myself of this—that he did all this work after he'd been ill. I've seen him grovelling about on mats under cars in our back yard with his legs dragging about behind him. I've held torches and lamps for him to see into the innards of the cars he has worked on. I've passed him spanners and wrenches, nuts and bolts. I've squirted oil where he pointed with his shaky finger and I slid my skinny arms into spaces that he couldn't reach and even held the hair out of his eyes. But always it's been to repair something that was broken or damaged. He gets it done; but it makes him exhausted, he's out of breath and it hurts a lot. I just can't imagine he made this car from nothing, and yet he did. But it isn't finished and I've never seen him do anything to it.

'It is beautiful, isn't it?' Grannie smiles at my enjoyment. 'I keep the tyres pumped up so that the rubber doesn't perish.'

'Why didn't he ever finish it?' I ask for the first time.

'Because of you.' She looks at me and smiles.

'Me?'

Grannie picks up the dust sheet again and gives me an edge. I take it and stand at the back of the car. 'When you were born, I think he didn't have anything to prove any more so he didn't need the Special. Now, hold tight.' She flips the dust sheet open and together we let it float down to cover the car again and turn it once more into a checked shape crouching on the ground. Then we climb into the Maxi and, gears grating horribly, we roll down the drive towards Diss and the Co-op in search of lemon-flavoured Pennywise biscuits.

Present: April

After talking with my mother, I went back to opening cartons. I found one containing a number of rather smart yellow and gold State Express 555 cigarette boxes. Inside there were numerous official letters written on war-time sized note paper measuring just 17.5 x 11 cms each.

The last item in the box was an undated postcard acknowledging receipt of ten shillings, the remittance due for a driving test starting from Mile Cross Lane in Norwich. If my father had known that driving would again one day become a reality, I wondered if we would still have had his Aston.

Prior to this test, I knew that my father had practised

hill-starts on the cobbled surface of Timber Hill, a street that had become fully pedestrianised in the 1990s lined with fashionable boutiques and restaurants. Timber Hill was the route I took most often into the centre of Norwich and I sometimes imagined my father learning to drive all over again when he was finally well enough to consider buying another car and have it converted to hand controls. The stones and cobbles in the road echoed to the sound of many footsteps where once my father's tyres ran. He could not have dreamed then that his own daughter might one day walk with his grandchildren down that same street or that eventually he'd be able to drive his family in his car.

Driving gave my father liberation and, when he drove alone, it was the only time that nobody knew exactly where he was. Once, he told me that he sometimes took unusual routes home from work or spontaneously travelled to look at something just so he could feel let off the leash. When my father drove his car he looked like every other driver on the road; driving gave him anonymity.

West Country: 1967

Daddie's new car is a metallic lime-green Ford Cortina GT Estate, and he's very proud of it. Mr Prime himself drove it up from Prime and Cowles to deliver it in person. He is short, has a small white moustache, wears a green tweed suit and a matching cap and my father calls him Herbie. He said there'd been some difficulties fitting the hand controls but everything seems to work now.

There is obviously something to be admired about this car but all Will and I noticed when we squeezed into our seats beside the holiday luggage on the back seat was the horrible smell of vinyl. It is thick and plasticky and has got worse as the day's got hotter. The seats stick to the back of my legs and it hurts when I fidget about. We roll our windows down a little to let in some fresh air.

'There's a draught in here,' Daddie complains immediately, rubbing his neck. 'Who's got their window open?'

We roll them back up.

'There's a smell,' Mummie says.

'It's not a very nice smell,' I say, relieved that someone has mentioned it at last.

'Oh, don't worry about that. It's just a new-car smell. It'll soon go away.'

But it hasn't and Mummie and Will have had to take seasick pills and I'm sucking lemon flavoured travel sweets as though my life depended on it and not a thought to what Dr Guthrie will find when I go for my next check-up at the dentist. But Daddie really loves his new car and he especially loves the extra power he has to play with, and because he's so excited by it, we're all beginning to love it too, despite the smell. It is a pretty colour and, in any case, we're on our way to Cornwall, Gunwalloe, the Hockings, our friends the Vaughans who knew our parents in Iver, and three weeks of sun, sea and sand. We can cope with anything.

After a night spent with Grannie Latta in Berkhamsted we've got to the sign that says *Okehampton, Gateway to the Moors*. Our hearts leap with excitement.

This is the beginning of the West Country but then everything slows right down and finally we stop. It is midday
and we're really hot and soon the vinyl smell creeps around
us like a disgusting fog. Mummie's the first to crack.

'I'm sorry, Push. I just have to open the window. We
can't breath in here.'

'Good idea.' As though he's never been annoyed
about a draught.

We've been watching the clock but nobody's moved
an inch in over ten minutes. Daddie turns the engine off
and suddenly it all seems very quiet. Before we came into
Okehampton Daddie had started making 'We'll soon look
for a picnic spot' noises. Everyone knows this really means
'my backside is beginning to hurt and I need to stop and
stretch out on the Lay-About'. He starts to shift about in his
seat, pulling the loose folds of his trousers about and lifting
himself up on his hands. Then he puts his hands under each
leg to move it about in the little space beside the pedals. He
takes his cap off his head, then puts it back on again. He
leans his elbow out of the window and peers up the line of
cars. A policeman on a motorcycle comes slowly down the
empty lane towards us so he pulls his head back in.

'I think there may have been an accident.' He sounds
calm, but he starts wriggling about even more.

'I think I'll get out and see what's going on.' Mummie
can't bear to see Daddie in pain and she gets bored very
quickly. She reaches for the door handle.

'Don't, Didie. There won't be anything we can do
about it.' Daddie puts a hand on her arm.

'No, I will. I might be able to see how long we're

174

likely to be.' She leaps out and starts striding up the side of the traffic. She's wearing a blue and white T-shirt and the stripes wobble in the heat and fumes.

We wait and we wait. Other people start to get out of cars further up the queue but they don't walk up the road like our mother; they sit on the grass in the sun and open Thermoses and have cups of tea. We've some Corona lemonade in the boot and the thought of it makes me thirsty. Daddie wriggles and heaves his shoulders about and drums his fingers on the steering wheel or hangs his arm out of the car and thrums the side. Eventually, he turns around to give me a wide smile. 'You all right, Sarie?'

I nod and grin back.

'You too, Willie?'

'Yes, Daddie. Look I'm making my Action Man fly.' He hangs it out of the window and then drops it on the road. 'Oh.'

'Yes, oh! You'd better pick it up. But watch out for the motorbike.' Daddie looks both ways before letting Will open the door and suddenly we see our mother's stripy T-shirt appearing down the other side of the line of cars. When she gets to the car, she leans on the roof and talks to Daddie through the open window.

'I've been right up to the top of the queue. You're right, there's been an accident over there. They're taking forever to tow it away.' She waves her arm and points to the left. She's always pointing at something and it embarrasses me. Everyone in the car behind us and the children in the car ahead are all staring at us. I get my book out and start reading. If we're not moving, I won't feel sick, and the vinyl smell is not nearly so bad now the windows are open.

Then all at once, the door opens, Mummie jumps in and pulls the door shut with a loud clunk.

'Nothing's blocking the way and there's acres of open road. Go now before everyone gets the same idea.'

Daddie hesitates and peers up the road. Absolutely nothing has changed for what seems like hours.

'Go now, Push. You need your rest.'

'I need to take a leak.' Daddie starts the car and pulls out into the empty lane beside us. The cars behind us start to inch forward. He looks, then we start to drive up the line of cars.

'It's fine, Push,' says Mummie in a soothing voice. 'We want to go to the right to find a picnic place, so you'll be fine. Keep going.'

He goes faster and moves from one side of the road to the other indicated by lines of traffic cones. The motorcycling policeman draws alongside. He looks into the car and shows his teeth in a threatening grin. 'They'll show you no mercy,' he says to Daddie before roaring off with a big noise and lots of dust.

And then we arrive at the junction. A lorry with high, rattling, green sides is inches from my face. On the other side, cars have suddenly started moving towards us, then everything seems to come from everywhere and it's all too confusing to work out what's coming from where. Something large and white is almost on top of us. Daddie's trying to get round the traffic circle. I think we might be facing the wrong way. No we can't be. Daddie whirls his head about, grips the wheel hard with his thumb and juggles his fingers on the hand controls, whilst pushing the brake with his left hand. For a moment it feels as if he's left the car to fend for itself, then he jams his finger as tight as he can against the side of the wheel, pushing with his hand so that the engine roars really loudly and we surge forward in front of the green lorry and away from the rest of the traffic. The lorry accelerates too; he seems to be doing it on purpose to stop us from overtaking, and pushes us towards a red truck on the other side of us. I squeeze my eyes shut and cover my ears and wait for the crunch. Our engine roars even louder, I open my eyes again and, I can't believe it, Daddie seems to have danced us through an impossibly small gap. We skate right in front of the lorry, bump up over the kerb, then stop on the grass at the side of the road. My heart is thumping so hard, I slap my hands over my chest to try and stop it leaping out of my mouth.

Daddie is livid. 'Did you see …?' he starts to say, then flings his door open and falls out of the car.

Mummie is so shocked that she can't say anything. Will and I start to cry.

We look at Daddie lying half on the grass, his legs still left jammed under the pedals. It's so scary and all we can do is watch in a terrible sobbing silence. He scrabbles for the kerb and tries to heave himself upright. Cars are swerving around him although he isn't exactly in the way. His cap is still on his head and I'm so glad that it isn't lying in the road being run over, but his hand is dirty and blood-stained. We know he wouldn't want us to help, so all we can do is watch, Mummie too, as he makes a huge effort to inch himself away from the edge of the road. Then we wait while he braces his arm, reaches for the door frame, and with a big noise, he's back in the car at last.

Finally he closes the door and things feel almost normal again. We sit and wait for what happens next. Apart from Daddie trying to catch his breath, and the steady swirl of traffic outside on the road, we're all sitting frozen-still and quiet.

Then Daddie starts to laugh.

It's completely horrible. Will and I grip each other's hands so hard our nails dig right in. Will roars out with fright; he's only six. I can't move a muscle.

Daddy looks at our mother and starts to shake his head. He is still laughing. In fact he's laughing so hard that tears begin to roll down his cheeks. Maybe he's crying. She takes his hand all bloody in hers. Then gently smoothes the tears away with her other thumb. He turns to glance at us for a moment, then sighs and looks back to her.

'Jesus!' He closes his eyes and takes a great shuddering breath. 'For a moment I forgot I couldn't walk. I was going to get out and give that driver a piece of my mind.' He shakes his head as though he really can't believe what happened although we all saw it and his hand is all grazed and dirty. Then he starts the engine and we gently move forward into the road. 'Right, everyone look for a place with a view where we can eat our picnic.'

1. *Thelveton Grange, Norfolk*
2. *Push's parents, William Prockter and Mary Pulman. Drakes Place, Wellington, before the sale*
- post WW2.

3

4

5

3. *The Olympic Trial Pair: M.E.O'Brien & P.T.Pulman Winners Silver Pairs - 1950*
4. *Push rowing for London Rowing Club*
5. *Push and Diana. Norfolk Broads holiday - 1951*

6. Push and Diana with mushrooms. Thelveton Grange, Norfolk - Summer,1952
7. Push and Diana on their wedding day. London - 6th September, 1952

8. *Push during walking practice - probably February, 1953*
9. *TB lesions suspected but not admitted. Response to Diana's enquiry - May, 1953*
10. *Card enclosed with first wedding anniversary bouquet - Sept, 1953. Almost one year of separation*

MR. H. OSMOND-CLARKE

15th May, 1953.

Dear *Mrs Pulman*

    I am sorry for the delay in replying to your letter. Our reason for not transferring your husband was that he developed this abscess which required treatment by Mr Butler and it seemed advisable to have this thoroughly healed before going to Stanmore. Your husband has now developed a chest complication which requires further investigation and treatment and this, I am afraid, is a further cause of delay. Furthermore, there is a tremendous waiting list at Stanmore and I am afraid no private beds. However, the main immediate thing is to get him over his most recent complications.

Yours sincerely,

Osmond - Clarke.

Mrs D. F. D. Pulman,
Larchmoor,
Shootersway Lane,
BERKHAMSTED.

To Push,
Clove Carnations for our
First Wedding Anniversary.
With all my love,
Didle.

Cascade Florists
BRENTWOOD 751

11

12

her attention to God and asked for miracles. She even listened to a Billy Graham broadcast on the wireless by herself, comforted in the knowledge that Push was listening too.

At a cocktail party after Easter she had several people tell her that she and Push were 'so brave.' She thought about this for a time, then put pen to paper.

People say we have been brave about all this—but I know I couldn't myself have coped without the implicit belief that God was there helping me and I know he wouldn't leave you that way.

However, despite all her efforts to be positive for Push, it was almost as if in thinking, writing and speaking these words, she could make something that, perhaps in the very deep recesses of her mind she feared wasn't happening, real and concrete. When Push was walking he had seemed so tall, so full of life and focus. Now, out of the corner of her eye, Diana perceived a waver which she refused to give in to for a single second. She would make Push walk again through the sheer strength of positive thinking and if Push wanted her to do that through God's will, then through God she would do it.

Present: May

We returned from a few days visiting my brother. As we were leaving he'd handed me yet another carton and I'd groaned. 'How many more of these things have you got in your attic?'

'Oo, dozens!' Even as a child Will would never give me a straight answer, so I just made a face and took it. 'I think you may be surprised at some of the contents,' he'd added, suddenly serious.

I found the surprise in a box that had once contained Rothmans's Gold Flake cigarettes, still bright as a daffodil. It revealed a depth to my father's vulnerability and evidence of his desperation that astounded me. It had KEEP written in my father's unmistakable hand on the top left corner. Will's post-it note stuck to the lid informed me that the contents were 'Letters from Harry Edwards (Spiritual Healer) to PTP in hospital'.

My paternal great-grandfather and his father before him were both Church of England clergymen; my grandfather would have been too, had he made as much effort in the university lecture theatres as he did on the river Cam.

Our grandfather, despite failing to follow his father into the church, continued to enjoy a profound Christian faith and, although he didn't go so far as to say Grace before meals at Thelveton, everything he did was underpinned with an implicit understanding that God was beside us and that Judgement Day would ultimately find us out. Bad behaviour of any sort was simply far too risky to contemplate. When we moved from living with our grandparents at Thelveton to our new home in Suffolk, we took the family values and routines with us. My parents continued with their regular Sunday worship, but my father never talked about his faith and we never questioned it. That he had held such a profound and unwavering belief at any time during his life was news to me.

Yet, in this little yellow box, I held the evidence that my father had sent reports to Harry Edwards of Burrows Lea for distance healing; and every week he received a short reply. They all said much the same thing, just variations of: *As we continue our intercessions with our Spirit doctors so I know the flow of healing will go on. We can therefore look confidently to the future and the overcoming of all the causes of weakness and happier days to be.* There were two batches, six months worth in each, ending November, 1954. They infuriated me.

I put the box with another relic that I'd also found disturbing when I came across it a couple of weeks before, tucked in behind the application for my father's first wheel-chair. Foxed and brittle, this small cutting had been clipped to the exact size of the article: there was no date and no clue as to the newspaper it was taken from.

Joan has battled on to a Sunday stroll. AFTER 28 YEARS—SHE WINS. Joan was one year and eight months when she caught polio. Twenty-eight years and twelve operations later she walked, or so the article said. Joan Osborn's 'Sunday stroll' was taken between the beds of Ward 10 at the Royal National Orthopaedic Hospital, Stanmore, Middlesex, using crutches. Between the beds! Hardly a stroll.

'She didn't win!' I burst out loud.

Did my father find the cutting himself and keep it? Was it sent by a well-wisher? Did it represent an import-ant hope to cling to, or realistic evidence of the futility of dreams? Was all of it preying on the vulnerable? I felt heat rush into my throat and my heart race with anger.

I detested the idea that illness should be a battle to be fought like a war. When talking about my father, I disliked the word suffer but I especially hated the word victim.

I took a last look at the cutting and folded it carefully along the lines it had lain in for fifty years before returning it to the cigarette box. Then I closed the lid.

Unaccountably, the garden was full of magpies. It had started to drizzle. The sky was light and the fine bands of spring rain, sparkling in the sunshine, could be mistaken for nylon fishing lines connecting earth and heaven. In heaven they were fishing for men. In my garden the only creatures to be had were the magpies. I thought I counted seven but they were constantly changing position; flashing white bars against an iridescent midnight blue and fanning their tails in the air. They hopped and strutted with attitude, pecking at the grass, flying to the roof above my head where I heard them stomping on the old clay roofing tiles, then off again to perch in the high branches of the gleditsia tree while throwing back their heads, opening their black bills and laughing coarsely.

I stood and watched them for a while and felt my anger subside. I wished the letters my father had received from The Sanctuary hadn't been so patently written from a script. My father was far from stupid, he'd have known that they weren't really from Harry Edwards himself. Did he mind? Was the importance of sending in the reports a way of giving him back control?

If I were to ask my mother what she felt about the Harry Edwards episode now, I guessed that she'd simply tell me that they'd wanted to try everything they could. No stone left unturned.

It wasn't complicated; there was no reason to feel this young couple were in some way exploited, or for me to be angry. After all, it was their choice and Harry Edwards made no charge. Burrows Lea offered hope, perhaps no more than that. Curious, I sat down at my laptop, put Harry Edwards into a search engine and discovered that The Sanctuary had opened in 1946 and was still open for business, having fully embraced the internet age.

My ancestors—as did many of their peers—undoubtedly felt a responsibility to hand on spiritual values and my grandfather certainly succeeded in giving me a deep connection with the natural world, another kind of spirituality, but you can't determine what your children will believe. My father had religious faith to the end, although his brother's wavered. I was sad that mine was also wavering. I should have loved to have my father's certainty but belief, or perhaps I was looking for trust, is one thing that can't be inherited.

Chapter Thirteen

Home, Suffolk: 1967

There's an owl in one of the box rooms and I've been sent to deal with it. It came down the chimney covered in soot, leaving a pile of dirt and sticks in front of the grate. Now it's sitting high up on a stack of cardboard boxes in a corner.

Mummie likes birds but she can't stand to touch them; their bony bodies and stiff feathers give her the creeps. In early summer lots of rook babies flop out of their nurseries in the Scots pines onto the ground in front of the house. They flap around prodding the earth for worms, or wait to be fed by their parents, and Mummie keeps well out of the way. Sometimes they get themselves onto the tennis court and stuff their heads through the wire netting round the edges, pushing forwards and hurting themselves. And sometimes they die if nobody rescues them.

I love the rooks, but they're not very grateful. They stab their rescuers with their long black bills and scratch with their claws. Daddie isn't able to catch them, Mummie won't and Will is too little. I've learned that throwing a towel over them before walking back to the rookery to let them go, is the only safe way. They scream and complain at the tops of their voices for the whole journey, then sit hunched on the ground shouting some more before I back away. Eventually they calm down and go back to their usual clicking and wheezing.

The owl is watching me from its perch with round dark eyes all glittery from the sun, and specks of dust and ashes are dancing in the air from all its flying around. It's covered in soot, but I can see that it's a tawny owl and it's terrified. Its chest is heaving and there are bird droppings all over the room. Stacks of boxes have fallen onto the floor and everything is spilled out. Then it lifts its tail and squirts out another splatter of muck.

The box room is bare and hasn't been painted for an age. Mummie's latest haul from the Cash 'n Carry sits on a creaky old dining table in the middle of the room. She likes a bargain, although there's not much that anyone likes to eat. Fray Bentos pies, Tyne Brand tinned meat (which Daddie calls sour mince), giant tins of strawberry jam that grow mould before we can finish them, tinned vegetables that are never used because we grow everything we need in the kitchen garden, Oxo cubes that are all damp and have burst out of their boxes leaving a dark brown stain and dozens and dozens and dozens of tartan tins of Jock dog food.

I tiptoe to the window and reach the catch by standing on an old trunk. It's very stiff but I can just push up the bottom sash. The owl doesn't wait for me to get out of the way. She leans forward, opens her wings and glides through the open window without her sooty feathers touching anywhere. I stand still and watch her go. In a second she's flown over the tops of the horse chestnuts and I can't see her anymore.

'Has it gone?' Mummie rattles the handle of the door a little but she doesn't open it. 'Sarie? Have you got rid of it?'

'Yes.' I can't help feeling a bit sad. I liked being in the room with the owl, it reminds me of feeding Grannie's owls at Thelveton. 'There's no more owl. You can come in now.'

The door opens slowly and Mummie's head appears. She checks that the owl has really gone. She looks around and tuts. 'What a mess.' She's back to being proper Mummie now the bird is nowhere to be seen. 'I'd better get a wet cloth. You can start by putting some of these papers back.' She makes a swirling motion with her finger, then goes.

I seem to be standing on lots of saved bits of wrapping paper from the Present Box. I carefully flatten them out again and pack them away for another day.

By the time Mummie comes back I'm collecting escaped brown envelopes into a pile. A sheet of partly see-through plastic slips out and floats across the floor like a sail-plane and finishes up half under an old mattress propped on its side under the window.

'What's this?' I lunge across and grab it by one corner, then hold it up to the light and peer at the grey film.

Mummie looks around from wiping old oar handles with her floor cloth. 'It's an X-ray.'

'An X-ray. What's it for?' The only X-rays I know about are to see if you've broken a bone and although we've had plenty of spills, none of us has broken anything.

Mummie kneels down beside me on the carpet of papers and takes the X-ray from me. 'It's Push's chest. When he had TB.' She reaches for the envelope and I pass it to her. It's stiff with a cardboard back. She looks inside, then reads the words on the front. She holds the X-ray in the air.

'Let me see,' I say.

We look at the X-ray together in the light of the open window. It doesn't look like anything I've ever seen before. I can't really make sense of it even when Mummie points out the ribs and lungs. We feed the cats lungs, which the butcher calls lights, but they don't look like this, even when they're raw and red and wobbly. I want to keep the X-ray and take it to school, so we tidy up quickly and take it downstairs to the kitchen.

'What've you got there, Sarie?' Daddie's finishing his breakfast. We tell him about the owl and the mess.

'It's your X-ray,' says Mummie.

'Can I take it to school when I go back?' I don't really know why I want it but I like things to do with science and I think it might be rather special to have this picture of my father's insides.

Daddie takes the envelope off the kitchen table and puts it on his lap. He takes his glasses off his nose, folds them into their case and puts it on top of the envelope. 'I don't think that would be very wise, Didie. Do you?' He looks very grave and I wonder if he's going to be cross with us. 'Where did this come from?'

'From one of those boxes full of all your hospital

stuff.'

'Did you touch the things inside?'

'Of course,' she says looking surprised. 'The owl knocked the boxes over. We couldn't leave everything all over the floor.'

'Then I think this should go back there and then you had both better wash your hands very carefully.' He gives the envelope to Mummie.

'Is that really necessary?' But she doesn't really mean him to answer, we always do what he says. She shuts her mouth into a tight line and soon we hear her footsteps on the back staircase.

'Wash your hands now, Sarie. In hot water. With soap.'

Daddie wheels over to the kitchen sink and watches me while I do it. 'Really thoroughly. That's right. Round and round and at the base of your thumbs, like this.' Daddie shows me on his dry hands and I copy him until the lather goes all white and covers my hands all the way up past my wrists. 'Now rinse them off under running water. As hot as you can stand.' I do what he says until my hands are red and smarting.

'Why?' I say, wanting to stop.

'Just in case.' Then he points at the roller towel on the back of the door to the pantry. 'And dry them really well.'

Present: May

For a brief while, between the arrival of our two daughters, it was part of my job within the local Environmental Health department to keep the infectious diseases records for the region and pass them on to the relevant authorities. I never once saw the word polio cross my desk, but the appearance of tuberculosis on a report card was an infrequent reminder that TB hadn't yet been eradicated.

Reading of life on the TB ward through my parents' letters and the written dialogue with Anne Johnson, gave me a new understanding of the livid sickle-shaped slash down my father's back, so rarely seen and even more rarely spoken of, as well as his obsession with germs. Even so, my knowledge of TB remained sketchy compared with that of polio.

When my mother's grandmother died from TB in the late 1800s it was likely to have been known as consumption. The disease consumed the body, frequently causing its victim to literally waste away; diagnosis didn't have to be a death sentence but there was no cure other than good nursing, a nourishing diet and plenty of sunshine. TB sanatoria were effective as much for taking infectious cases out of general circulation as they were for improving the quality of life for victims of a life-threatening disease.

But by 1953, the introduction of effective drugs and a new immunisation programme had radically improved the outcome for tuberculosis patients. The mortality rates dropped from 50% in the 1940s to around 9% by mid-1950. But it was by no means a quick cure. Anything from eighteen months to two years could be expected for the combined drugs—streptomycin and para-aminosalicylic acid, known as PAS—to begin to penetrate the grainy deposits of dead tissue that surround the live TB bacilli. Anyone entering TB sanatoria should expect a lengthy stay.

The very year that my father caught TB was the same year that the BCG vaccination was first used in the UK.

In the 1970s, I lined up with the rest of the thirteen-year-olds at my boarding school, shirts and jumpers rolled up to our elbows, eyes squeezed tight shut against the anticipated, but unrealised, pain of the Heaf test. A week or two later those who'd had no reaction again lined up, this time for our BCGs. Both my father and I thought I was protected from TB for life.

The London Hospital Annexe: August, 1953

Willie Pulman continued to visit his brother as often as possible but he'd noticed that behind Push's usual good humour, he appeared restless and fractious. Push wasn't alone. As mid-summer came and went, the mercury rose ever higher and tempers throughout the ward became frayed. Thunder storms broke the endless run of hot weather, but fresher weather lasted only a day or two and the positive atmosphere of the ward that Anne Johnson had worked so hard to build, began to break down.

One day Willie came in to find the bare, oyster painted walls of the ward transformed with brightly coloured travel posters. Anne had found a new way to lift the dreary atmosphere, engaging patients' interests and providing something different to talk about. Interfering with the clinically clean decoration of the hospital was unheard of but Anne told Willie that she'd been quite prepared to challenge the strict rules for the sake of her patients. However, she was relieved that she had won the day without putting any argument to the test. Willie reciprocated by bringing some huge tubs the next time he drove to Brentwood, and arranged for his mother to fill them with flowers.

So far as the Pulman family were concerned, everyone had quickly come to rely on Anne. The family was always included in Push's treatment plans and they trusted him to her care implicitly. Soon they began to look for ways they could help her.

While other TB patients were taken out for walks in the grounds, Push's paralysis meant he couldn't leave his bed and was often one of the few patients left on the ward. All the visitors in the world could not make up for the fact that while others were out enjoying a taste of the real world, he had to stay trapped within his own four walls.

Willie often discussed the situation with Diana and they felt that the ideal would be for Push to get into a car, then they'd be able to take him for drives, but Anne explained that realistically it would still be many months before Push would be able to support his back enough to enjoy being driven.

While Miss Hillier, the physical therapist, made a car journey Push's physical goal and faith in distant healing with Harry Edwards his spiritual ambition, Anne Johnson had ideas for his mental health. Willie found himself hijacked on his way to see Push one Wednesday evening.

'Those beautiful flower tubs you gave us: I want to be able to move them into the wards to brighten the place up and move them out again when they need watering or if head office comes snooping, but since your mother kindly planted them up, they're just too heavy for us to shift.'

'I can't see that being a problem.' Willie said. 'I can make something so you just roll them about.'

'I'm jolly sure you can but you see, I want Pete to be involved. I think he should design us something and then maybe you could make it.'

Willie stood, thinking for a moment, his pinstriped suit and gold watch chain belying his willingness to get stuck into the practicalities of life. 'You want him to have something to do.'

'Don't you think this would be a start?'

Willie nodded. 'He'll come up with the perfect solution.'

'Exactly what I thought. Now, don't keep your big brother waiting any longer, he's looking forward to seeing you. Oh, and keep those chocolates to yourself, he's on a diet...'

'I'll report back to you later,' said Willie and walked into the ward to see Push.

Push was sitting up and staring at the door.

'Hello Beppo. Happy birthday for tomorrow.' Willie fished a card out of his inside jacket pocket and threw it on the bed. 'Bad news about your present, though. I've had to promise that I'll eat this fantastically expensive box of chocolates all by myself and that you're to have none of them.'

194

Push laughed but said nothing.

'What've you done to look so sheepish for?'

'Just trying to put on some weight and keep every-one happy.'

'I don't think the saintly Sister is very happy.'

'I might have overdone it a bit.' Push swept his hair out of his eyes with one hand and pointed at his locker. 'Only fruit from now on.' There was a large wooden bowl of apples and plums beside his jug of water and empty glass. The ubiquitous box of marrons glacés and empty tissue paper cases was missing. 'Seems everyone was doing such a fine job of bringing me all my favourites to fatten me up that I caused a bit of a fright after my last blood tests. Not so much blood in my circulation as liquid glucose. Point of fact, there was so much that they thought I'd developed diabetes to add to my list of problems.'

'You haven't, though?'

'No, Willie, I really haven't. It was a false alarm. I'm afraid that I can't eat your chocolates, though. But I'll keep the lid; the kitty on the right looks just like 'Swald. I hope you enjoy them.'

Willie scraped a chair close to his brother's bed.

'Now, big brother, we've been given an assignment. Your rebellious ward sister is planning an assault-by-horti-culture. We have to design some sort transport for the tubs I brought in last week. I've had an idea using some spare bed castors I might find at work but I think we need your superior engineering skills at work here. They're so fright-fully heavy.'

Present: May

Gradually, I came to understand a little of my father's insecurities and a need for vigilance that verged on the compulsive. At the time his actions had often seemed pedantic and unnecessary, although we rarely questioned his decisions. When we did, he gave a reasoned answer.

Although child-rearing was beginning to be a shared activity by the nineteen-sixties and women were going out to work, taking responsibility for family planning and making tentative demands for equality, my father was still profoundly influenced by his father's generation. He took a patriarchal view that providing for his family, keeping them safe and having ultimate authority over his wife and children, was his role and duty. Given what had happened to him at an age when young men typically feel invincible, it was understandable that he was so cautious on our behalf. He prepared us for all sorts of eventualities and catastrophes, but he feared—perhaps above all other fears—any one of us having to endure prolonged illness or injury. He knew more than most, how a sudden breakdown in health could affect the future.

My mother rarely mentions returning to Thelveton in the early letters—she'd only known it as a visitor—and probably assumed that her husband would return to their marital home at Burnage. But how my father's confinement must have dragged, and how he must have longed for home. His home. The one he'd shared with his family, filled with friends and neighbours. Not Burnage, where he'd only spent a few weeks and which must have been almost forgotten, not the digs in Boston Road, London, where he'd lived until his marriage, but the glorious mix of chaos and serenity that was Thelveton.

Children suffering from polio or TB were routinely kept in hospital away from their families for years at a time. It was thought kinder to avoid the regular pain of departing loved ones, however, many returned traumatised and alienated from their families forever.

My father was just twenty-six when he became ill. By the time his twenty-seventh birthday came around in August, 1953, he was still suffering the complications of paralytic polio and had been in the TB hospital for nearly three months with no predicted date of release.

In September my parents celebrated (if it could be called a celebration) their first wedding anniversary and by mid October my father had been in hospital for a year without respite. He may not have been a child hospitalised in isolation from his family but still, he was traumatised, as well as thoroughly institutionalised.

Between a letter from my mother in late May, 1953, shortly after my father had been admitted as a TB patient, and one dated 13 December, 1954, there was a frustrating gap of over eighteen months with no letters. But in the daffodil yellow box containing Harry Edwards' letters I found some clues to what was going on.

The tone had changed since the previous message. It started "Dear Mr. Pulman", instead of "Dear Friend". The type was darker and the words more personal.

We do not cease in our intercessions for your legs.

*In ways we cannot see, the Divine power of healing... etc.
etc. Only good can come of this and I shall await your letters to tell of signs of betterment. I am so glad to hear you
are able to get out in your chair.*

Alleluia! Something tangible and authentic at last. I
read the last line again. ...*get out in your chair* must mean
that my father's back was finally strong enough to support
him getting about in a wheelchair. Enough to go outside.
Perhaps even to go out in the car. I looked at the date: 1st
October, 1953. I wondered how long he'd been able to use
a chair and if the weather had been good enough for him to
enjoy feeling the breeze on his face, hear the birds.

Dated around ten months later, 12th August, 1954,
there was another letter in the same dark type.

...*The toning up of the general health state will
play its part in the overcoming of the symptoms of stress
and I look for these breaking down as the healing goes on,
and for your letters to tell me so. I expect them to do so.*

I flicked through the box of my mother's letters. On
the 13th December, 1954, my mother wrote that she was
longing for Christmas—surely not so that they could celebrate a third Christmas on a hospital ward?

Larchmoor: December, 1954

Diana ran upstairs and threw her case on her bed. She
didn't bother to unpack, but sat down at her dressing table,
opened her leather writing case and took out a page of pale
blue Basildon Bond headed with the Larchmoor address

printed in red that was available in almost every room of the house.

Although she'd had to drop Push back at the Annexe in Brentwood, and make the rest of the journey to Berkhamsted alone, she couldn't remember when she had been more happy.

My darling Honey, she wrote, *Thank you for a perfect four days—I had forgotten how wonderful it is to be in your company for long periods & surrounded by friends— also to be at Thelveton, which I always consider as having the most homey atmosphere of any house I know.*

Darling, I only hope I didn't tire you too much with our late nights—it was rather a case of fighting against time & I felt I shouldn't waste a single minute of you! My conscience told me that I should have given you a clear night's rest, but my heart told me otherwise...

She sat back in her chair, untied her favourite red silk scarf from round her neck and kicked off her shoes. She stretched out her stockinged feet, welcoming the central heating that her mother insisted should be turned high enough to enjoy. She loved Thelveton, but it was a very large house and comfort wasn't a priority; layers had definitely been the order of the day. But four whole days together! She luxuriated in her memories of a Christmas that had been nothing but a dream for the past two years. She picked up her pen again.

If your visit home was half as wonderful for you as it was for me, it will certainly have done you the power of good—

Chapter Fourteen

Present: May

My mother relaxed back into her chair, pulled a footstool towards her with the toe of her shoe and rested both feet on it. She crossed her legs at the ankles and looked at me expectantly.

'Can you think back to when Daddie was first allowed to come out of hospital?'

'Yes,' she said, immediately. 'We went to Thelveton to live and it was the day before Uncle Willie's...'

'No, before then. I'd like you to describe what it was like when he was allowed to go out for the day. On outings.'

'Oh.' She stopped and pulled at her bottom lip.

'I'm talking about the first time he would have left the hospital. Perhaps even been outside. It must have been a pretty big thing for him.'

'Oh, it was,' she said, suddenly remembering. 'I brought Daddie's big car over specially and it became the highlight of Push's week.' She paused. 'Our week, really. He'd got himself a book of maps and he'd spend hours studying them and planning every outing.'

At last, I thought. Here was something he could

have control over.

'He always found some special place for us to visit.'

Something occurred to me. 'When you started to go out. It must have been the first time Daddie had got dressed and worn proper clothes in years.'

My mother nodded slowly. 'I suppose it must. I only remember him wearing pyjamas in hospital.'

I tried to imagine my father looking at the clothes that she would have brought with her: shirt, trousers, jacket, possibly even a tie—he always wore a tie except when he was on holiday. Clothes he had last worn when he walked. I wondered about his shoes. I only remember him wearing soft, Hush Puppy suede boots. They accommodated his swollen ankles and were easy for him to put on while sitting on his bed, pulling his foot right up into his groin like a yoga master, to give him access to the laces without toppling forward. I sighed as I remembered the photograph with him wearing pyjamas and traditional hard, leather Oxfords.

'It must have been really nerve-wracking when you first went off in the car by yourselves. I mean, you hadn't any idea how he would manage.'

My mother smiled. 'No,' she said gently. 'Not nerve-wracking at all. It was really exciting. We still felt we were newlyweds and we had a lot of time to make up.' She looked up towards the ceiling. 'We found a golf club with very big grounds. We used to park somewhere private and have a canoodle in the car.' She glanced at me to ensure I understood what she was saying. 'It was lovely to be on our own at last. Until then, we'd only been able to see each other when there were other people around.'

There was a line in one of her letters where she asked my father if he thought they should be better behaved when they go out, but it was written in such a way as to suggest they should be anything but. I let my imagination take them to a secluded spot on the golf course. For some reason, I saw gorse bushes in full bloom, a shimmering yellow partially obscuring fairways in the distance mown tight to the ground, I heard skylarks way above. My father opens the door to let the warmth from the sun inside his father-in-law's car, my mother reaches across to kiss him, he slips an arm about her waist and pulls her close. And there I left them in the privacy they craved.

I allowed my mother time with her memories. Ten seconds. Twenty. Then she looked at me.

'How did he get from the hospital to the car?' I asked.

'In his wheelchair, of course.'

'Did he have one then?'

'Well, he must have done. It was a ghastly, huge, wooden chair with a sort of basket work affair.' She put her arms out in a circle to show me how big it was.

'Wicker-work?'

'Yes, that's right. It didn't fold up and it had a sort of trundly wheel at the back.' She paused. 'Or maybe it was at the front. Anyway, it was a frightful thing.'

'I've found a letter dated 29th December, 1954,' I said. 'It shows you both went to stay at Thelveton for four days over Christmas.'

'Did we?'

'How did you manage at Thelveton?'

'We had the wooden chair there for a long time.'

'Oh my goodness!' I uncrossed my legs and leaned forward. 'Was that the old wooden chair near the lavatory by the back kitchen?'

'Might have been. Yes, it probably was.'

The chair was quite clear in my memory. A wicker-work seat with semicircular back and sides, like an open-work Lloyd loom chair from the thirties, connected to large curved handles at the back rather like hockey sticks, all suspended over two vast wooden wheels and smaller wheels at the front.

'The metal Everest and Jennings chair was a revelation when he finally got one. There were the most amazing claims: you could tip it and turn it, jump up steps, hop in it. They had to tone the claims down after a while in case anyone injured themselves and sued. But they were wonderful chairs. Made by two American engineers.' She suddenly laughed out loud. 'I remember when Push was learning how to use his and working out what he could do, he tipped it right up and landed on the sofa at Thelveton with the chair on top of him. Pa P rushed into the drawing room and asked him "What are you trying to do, lad?" and Push said, "I've done it, Pa." He was frightfully pleased at being able to do tricks with it.'

I never saw him do tricks in his chair. In fact, this was the first time anyone had talked at length about wheelchairs. My father constantly checked its whereabouts if he wasn't in his chair, and would ask us to move it so it was always within reach. He sat in his chair, he was mobile in his chair. He repaired it, looked after it and occasionally replaced it, but unless he mentioned it, we never referred to it. I thought he hated his chair. He certainly never played with his chair. And neither did anyone else. It was one of the many taboos.

Home, Suffolk: 1965

I've been wanting Emma to come to my house to play for ages. We're almost best friends but not exactly because she lives too far away, and, in any case, it usually works out that I go to hers. Mummie thought we could play tennis but we decided to go for a ride on Fanfair, if we can catch her. Not out anywhere, just in the field riding bareback and then we'd have had time to play with my tricycle. It has yellow mudguards and a white bag for shopping on the back that closes with two silver metal buckles. But it started to pour with rain as Emma got out of the car, and it hasn't stopped yet, so we're going to play with my dolls' house instead.

Daddie made me the house and it's my pride and joy. Nobody else's father can make the wonderful things that he can make and I love showing them to people. One Christmas, when we were very small, my parents made us a model of a merry-go-round. Daddie drew a picture of it, then made it from stiff card. It has a pointed roof like a tent, striped red and white. Mummie has stuck pictures around the top that she cut from old cards, and painted the words: Pulman's Christmas Fair, very carefully. Down the middle is a core like in an apple. There's a mirror on each of the six sides made from silver foil with a painted frame, and hanging from tiny wire hooks made from paper clips she's hung six galloping horses and six running ostriches. When we came down for breakfast on Christmas morning, Daddie had arranged the merry-go-round on the record player so that it spun round and around, with the horses and ostriches flying out to the side with something that he explained was centrifugal force. Uncle Willie spins us by our hands using centrifugal force. If he were to let go, you might fly to the other side of the world. Mummie's very good at drawing and painting. She made all the animals, they're very pretty, with red and green bridles, gold bits and flowing manes or feathers. It lives in the box rooms with my dolls' house, and we don't get to see it very often in case it gets broken.

My dolls' house isn't like any I've ever seen. Daddie copied a real bungalow that he visited when his job was working out central heating systems. He said that he'd 'admired its compact design and clever use of space and light'. I'd love to have the dolls' house in my bedroom or in the nursery, but it has to live in the box rooms. If I want to play with it, Mummie brings it downstairs. She says I can feel as if I'm getting it for the first time all over again.

Emma and I stand in the hall watching Mummie walk down the stairs, carrying the house like a crown on a cushion. Daddie built it on a big base and Mummie's arms only just stretch wide enough to pick it up. It's heavier than it looks and she puts her feet very carefully on each step, feeling for the edge because she can't see where she's going.

She creeps past us sideways while I hold the drawing room door open for her. She puts the house on the floor in front of the window behind the sofa, bending her knees as she's been told, to take care of her back.

I show Emma how to hold the roof under the edge and together we lift it off and put it down on the floor.

'My Daddie made it.' I can't help saying this even though I think it might be showing off a bit.

Emma kneels down and peeps into each room in turn. There's a bird's eye view of the house, not sideways like most dolls' houses.

'All of it?'

'Not the furniture. Mummie bought the furniture at Hamley's in London. And the dolls.' I pick them up and give them to her, one by one. There's a family of three: a mother, father and a little girl. They have bendy arms and legs like pipe cleaners, which makes it easy to sit them on the chairs.

We play for most of the afternoon as it rains and rains outside. We arrange and re-arrange each room. Emma really likes the kitchen with its black-and-white tiled floor and grey-and-white striped wallpaper. I like it too. There's a dresser like the one at Thelveton, a sink bit with a cupboard that opens, an ironing board and a chair.

'There's no table,' Emma says, but I tell her that they don't eat in the kitchen. There's a polished table with a bit you can take out to make it smaller, a matching sideboard and six ivory-coloured chairs, all made of plastic, in the dining room. In the walk-through sitting room there are a sofa and two chairs There's also a side table with sliding doors and a fireplace with a painted plaster surround. We try the fireplace out on different walls until Emma says it has to go on an outside wall and I secretly study the roof to find that Daddie has forgotten the chimney.

We put the little girl to bed using some hankies that Mummie gave me to make sheets and leave the Mummie and Daddie sitting together on the hairy orange sofa. Emma put them like that; my parents never sit together on the sofa. Then we drew pictures and cut them out for the walls.

After a while, Daddie comes in to see how we're getting on and Mummie brings him a cup of tea. There are two glasses of milk for us and a plate of fairy cakes with pink and yellow icing. He talks to us for a bit and tells us a joke which makes us laugh. We show him the pictures and he says we've done well, then he heaves himself out of his chair onto the sofa so he can lie out and rest his bottom. He pushes his chair away, as always, towards the foot of the sofa, shakes out the newspaper and starts to read.

Emma watches what he's doing, then she gets up from where she's been kneeling beside the dolls' house, pulls at her green-and-white striped skirt and smoothes it down carefully. Her thick, red hair swings in front of her face and I wish mine was thick enough to do that. She's wearing long white socks and brown Clarke's sandals like mine and I watch her walk round the back of the sofa towards Daddie's chair and stand in front of it.

Then, in a second, I know what she's about to do. I should have seen what was coming and warned her, but I never thought that she'd do it.

I stop right where I am, leaning half over the house,

little girl in one hand and fairy cake in the other.

Time has screeched to a stop. My legs and arms are frozen, I'm not breathing. I can't get my voice out, I can only watch. Emma grips both wheelchair arms in her hands and swings herself up and round over the foot-plates, and sits neatly on the pile of sorbo-rubber cushions.

And I want to scream and scream and scream at her.

Daddie turns the page.

Emma turns to look at me at the same moment that Daddie looks up from his newspaper. She starts to smile but, as she catches my eye, the smile wobbles and slides off her face like melting ice cream.

There's no sound in the room at all except the thumping of my heart, which is so hard that I want to be sick.

Emma looks at Daddie. He has his back to me but I can tell by his shoulders what his face will look like.

'Get. Out. Of. My. Chair.' He's actually speaking quite quietly, but his voice is cold as ice. Emma slips out of the chair without a word. She can't take her eyes off me. She's hurt beyond infinity that I didn't say anything. Didn't stop her.

Daddie's hands are shaking and the paper rustles. He drops his head and I think he's reading again but the corner of the paper continues to rustle. Emma stands stock still, blinking back tears.

Then the sound of the swing door, the approach of footsteps and voices growing louder as they get to the drawing room and all at once both our mothers are standing there in the doorway smiling.

I seem to have got to my feet and Emma and I are already moving towards the door.

'They've had a super time playing with Sarie's dolls' house. Haven't you?' Mummie has her big smile on.

'How lovely,' Emma's mother says. 'Hello, Push.'

I hear Daddie put his paper down, but I can't look at him. At the door to the back yard we stop and say our good-byes. It's stopped raining and the sun has come out. The cobbles in the back yard are beginning to steam. Emma thanks Mummie politely for a lovely afternoon. I agree with Emma's mother that we can go riding next time and that hopefully we'll chose a day when it won't rain all day.

Emma and I stand beside each other and smile and nod. We never catch each other's eye. We don't touch. There can never be a next time.

Present: May

My father had several chairs: the wooden one at Thelveton, which I never remembering him using; a second Everest & Jennings that stayed in the car as a spare, was used for work or when he went out; and two more chairs in the house, one for upstairs and one for downstairs. He had his little chair for upstairs, as the comfortable E & J chair that he used every day wouldn't fit in the lift my parents had bought second-hand from a small hotel in the early 1960s, shortly after we'd moved from Thelveton. It was a terrible piece of engineering with a canvas back that didn't support him properly, had black inflatable tyres prone to punctures and stuck to the floor.

'Are you listening?' My mother's interruption made me jump.

'Yes, of course. Only, I was just thinking how quiet it is here.' My father had been a man with a big personality and a voice that was distinctive rather than loud but he was also accompanied by a full orchestra of creaks, squeaks, rattles and bumps that signalled every entry and every departure like a salute. After polio, he became incapable of being stealthy. 'I always expect to hear the swing door bang, and squeaks from tyres on the floor. Or the lift.'

Our family home was almost perfectly designed for wheelchairs, with no thresh-holds and wider-than-standard doorways leading to large, square rooms. Any adaptations were made unobtrusively: a small ramp at the backdoor, short-pile carpets with no rugs or mats to snag wheels, and few surfaces above waist height. The lift was the most obvious addition, but it was hidden away in the corner of my father's study, along with his little chair during the day, and rarely seen by anyone else.

My mother looked at the door as if she expected it to jerk open and my father to follow. 'The wheelchair was just a temporary measure,' she said after a moment. 'Push really believed that he would walk again. When the place on his lung closed up he was able to get going with his exercises again.' She cupped her hands and patted them together to illustrate the lung healing. 'Russ thought it was extraordinary. That's Mr Rusby.'

I nodded to show I knew that Russ had been my

father's consultant.

'He said that he never thought it would close so quickly. Miss Hillier took it as a sign from God and convinced Push that it was a miracle. She had complete faith that he would walk again.' She paused. 'Looking back... I don't think Anne Johnson did.'

'She was more of a realist?'

'She probably thought Push should accept that he'd never walk again.' She shrugged. 'At the time, you hear what you want to hear and Miss Hillier was working with Push every day. Every day.' She bent towards me and gave a slight shake of her head. 'The NHS then was absolutely fantastic. If we'd had to pay for all the physio he got, we'd have been bankrupt.' She smoothed her hands over her legs then leant back into the cushion. 'Well, we couldn't have done it.'

A silence grew between us as I realised that, although I longed for my father to be *better* when I was a child, I'd never really considered what that might mean; I never imagined him walking. The young man in photographs standing tall in rowing whites holding a blade upright beside him, was a different man from the one I knew as Daddie. I wondered if my mother had been with Miss Hillier or with Anne. Did she believe my father would walk again if he put in enough effort, or did she see it as a journey that had to be made but could only end one way?

I caught her glancing at the clock.

'You stayed at Coopers longer than you initially thought. Weren't you there almost until Daddie came out of hospital the first time?'

She nodded while she thought. 'I was there a long time. Although, my parents wanted me to rent a flat in Brentwood, get a job and live near Push.'

'Why?'

'They just thought it was what I should do. The duty of a married woman, I suppose.' She lifted her hands off her knees. 'I didn't want to. I really didn't want to be living away from all my friends.'

'It wouldn't have made much difference to Daddie, and you wouldn't have been able to see him any more often.'

'They were pretty mean about visiting hours, and I thought I'd be very lonely. When I asked Push and he said I must stay in Berkhamsted, I was so relieved.'

The ormolu clock in the corner behind my head delicately chimed eleven. It used to stand on a bracket at the top of the front stairs at Thelveton and reminded me that I still had to ask about their first Christmas together.

'That first visit to Thelveton must have been a momentous occasion. How did that work?'

'What do you mean?'

'Well, how did you arrange your room, for instance? And what about all the hospital paraphernalia? You'd had no training, no idea...' I really didn't know how to say the next bit. '...how to care for him.'

My mother's eyes widened momentarily. We had never, ever described my mother as a carer. But that was what she was. All the NHS pamphlets, visits from support organisations, home care agencies—the whole clapdoodle that surrounded disability in the UK—none of that was for us. My father didn't have a label. I was always furious if my friends called him disabled, or talked about The Disabled, or gave me *that look*. He didn't come under any of those umbrellas. We didn't need help. We didn't want help. We could do it all ourselves. It was only after he'd gone that I realised we made compromises all the time, and I felt guilty that I hadn't offered to help more. But between them, my parents had made it all seem so effortless. Of course, it wasn't, but they didn't want help even from me and Will. All the same, I needed to know how my parents had settled into such determined and furious independence.

'No, I had no training, but you know your father. He was in control.' She arched her eyebrows slightly. She knew that I understood exactly; it was the closest she'd ever come to saying that he could be peremptory and autocratic, especially concerning his own needs. 'He knew everything from top-to-toe. He told me everything he needed and what I should do. And I just did it.'

Thelveton: Christmas, 1954

'It all looks different, somehow,' said Push as they drove through Scole. It was half-past three and dusk was falling fast.

'Different? In what way?' Diana steered the car carefully up the main street as Push hung onto the strap above the window and turned his head from side to side. Every time he shifted in his seat, his shoulders jogged her arm or his head got in the way of where she needed to look. She'd given up asking Push to keep still; she was enjoying his pleasure in the drive too much.

'That shop, for instance. I'm sure that's new. Or maybe it's had a lick of paint.' He whirled around again to get a better look at someone cycling past, very upright and dignified on a black bicycle. 'It's Foggy!'

'Foggy?' said Diana, laughing.

Push watched as the man slowly negotiated the corner by Pettitt's Stores. 'Foggy Dew, on account of his runny eye.'

They turned left at the T junction and passed the Scole Inn. 'Ah,' said Push, at the sight of its distinctive Jacobean architecture. 'Now I know I'm nearly home.'

They left Scole on the Norwich Road and soon the low, red-brick lodge of Thelveton Hall appeared, rising above a red brick wall with curiously designed bell-shaped holes. Diana hit the indicator to turn left.

'What day is it?'

'Christmas Eve.'

'I know that, Didie. I've forgotten the day of the week.'

'It's Friday, lovey.'

'Then it's fine to use the drive. Christmas Eve doesn't count. Jack asks for peace only on Sundays and Christmas Day.'

Diana smiled and turned left between the open gates. 'Jack told Ma P that you were to use the drive whenever you needed. In fact, he said that he expected you to use it. It would save you being slung around the corners on the back road.'

'I can't say I'm unhappy about not having to bump over those pot-holes. I don't suppose they've improved in the time I've been away.' Push pulled himself up on the strap again and Diana caught him closing his eyes and grimacing as he shifted his weight and pulled at his trousers to prevent creases forming underneath.

She turned to smile at him again. 'I bet you can't wait to get out of this car.'

'Believe me, Didie, I'd travel four times this distance if it meant being at Thelveton with you at the end of it. Oh, I say! Just look at the Hall. That's some wreath on the front door.'

As they moved out from under the avenue of beech trees, the Hall appeared like a denser patch of dusk set back from the drive, the lawn to the front so flat and black it could have been a lake. Diana slowed almost to a standstill so Push could absorb it. The huge frontage of Sir Jack Mann's house was in total darkness apart from the carriage lamps either side of the front door, highlighting a great circle of greenery.

'That looks like Mother's handiwork,' said Push, laughing. 'I can't imagine Jack organising such a decoration himself.'

'I imagine she'll have really pushed the boat out for you this year.' Diana let the clutch out and drew away gently. The avenue of trees resumed and they left the Hall behind them. A couple of late-to-roost pheasants were spooked by the car and flew up into the trees with a cackle. A horse, rugged and dozing by the fence on the right, threw up its head at the light of the headlamps, the bristles on its muzzle and pupils of its eyes gleaming momentarily as though struck by a sudden hoar-frost. Night had fallen completely.

As they drove in through the gates of Thelveton Grange a second or two later, in contrast to Thelveton Hall, every window of Push's family home seemed to be glowing. The arch over the porch was flickering inside with a dozen or more night-lights in jam-jars suspended within the delicate leaves of an evergreen jasmine, and on the door, wrapped in yards of red silk ribbon, was nailed the largest and most exuberant wreath of ivy and holly that Diana had ever seen.

'I see Ma P saved the best in your honour.'

She swung the car around in a wide curve and parked it as close to the house as she could. Immediately the front door opened, light flooded into the drive and a crowd of people spilled out into the chilly air, all talking at once and grabbing every door to the car and pulling them open.

'My, my. What a turnout!' said Push, obviously delighted. 'Who have we here? Mother, Mrs B, Willie. And Marjy. Marjy's here, Didie.'

'Hello, PT.' Marjy peered at Push through the open door, her eyes huge behind her bottle-bottom glasses. 'Isn't this a splendid day for you both? We've been busy for days getting everything ready.'

'Just a simple matter of re-arranging,' said Ma P, over Marjy's shoulder. 'We did it in a trice.'

'Hello, Mother.'

'Oh, Bime!' said Push's mother, using his childhood nickname, and Diana watched as Ma P gripped Push's hand and held it as she kissed him on the cheek. 'I can't tell you how good it is to have you home.' She pulled back slightly and looked at Push intently, as though he might be a mirage and a quirk of fate might take him away from her again at any moment. Diana couldn't help but wish her own mother showed affection in such an uncomplicated and natural fashion. Push squeezed his mother's hand hard, as she turned to Diana still sitting behind the wheel.

'I hope your parents weren't too cross with us, kidnapping the two of you for every day of your leave.'

'Not at all. To be honest, I think Mummy thought we'd be much better off here for our first overnight trip.'

'You tell her, Didie, that I'm very grateful. But you will see them sometime over Christmas, won't you?'

'I saw them yesterday. We had a bit of an early celebration then.' Diana got out of the car and walked round to kiss her mother-in-law.

Last out of the house, pipe clamped firmly between his teeth, was Pa P behind a large, wooden wheeled chair. He trundled it over the gravel and brought it in tight to the passenger side of the car.

'Told you we'd manage to find something to tide you over. How did Didie do? Managed her precious cargo all right, did she?' He leaned over the chair to see into the car.

'Hello, Pa,' said Push. 'I have to admit, she drove beautifully. And here we are, almost dead on time.'

It seemed that everyone had something to say, but Diana knew Push needed to get out of the car and rest as soon as he could. She was relieved when Ma P seemed to read her mind.

'Now, why don't we take the suitcases and let you two get Push out of the car without us all getting under your feet,' Ma P suggested. 'Marjy, you put the kettle on again, I'll break out the cake and we'll get some tea ready in the drawing room. They must be starving.'

Diana waited until Push had had a proper look at the wheelchair that his father had found. His face, in the borrowed light from the front door, looked white and strained. He was clearly delighted to be back at his family home, but Diana knew the fear of being away from the security of the hospital was only just under the surface.

'A very good idea, Pa, to put those cushions on, but I've brought my own.' Push pulled the drawing room cushions off the seat, handing them to Diana. 'We'll get that a little closer if we can.' He grabbed one wooden arm and hauled the chair at right angles to the car, getting it as tight to the door as he could with a series of jerks. 'Then, if you stand behind as a kind of brake, to stop it skittering away, I'll swing myself on like this,' and, matching motion to intention, Push lifted himself up by one arm with an astonishing display of strength and swung his body round from the car into the seat of the chair. 'Now, Didie, if I lift myself up again...' he pushed hard with his hands on the arms of the chair and lifted himself clear of the seat. 'You can shove my cushions under me here.' Diana was used to this after so many recent outings and no sooner had Push given his directions, than she passed Pa P the unwanted drawing room cushions and had grabbed Push's sorbo pads—one large and square, one like a doughnut— and slid them beneath him. Push lowered himself down slowly, then looked around at his new transport. 'Good Lord! You seem to have stuffed me into a basket. Hang on, I know where this came from.' He peered over the edge and tapped the sides of the wickerwork. 'This was Grandpa's.'

'Absolutely correct. Willie's oiled it, polished it and checked it for worm and it's running as good as new,' Pa P said.

Diana leaned into the car to collect a pile of presents off the back seat before following them into the house.

'Mm.' Push spoke softly as the front door closed behind them. 'I've dreamed of this moment more times than I can count.'

Diana started to walk towards the drawing room but Push put his hand out to stop her. 'Can we just go over a couple of things while we have a moment, Pa?'

'Of course, lad. What d'you want to know?'

'You got the frame to go over my legs made up all right?'

'William Pretty did it. All metal cut and braised to your exact specification. It's upstairs now. And he made the monkey pole to go above your bed too. Excellent engineer, William Pretty. Excellent engineer. You'd have been proud to have made it yourself.'

'And you're sure the pole can support me.'

'As God made little apples.'

'All this work for just a few days. I can't thank you enough, Pa.'

'You could do with a rest now, Push,' Diana said, worried that the crowd behind the drawing room door was going to prove too exhausting.

'Maybe a short rest before dinner. A change of seat is as good as anything. Anyway, I can't miss a slice of Christmas cake.' He put his hand on the doorknob then pulled back again. 'Mother's sorted somewhere out for my rests, has she, Pa?'

'Yes, lad. You mustn't worry. Your ma made copious notes last time she came to see you and she and Didie have nearly bankrupted me with telephone calls.' He winked at Diana, and she felt a rush of gratitude for her new family.

'We've made the back kitchen into a very comfortable day room with a bed and a couple of arm-chairs for Didie or visitors.' Push's father sucked on his pipe. 'Bit too comfortable, I should say. We'll need a crow bar to get you out of there, but it'll be ready for when you come home for good. And, upstairs is just as you suggested, with the two of you in the connecting rooms opposite the morning room.' He contemplated his pipe for a moment. 'Clem's going to come in each evening to help you up the stairs.'

'There's plenty of time to sort it out,' Diana said. 'We'll get it all just the way you want it.'

Push nodded several times but Diana could see him thinking and worrying.

'You know we've brought everything you could possibly need with us. We'll manage.'

'Perhaps Diana might like to powder her nose before she meets her public.' Pa P took his pipe out from between his teeth and pointed towards the stairs with it.

'Would I?' asked Diana. 'Oh, yes, I would. What a good idea. Won't be a tick, Push.' She put the pile of presents on Push's lap. He steadied them, then turned the door handle, shoved the drawing room door open and rolled inside amid cries of approval and excitement.

Diana turned to walk down the hall.

'I should take the long way back, if I were you,' said Pa P.

'The long way back?' Diana stopped and looked at him, confused.

'Via the back kitchen, if you catch my drift.' He looked into the bowl of his pipe, then stuck his hand in his waistcoat pocket and fished about for his tobacco pouch. 'You know where it is?'

'Yes, I think so. Near the back door.'

'That's right. Have a bit of a recce and report back. Put his mind at rest.'

Present: May

'Was that the cage that we had here?' I asked when my mother mentioned the metal frame that had been made to keep the weight of bedclothes off my father's feet while he was sleeping.

'I think it must have been,' she said. 'Yes, I'm sure it was.'

I remembered it well although he hadn't used it for years, not since he decided that the continental quilt he was given in a hotel he once stayed in was the lightest and most comfortable form of bed cover he'd ever experienced. From that moment, he was an instant convert and the cumbersome metal frame—made from tubular steel with braised joints and shaped like a tent, nearly three feet wide and two feet high at its apex—used routinely since he came out of hospital, became as obsolete as the sheets and blankets he'd used all his life. I wondered what had happened to it.

I couldn't remember ever seeing the monkey pole; we never had one around when we were children. Only in his last few years, when my father had lost much of the upper body strength that he'd relied on for his mobility, did he resort to having a bedside device to help heave himself around in bed. I recall the shock when I first saw the hoist in my parents' bedroom. I'd become blind to the implications of his chair, conspicuous as it was—after nearly fifty years, his wheelchair had grown into a part of my father's own physicality—but the hoist was proof of his waning ability; evidence so sharp it was like a punch in the face.

I missed seeing his chairs around the place. The house seemed a bit hollow. In the garage, if his car was missing, his house chair was left waiting in the centre like the hub of a wheel and we had to be careful getting in and out of the cars not to knock it out of position. When my father drove in, he needed to be able to park alongside his chair in order to reverse the whole complicated process of getting into the car. Teaching us to leave everything, not only his chairs, exactly as he'd left them helped maintain his independence without drawing attention to potential difficulties. He made the move from bed to chair, chair to sofa, chair to car, nine or ten times a day or more.

'How come we didn't have the monkey pole here?'

'He found other ways of coping. He had enormously strong arms right from the beginning. You have to remember how fit he'd been. Rowing makes you very strong.'

'It'd been a long time since he rowed.' I knew how quickly I lost fitness in the winter when I stopped running so frequently.

'Yes, but all the physio he was getting. Working on the bars...'

The wheelchair user's arms became their legs, which made the health and strength of their arms doubly important. An able-bodied person very rarely took the full weight of their body on their hands, arms and shoulders; arms were designed for torque and leverage, not to support weight. Increased use brought increased ability, but when my father fell out of his chair in the backyard and pulled the muscles in his shoulder, it took months and months to heal. He couldn't ever rest his arms, he relied on them for everything, and eventually they wore out. But when he was younger, we gloried in his strength and so did he.

Home, Suffolk: 1964

'Daddie, Daddie! Look at me!' The world's gone up-side down for an exciting two seconds; the roses and mock orange have flowers instead of roots, the ponies are walking about behind the tennis court with their feet stuck to a green ceiling and I can see Daddie sitting with his head in the sky. I do two whole steps on my hands with my hair all over my face before I fall over.

'You didn't see me.' I crumple to the grass and the world turns the right way round.

'I did, Sarie,' he calls. 'But I need a shove from you two, then I can see you properly.'

'Look at what I can do.' Will arches his back into a bridge and moves on his hands and feet towards the edge of the lawn. He looks like a crab.

'Mind the ditch!' Daddie warns.

Will turns his head to look and falls flat on his back. We both stare at the sky above our heads.

'Hoo-wee!' Daddie has a brilliant whistle. 'Who wants to give me a shove up to the hut?' He's sitting at the bottom of the long slope that leads down the bank from the lawn by the tennis court where we're dancing about. We used to have to scramble up the bank using three very thin stone steps which were tricky for the chair to roll up, even with a lot of help. Then an orange digger came to make a proper bridge over the ditch. It scraped the earth smooth and the driver dropped dark-grey cinders all over it and banged it flat. Now all we have to do is give an extra push from behind and Daddie's up by the tennis hut in seconds.

I turn a cart-wheel, stretching my legs and arms as wide as I possibly can to make a proper circle. Will lifts himself up into a crab again, and starts moving sideways. Daddie sits waiting in the yard with the newspaper and his cap on his lap. I get to the top of the slope, stand upright and wobble a bit, then run down towards him.

Daddie jams his cap on his head so it won't blow away, then he tucks the paper down the side of his cush-ions. I grab the white plastic handles at the back of the

224

chair, push my bare feet into the scratchy cinders and shove really, really hard. Daddie pushes his wheels around too and together we get faster and faster until we're flying up the slope and Daddie gets to the edge of the lawn.

'Steady now, Sarie!' I have to be careful that I don't dig in the little wheels at the front of his chair or jab his toes into the ground. I don't want to tip him onto the grass. In the last weeks we've practised this loads of times and we pause to get things really straight before shoving our way to the hut. Daddie could manage this part by himself, but it makes him puff so it's easier to keep pushing and I like to help him. In any case, my feet are sore from the cinders and the grass between my toes and under my feet feels cool and lovely.

'Let's see that handstand again,' Daddie says when we get to level ground, so I tip myself up again and manage three steps.

'Are they called steps if they're on your hands?' I manage to say before falling over again, but I don't think he's heard me.

'You're really getting the hang of that.' I squirm when Daddie is pleased with me.

I'm wearing my navy sun-ray pleated skirt (knickers attached) with white rickrack edging around the leg holes and the bottom of the skirt. Miss Ingate's school is closed for the summer holidays, it's been boiling all week, and now we have Daddie to ourselves for the afternoon. I'm very happy.

'Shall I get the Lay-about out?'

'In a minute.' Daddie looks around at Will, who is

still practising his crab-walking. His hair has turned almost white this summer and his legs and arms are burned brown like toast, but his face is as red as the wattles on Grannie's Muscovy ducks. James is wagging his tail and hitting Will with his nose as always. Last term we learned about space and the sun and the planets. James is attached to Will like the Moon is attached to the Earth.

'Let's teach you a circus trick before your mother comes home,' Daddie says and Will stops his crab-walking. We both stand waiting while Daddie tells us what to do. Soon, I'm lying on my back, legs and arms in the air with Will balanced on his tummy over my feet and gripping my hands. It hurts a bit, but not too much.

'Willie, you need to let go of Sarie's hands. Keep your legs absolutely still,' he says to me. Will lets one hand go and holds it out. We wobble, but keep our eyes fixed on each other and find our balance. Then I begin to uncurl my fingers from his other hand. Slowly, I lay both arms along the ground straight out from my body. Will rocks and I jerk a hand towards him but then, all at once, it works just right. He stretches his arms out above me and we are as still as still.

Will is flying!

'Very good!' says Daddie, which is not something he says unless he means it.

From the corner of my eye I see James get up from the shade beside the hut and wander towards us. He's panting in the heat.

My legs start to tremble and we grab for each other's hands. James nudges Will with his nose. Will shoves

226

him away with his elbow and puts a foot down but I grip his hands so he can't let go and push him back into the air with my feet. I want this to work.

'Buzz off!' Daddie says, firmly.

James backs away and lies down with a thud.

'She's hurting me.' Will whines. Then he dribbles. He always does this if he thinks I'm getting the better of him.

'Eew! He's spitting on me.' I roll over, tipping Will on his side. Will wipes the saliva off his chin and grins horribly at me so I kick him, hard, on the shin.

'Ow!'

'Now, now,' says Daddie. 'Stop bickering.' We lie, exhausted and giggling on the grass. James thumps his tail but stays in the shade.

'I've an idea,' Daddie says. 'Let's see if I can lift you.' He looks at us both. I'm six now and Mummie says I've shot up, but Will is only four and still small. 'Willie first.'

So I will have a turn. I let my breath out. Daddie grabs Will around the waist and swings him up onto his lap, his legs hanging down either side. 'Now, see if you can sit on my hand.'

Daddie folds his arm back and cups his hand so the fingers are touching his shoulder and his palm faces the sky. I listen hard so I can do exactly what he says when I have my chance. Soon Will is sitting on Daddie's hand, which is so big and wide, it looks like the scoop from the digger that made the slope. He hangs onto the arm rest with his other hand and slowly lifts Will into the air.

'Keep still,' Daddie warns and Will goes up high and

then comes down low. Daddie's chins wobble as his arm straightens. His face grows really pink, he must find it very difficult. He lets Will slide to the ground.

'Now you, Sarie.' Daddie shakes his arm. 'I think we'll use the other hand.'

I climb up and sit in his palm. He feels safe and comfortable. This is better than any fairground ride. 'Now, up we go!'

I can feel the muscles in his arm bulge under my weight then start to shake, and I can see the veins at the side of his forehead get big and purple. Slowly, I rise up until I'm way higher than his head and looking down at the top of his cap. My legs are long and swinging loose and I want to put a foot out on the arm of his chair but he hasn't said I can, so I leave them dangling.

Then it's over, and I'm sliding back to the grass. Daddie is grinning fit to bust.

'We've two tricks to show Mummie now, haven't we?' Will says.

Daddie is still shaking his arm and stretching his hands. 'We'll show her the flying trick.' He puffs his breath out. 'But I'm not sure I'm quite ready for another arm-lift today.'

Chapter Fifteen

Present: May

Doggedness was, without question, a family characteristic. I watched our daughters as toddlers attempt activities with purposefulness and admired their determined application, knowing my father would be proud of them. But I sometimes found myself wondering: when does persistence slide through obstinacy into intransigence?

My grandfather taught us the values of perseverance and we never attempted an activity without the expectation that we would see it through to the end. He disliked change, and especially pressure to change, to the extent that he kept Thelveton forever frozen in the style of his own youth. He spent the same week every summer at the same south coast resort, in the same 'fat' hotel (my grandmother's words). He wore the same pre-war style clothes–winter and summer—and pursued the same interests all his life.

At the root was fear.

My grandfather felt it, my uncle felt it, my father felt it. I felt it. There was safety in what we knew. When others around us were excited at the idea of something new, we felt anxious. What did we think would happen to us? For me, fear frustrated possibility and gnawed at my self-worth.

But as I watched my father try to leave his workshop,

rattling the door, checking his keys and returning to do it all over again, or saw my uncle pole-axed by debilitating anxieties brought on by stress at work, I wondered if my fear was a learned response, or genetic.

Frank Gardner, the BBC's Security Correspondent and a wheelchair user since being shot in the spine in 2004, wrote about travel being fraught with uncertainty, and yet he never considered giving it up. My father felt many activities were fraught with uncertainty so he planned and prepared obsessively. He had to balance the outcome with pain if it all went wrong. I had no such spectre waiting for me, yet I found myself behaving in the selfsame way.

As a young adult, bedevilled with nausea, headaches and panic attacks, tormented by phobias and sleeplessness, I swore I would never have children; the risk that I might bring another generation into the world to suffer the same imagined oppressions was unendurable. Yet, here they were: our girls, half me and half their father (a fearless and spontaneous man, if ever there was), both a mixed bag of anxieties and courage. And having children was to have an unexpected outcome; the delight and distraction of caring for them allowed many of the more extreme of my anxieties to dissolve and melt away.

The more I burrowed away at the events that motivated my father's choices when I was a child, the more I began to understand myself. Perhaps I was even beginning to lose the fear that I thought had supported me, but which others were wise enough to realise had restricted me; the difference between armature and barrier.

Fear is a primeval response. It keeps us safe, or we

imagine it does. As a young, fit athlete my father must have thought himself invincible, but polio, then tuberculosis swept through his life, forcing him to bend and break like a tree uprooted in a hurricane. He may never have felt safe again.

My father's fear ran through me like letters through a stick of rock, but so did the family persistence. It was that Pulman persistence that pulled my father through, that and the kindness of others. He worked in the knowledge that success was its own reward, but always with hope.

And there was no denying my father had courage. It was persistence in the face of fear, that had given my father courage.

'Why do you think there're only two letters for the eighteen months between May, 1953 to December, 1954? Do you think they may have just been lost?'

'Maybe.'

My mother didn't elaborate, so I tried something else. 'If visiting was so restricted, what did Daddie do all day while the other patients were out of the ward?'

'He worked hard at his exercises.'

'But he can't have done that all day, every day.'

My mother nodded. 'He did. He was determined. And Alan Muntz, his boss, was still paying Push a retainer. He didn't have to after all that time, of course.' She smiled and her face softened. 'He was so kind. He'd come and see Push and give him patent applications to go through. It was work of a sort, I suppose.' She paused. 'And then, of course, there was Deafy.'

'Deafy?' I couldn't imagine anyone being called Deafy.

'Deafy had lost his hearing because of a batch of faulty strep. Push was always worried that it might happen to him but he never told me about the risks until later.'

'How come they didn't all go deaf?' I frowned trying to understand the science and probability. With the difficulties at the time of keeping streptomycin stable, it had to be mixed fresh from the powdered form each time it was administered. Everyone on the ward would have had injections prepared from the same batch time and time again.

'I don't know. But they didn't. Some people lost their hearing a little but Deafy lost his completely.'

'Wasn't Daddie deaf in one ear?' He'd always preferred us to sit on his good side.

'That was from riveting aeroplanes during the Air Lift.' She dismissed the thought with a little shake of her head. 'Anyway Push spent hours helping Deafy learn to lip-read. And he started to do other things.'

'What other things?'

'All sorts of things. He had a small tool kit with him.'

This was so typical of my father that I couldn't help but smile. The tool kit—a brown leather (or maybe vinyl) zipped bag, bursting at the seams, and complete with all sizes of spanners, sockets, measures, screw drivers, Allen keys, ratchets, pliers, wrenches, spark plugs, connectors, and spare bulbs, just for starters—was as much a part of my father as his wheelchair.

'Anne Johnson asked him if he could help other

patients at Brentwood. You know? That chap who'd been in Africa who had his elbow shied off.' She made a chopping motion on her arm.

I remembered this very well. It was another of my father's awful warning stories, stories he told when he wanted to pass on important information. 'The man who was driving his car resting his elbow on the sill of the open window?'

My mother nodded again. 'Push made a special fork so he didn't have to bend his elbow after he'd had some big operation. They let him have a soldering iron and all sorts. They really were very good in that hospital, but then some of them, like Push, were there for an awfully long time.'

Always happy to help others, I thought, remembering another letter describing an electronic toy he'd made for a couple of the children stuck in the TB hospital with him. But my father wasn't so quick to help himself. Another thing we had in common. Perhaps that was born of fear, too; the tighter we kept control, the less likely we were to be coaxed out of our comfort zone.

'I found a little card the other day,' I said as my mother walked with me to the yard. 'It was from the Cascade Florists in Brentwood. It said, To Push. Clove Carnations for our First Wedding Anniversary, With all my love, Didie.'

'Did it? I don't remember.'

'That must have been a difficult day to get through.'

'They were all difficult.'

The London Hospital Annexe: February, 1955

'Oh, Didie. What have you done?' Push had his hands over his face and was shaking his head from side to side. 'It wasn't for you to say that I was ready. Especially not for a full assessment.'

'I know, but you're such a perfectionist, you were never going to do it, and we can't risk losing Miss Hillier.' Di had feared that Push might react like this but she had suggested that they might bring in an independent specialist to give a second opinion, and thought he'd given it his tacit consent. They'd even decided the best person for the job, so she was determined to stand her ground. 'And you don't know what it's like having my family constantly on my back saying you're not going to make it.'

Push lifted his head out of his hands. 'Is that what they say?'

'Well, no, not exactly. I didn't mean...'

'That I'm not going to make it? Make what, precisely?'

Diana dug her hands deep into the pockets of her skirt. She felt a tiny hole in one corner and deliberately pushed a finger through. She felt the stitches rip, a thread caught under her nail and tore the skin; it was a relief of a sort. Push's eyes were glassy-grey and two high spots of colour had appeared on his cheekbones; she'd seen those enough times to be wary. 'It's only that Daddie keeps saying that you might be wasting your time trying to walk when time might be better spent...' Diana took a quick breath, pulled a hand out of her pocket and rubbed her forehead.

'It isn't that I don't believe you can do it. I wouldn't have asked Dr Tegner to come if I wasn't absolutely sure that you'd pass with flying colours.' Diana felt herself misunderstood and on the point of being treated unfairly. 'Oh, I can't say it properly. I'm going to get some tea.'

She left Push sitting in his bed while she walked the length of the ward, all the while feeling his eyes burning into her back. She stopped near the door where a table had been set with a large Brown-Betty tea pot and about twenty pale blue and green china cups and saucers. There was a draft from the door and Diana pulled her cardigan tightly around her.

'Two teas, please,' she said to the girl in the flowery pinny who was carefully pouring a little milk into the bottom of each cup from a blue and white milk jug.

Diana looked quickly over her shoulder. Push appeared to be reading a letter; he wasn't smiling.

She took the cups of tea and walked back towards Push's bed.

'Thank you,' Push said as she handed him his cup. 'I'm sorry, Didie, I shouldn't have questioned you. It was a shock, that's all. Especially as I wasn't expecting to hear from him.' He took a sip from his cup and then put it on his locker.

Diana looked around the ward at the other beds, most of which were empty. 'Why aren't you in your chair today?' She was still smarting from Push's earlier accusations and was reluctant to be drawn into a further conversation about Dr Tegner. 'I knew we wouldn't be going out because of the weather, but I didn't expect to see you in bed.'

'That's the trouble. It isn't just the rain. I should have told you before, so all this is really my fault.'

Diana sat on the chair beside Push's bed and held her cup and saucer in her lap.

'The drive to Thelveton and all our other driving about was probably a bit much,' he said. 'It seems my fistula has broken open again.'

Diana closed her eyes and felt her shoulders collapse. She didn't know what to say.

'I'm not supposed to sit for so long.'

'What about the walking?' Diana said in a whisper.

Push made a face. 'I told Russ that I wasn't going to give that up for anything.'

'So Tegner coming is a disaster.'

'It's certainly not the best time to see what we've achieved.' He looked at the letter in his hand. 'They've set my assessment for the second week of next month. That's about three weeks away.'

'Can't they put him off?'

Push shook his head. 'It won't help anyway. It's been decreed that Miss Hillier should return to Whitechapel Road at the end of the month.'

'I'm so sorry.'

Push brushed his hair back from his forehead. 'It was going to happen some time,' he said. 'I think we were rather naive to think I could have this amount of therapy for ever. It may have been a case of out of sight, out of mind for Miss Hillier.'

'You mean, they'd sort of forgotten about her?'

Push lifted his hands off the bed for a moment.

'Could be.'

'But she was working with Russ. He knew all about what she's been doing. What does he think about it?'

'Ah.' Push paused, looked at Diana and narrowed his eyes. 'I suspect Russ is part of the problem.' He glanced around the ward and dropped his voice. 'Look, Didie, I didn't want to have to tell you this because it's a preposterous suggestion, but I don't want you to hear it from anyone else.'

Diana felt her heart jump. She couldn't imagine what was coming next. 'Whatever it is, Push, just say it. You're frightening me now.'

'The houseman here thinks...' Push took a deep breath. 'It's ridiculous, but he thinks that Miss Hillier's interest in me is... Has, I mean. Has gone beyond the professional.'

Diana stared at him.

'And I think that's why Russ wants her to go. For her own good.' His grey eyes narrowed further. 'He's completely mad of course.'

'It isn't that he thinks you're not making any more progress, then?' Diana was confused.

'Oh, he's convinced himself that I won't walk. But he probably thought it did no harm to let me try while I had to be in hospital to get my lungs better. Now that there's this talk perhaps he's not prepared to turn a blind eye anymore.'

'You mean he thinks you and...?' Diana looked around the ward again and everything seemed just as it had a minute ago. The curtains were still blowing in the breeze from the perpetually open windows, patients were walking about, visitors were talking in low voices and the doors beside the tea table were still opening and closing as visitors came and went. And yet, she couldn't make sense of what she was hearing. She turned to Push.

'But, Miss Hillier's Plymouth Brethren! You said so yourself.'

For a second Push appeared completely nonplussed, then he roared with laughter, making Diana jump and slosh her tea into its saucer. 'Oh, Didie, that's what I love about you. You're so straightforward. Totally black and white.'

'But how can he say that? It's absolutely appalling that anyone could think like that. It's downright libellous.' Push grabbed her hand and held it hard. 'You're absolutely right, of course. Although not for the reason you may think. Miss Hillier's religion doesn't make her incapable of romantic feelings. Not that she has any for me, I'm absolutely certain,' he added quickly, seeing Diana's expression. 'No, her religion means her professionalism can never be compromised.'

Diana still didn't really understand.

'She is utterly committed to her work. She works beyond the call of duty because her religion teaches her to be one hundred percent dedicated to what she believes to be right. With all her patients, not just me.' Push paused for breath. He made his free hand straight and rigid and brought it down like an axe on the side of his bed. 'That man has it totally wrong. Miss Hillier is more professional than anyone I know. Her faith in God and belief in me is what helps me keep at it. He's an idiot if he thinks it's any more than that.' He stroked Diana's fingers and she sandwiched his hand between hers. 'I've been giving it a great deal of thought.' He reached for Diana's face, pushed her fringe away from her eyes and ran a finger down her cheek. He spoke more gently. 'Doctors are scientists. I can see how they might be frightened by Miss Hillier's faith in God. She's a threat. She gets results and they don't know how.'

'But you're a research and development engineer. That's a scientist of a kind.' Diana loved hearing Push talk about his convictions.

'But an engineer originates,' said Push, softly. 'Engineers have to know why things work, not only how, and that's why I know we have a creator.'

'We can't betray our belief in Miss Hillier or in God.'

'I couldn't have put it better myself.'

'What will you do?'

'I'll carry on without her. Now I'm up on my feet, there's a lot I can do. I'll show Tegner just how much we've achieved.'

'Oh, Push, you will.' Diana watched the fire come back into Push's eyes. 'And when Tegner sees how well your walking has come on, Russ'll have to agree for her to come back.' She looked down at her cup. 'I just wish your poor tail hadn't chosen now to misbehave.'

'Yes, that is a shame, but maybe this will turn out better than we thought.' He smiled. 'Come on, drink your tea.'

Present: May

After the apparent success of their liberation over Christmas, my mother was deeply disappointed that their afternoon drives had to cease with immediate effect. However, my father saw this restriction as an opportunity for more walking practice. He didn't hide from her that he'd argued with Russ. He claimed that while he was upright, he wasn't putting weight on his backside, therefore his exercises would help to heal the abscess in a way that constant pressure from sitting would not. It appeared that Dr Rusby was outmanoeuvred, and my father got his way.

This new confidence, much more recognisable as the father that I had known, would have been hard to overrule, and even though the abscessed fistula remained infected and open for weeks and weeks as it had in 1953, it didn't deter him from his routines. When Dr Tegner arrived for a *week of torture*, as my mother wrote, he noted the problem of the fistula and kindly left them for another fortnight before he made his assessment. When he returned, he was far more concerned about the abscess than he was about any walking progress that may, or may not have been made.

Dr WS Tegner had been the Hon. Secretary/Treasurer and administrator of the British Association of Sport and Medicine, an organisation set up in 1952 to offer medical advice to the Governing Bodies of sport. By 1955, the BASM (which later became the British Association of Sport Exercise and Medicine, BASEM) was working closely with the British Olympic Association and Dr Tegner would almost certainly have been known to several of my father's athlete friends; perhaps he'd even been recommended or approached by one of them. One way or another, he'd turned up at the London Hospital Annexe, and he couldn't have been better placed to weigh up the benefits of post-polio exercise over much needed rest to cure the abscess and heal the fistula.

In the end, Tegner's visit could be described as an anti-climax but for two things: the first was that he prescribed immediate surgery to cut the abscess right away in order for the fistula to heal without trapping further infection, and the second was that in early March, with no prior warning, Miss Hillier returned to oversee my father's walking exercises. It seemed that, either Miss Hillier's own efforts to be reinstated had born fruit, or Dr Rusby had taken pity on them and dismissed some badly-timed gossip as just that. Or perhaps it was a bit of both.

Surgery was scheduled for Tuesday 15 March, 1955. The operation wasn't plain sailing and my father spent two days being dreadfully sick as a reaction to the anaesthetic. As predicted, he was forced to spend his convalescence on his stomach. My mother bemoaned the lack of letters, but by the end of the month he was able to write calming messages. Recovery was painfully slow, and the sense of freedom and independence that my parents had enjoyed in the run up to Christmas was all but forgotten. My father remained in hospital over Easter which fell on the 10th April that year, while my mother went to Thelveton to spend the holiday weekend with her in-laws.

I could hardly bear to read the April letters, especially when my mother apologised for *making a dreadful fool of herself* after she found my father so racked with pain that he could hardly talk when she came to visit. For the most part, though, my mother kept up her relentless positivity, stressing that they had just *one more hill to climb*. But she also held herself responsible for the whole Tegner episode, convinced that the set back as a result of the surgery was all her fault. It wasn't, of course, and given the privilege of hindsight, I regretted that my father had been so persuasive and that Dr Rusby hadn't acted on his own instincts. I'd liked to have reassured her that the young wife I was reading about and whose life had been upended by unimaginably painful circumstances, had nothing to criticise herself for. I blamed hope for the delay, hope kept alive by Miss Hiller's ill-judged insistence that walking was the only goal.

Having the abscess operated on at such a late stage meant a much more serious procedure, with the risk that the infection might never be brought under control. My poor father was in constant pain, deeply frustrated at his enforced rest and lack of control. He was also tormented by persistent constipation and, as a consequence, a total loss of dignity; something he fought against for the whole of the rest of his life. Accepting help, any help, impugned his self-respect. We soon learned not to offer assistance without being asked, and if we did, we were left in no doubt that we'd overstepped the mark.

'Why don't you take an aspirin?' I'd once suggested to him when he was suffering from a painful form of the facial neurological condition sometimes known as Bell's Palsy. I was a mother by this time and used to making decisions about minor medical conditions and injuries. 'Give yourself some respite from the pain,' I'd urged.

'It bungs me up,' he said. 'And I can't risk that.'

'What about paracetamal?' But he just shook his head.

'Codeine?'

'All analgesics give you constipation.'

'Oh, come on, Daddie.' I was disappointed that he was dismissing my ideas. 'It's got to be better than sitting here with the nerves in your face on fire.'

And then he'd rounded on me. 'Have you had a faecal impaction? External evacuation?' His voice shook with emotion.

I said nothing, shocked at the aggression.

'Thought not.' I remembered how red he'd become, how shallow his breath, how frightening the Bell's Palsy had made him look with one side of his face dropped and his mouth working asymmetrically. 'Do you even know what it is?'

It was my turn to shake my head.

'Someone has to stick their whole arm up your backside and drag the contents out by hand.' He glared at me. 'Sounds like a whole lot of fun, doesn't it?'

'I was only trying to help.'

'Well, don't.'

Aldeburgh: 1967

It's the end of the film; everyone except Daddie stood for the National Anthem. Then the lights come up and he looks round at us with a big smile.

'The best, so far,' he says. *You Only Live Twice* is the first Bond film Will and I have seen but Daddie knows them all and has read all the books.

'Now, you two. Why don't you go and stand over there.' He points to a red curtain on the wall. 'And Mummie can help me into my chair.' We nod. He knows exactly what he needs so we follow Mummie to where Daddie's chair is leaning folded against the wall by the curtain, and wait near the exit we came in by. Mummie is the only one of us to use the front door to the cinema. She has to, to buy the tickets. We choose to walk beside Daddie. Entrances to cinemas, theatres, museums, galleries, hotels, restaurants all seem to be made with steps or revolving doors so we almost always get into buildings from the unseen places: stage doors, delivery slopes behind the dustbins, under fire escapes, through the staff rooms, past the kitchens or down long winding passages. We rather like it, the secret parts of buildings can be exciting, but sometimes we hear shouting and people running. Nobody wears a smile in these behind places.

I lean back against the wall and close my eyes to think about films. We don't often come to the cinema, which is a shame because I love movies, even the ancient ones shown on TV on Saturday Matinee, although Daddie feels watching television is a waste of time.

Last weekend, we were caught watching in the afternoon. Will was on the sofa, I sat on the carpet in front of the fire. We didn't notice that dusk was falling.

'Why's it all dark in here?' Daddie said as he flung open the door.

The fire was almost out because I'd forgotten to put more logs on and Daddie forced me to get up by rolling towards me with the unstoppable determination of a tank.

Not waiting to be told, Will got up and walked over to the television to switch it over to BBC One, ready for Daddie's News programme.

'Hang on, Will.' Daddie put up his hand. Will looked round in surprise, finger on the button. 'What are you watching?'

'A film.' It doesn't matter that I didn't know the title, I love them all. Or that it was black and white, because we don't have a colour telly and it's all we're used to.

'Just a minute. I know this,' Daddie had said, all excited. 'It's *The Third Man*. A wonderful film, wonderful!' He'd watched for a moment or two from about two feet away. His tweed jacket was half out over the right side of the chair where it came untucked when he was reaching for wood to throw on the fire, but he hadn't noticed and sat quite still looking at the screen with each hand spread over his knees as though they needed protecting.

'I remember going to see this with your Mum. In fact… Oh heavens! It was the last film I saw before I got ill.'

We stood beside him listening to the trancey plinky-plunky music, and watching the screen.

'I can't remember where we saw it. I don't think it

was in London, maybe it was Diss.'

He seemed to have forgotten us and the telly.

'I think I'd seen it before but it was so good, we went to see it again. Diss. Yes, it probably was Diss.' He paused and Will took the opportunity to sit down again on a chair beside the desk. Daddie looked at him. 'Do you know, I didn't see another film until I'd been out of hospital for a couple of years or so. And I remember that like yesterday; it was at the Aldeburgh cinema. Do you know what we went to see?'

'No.'

'It was James Bond. We went to see *Dr No*. I remember it being so loud and the opening sequence—there's a bit with silhouettes of girls dancing and looking down the barrel of a gun—was such a shock to me that I nearly fell off my seat. Can you imagine seeing this?' He'd pointed to the screen where Harry Lime was still creeping around in the shadows. 'And not seeing anything, anything at all until *Dr No*?' He sat there and shook his head. 'It must have been ten or eleven years.'

And here he is, back in the Aldeburgh cinema again, watching another Bond film.

Something is happening. I snap my eyes open and my heart jumps into my throat.

'Out of my way! I know all about this!'

A woman is running down the length of the almost empty cinema towards our parents and shrieking. The seats are on a slope and suddenly we understand the full meaning of the phrase breakneck speed. It's possible that an usherette has moved towards her, perhaps to interrupt her, but it's all happening so fast it's hard to be sure.

Mummie has been helping Daddie into his wheel-chair. The chair has been balanced at exactly the right angle to get his hand onto the seat before he grabs for the armrest. There'll be a moment of terrible effort to lift his dead-weight off the velvety cinema seat, hover over a doughnut-cushion and bang down into his chair. Then suddenly he'll be up, with cap, programme, and anything else he's brought with him pushed firmly onto his lap, and we'll be nodding at the smiling usherettes in their maroon uniforms who have crowded around ready to lock the doors behind us.

But this evening isn't going to be like that.

The woman has reached our parents and we watch open-mouthed as she elbows Mummie out of the way and grabs Daddie hard under one arm.

'Hey! What on earth d'you think you're doing?' My father's outrage would stop us at forty paces but this mad-woman doesn't seem to care.

'Just heave-ho! I understand this. My husband's blind!' she says sounding like my headmistress. She's strug-gling to reach over the wheelchair and, to our astonishment, she seems to think that she's able to help my father onto his feet. 'Let's get this moved,' she says suddenly and tries to throw Daddie's chair to one side into the aisle but it's very large and the little front wheels are stuck under the row of seats in front.

Last week I learned the word pandemonium, and I think this is it. Daddie cries out with real terror which shocks Mummie. Actually, it shocks us too.

'Get out of the way, you twit!' She shouts really loudly at the woman, and grabs the back of her coat. Will lets out a tiny high-pitched cry beside me but I'm too horrified and stunned to reach for him. How does this woman have the nerve to stand up to our parents like this? She obviously thinks she knows more than both of them. As she fights off Mummie's hand, her white handbag swinging wildly, she gets a hold on Daddie's waist and gives a great heave. His head comes up above the chairs for a second or two and then he crashes with an almighty bellow of pain into the dark space between the rows. The folding cinema seat snaps shut behind him and the wheelchair tips forward to jab him in the small of his back.

'Come to me!' commands the woman as though she were with a horse.

I can't stand it any more. I run forwards to join in the chaos between the seats. 'Leave him alone!' I shout. I'm no longer worried that Daddie will be embarrassed by this woman; I'm very afraid that he's about to be terribly hurt. The usherettes are like statues and doing nothing to help.

All at once a voice I recognise only too well cuts through the air like thunder.

'Everyone stop!'

It's Daddie taking control. His voice is icy with a furious calm. Will and I and the usherettes shrink back to our places against the wall.

'You!' he says to the nameless woman. 'You, bloody interfering fool! Go away! Get out!' An arm appears from above the seats with a pointed finger jerking towards the exit.

For a long moment we think she may ignore him and make a grab for his arm. She hesitates, and then glares at Mummie. All of a sudden she just walks away, past us children, down the aisle and out of the main door. Everyone watches her disappear in absolute silence.

I think Daddie is probably sitting in the dark between the seats taking a deep breath with his eyes closed. Then we hear his voice—gentle and quiet now, like he usually sounds—giving Mummie instructions which she follows to the letter, and eventually he's in his chair once more. He's a bit red-faced and sweaty, but he's safe. They don't say any more, and Will and I follow them through the only exit wide enough for Daddie's chair, straight outside into a narrow alley down the side of the cinema. The doors clang shut behind us and we walk into a cold drizzle, smelling of salt and the seaside and sparkling like firework trails in the light of the lamps on the High Street.

When we reach the road, the woman is nowhere to be seen. Daddie stops to straighten his trousers and wipe his face with a large hanky. He smooths his hair back from his forehead with one hand before putting on his cap with the other. Then he checks that nothing has fallen out of his pockets.

'Are you all right, Daddie?'

'Yes, thank you, honey,' he replies, with one of his heart-melting smiles. 'Now, who's for supper at the Festival House?' He catches sight of our mother's face. 'We're not going to let a stupid, interfering old…' He lets the word he hasn't said hang in the air like a threat, 'mess up our evening, now, are we?' And we walk down the street following his chair, skipping in and out of puddles, on our way to do battle with the Dover sole and, for the umpteenth time, hear the story about Grannie poisoning herself with home-made caper sauce, as though nothing had happened.

Chapter Sixteen

Present: June

...I had a pretty funny thing happen to me this morning. I was looking in a shop window at lunch-time with Bridget and Catherine when two strange looking types came up to us and asked if there was another shopping street in Berkhamsted. I said "No—what shop was he looking for?" He said "a draper's"—so I said "Oh. Are you going to start up a draper's shop here?" He said "No. I'm looking for an outlet for exquisite form brazeers (pronounced that way). I couldn't think what on earth he was talking about (Bridget and Catherine both did) so I said "Brazeer? What on earth is brazeers?" The other man gave an embarrassed simper and said "In English — Brassieres"!! Exquisite Form being a make! They were commercial travellers "looking for an outlet for Exquisite Form Brassieres!!"

There was a peppy insouciance present in all four pages of my mother's anecdotes. And a tangible mood of change. My father had been working the stock market, moving shares around and contacting his stockbroker on a weekly, sometimes daily, basis. I married up my mother's comments with the contents of yet another cardboard box full to the brim of statements and share reports but I could not for the life of me, understand why these had survived more than fifty years. It may have been simply due to a luxury of space that nobody thought to throw them away. But here was proof that my father was beginning to look towards a very real possibility that he might be leaving hospital all together in the next few months and playing the stock market, albeit with small amounts, may have been one way to make some money in the only way he felt able. And he had clearly recovered enough to finally be allowed out for weekend drives again.

Towards the end of the letter my mother talked of a prospective visit by Patrick Watson from Muntz Engineering, the company that my father had joined so full of hope at the time of his marriage nearly three years before. She suggested that they meet him at a local pub. *It would be nice if we could all get away from the hospital for a bit.*

There wasn't a single mention of TB anywhere in the remaining letters, but treatment must have still been a daily necessity. X-rays must have shown that the lesions in my father's lungs were closed and the programme of injections would have been expected to come to an end during the next few weeks. But none of this was mentioned in the excitement of my father getting up on his feet again to resume his physio and the fun to be had when they escaped the confines of the sanatorium at the weekends. In fact, my father persuaded my mother to get rid of her unreliable Ford and buy a new car. She called it Caramela.

May slipped by in a haze of preparations for rehabilitation into life outside hospital. Then, in early June, my mother wrote from Thelveton. Anne Johnson had also been a guest of the Pulman family and together they made plans for how my mother would manage when my father was discharged. It was decided that only Thelveton could offer the space and support necessary for my father's recuperation and the ever important exercises. Burnage was to remain rented out for short lets until my father finally dispensed with his wheelchair and normal life resumed.

My father was coming home, so walking, walking, walking became the whole focus.

London Hospital Annexe: End of June, 1955

'I didn't think I would get here in time,' Diana said as she ran down the length of the ward, leaving a trail of raindrops on the floor behind her. 'I thought you'd bound to be finished by now.' It was four forty-five, she was fifteen minutes late and had been delayed for a frustrating eternity at Wood Green bus station by flash floods that had broken a long spell of enervating heat.

Miss Hillier turned around and beamed at her. She was walking beside Push, guiding him along the outside of the parallel bars that ran across the far end of the ward. Push looked over Miss Hillier's head and winked at Diana then he returned to concentrating on relaxing his knees, resting between each step and starting the next movement from the hip.

'Meet Elizabeth and Brian.' Push nodded at two children sitting at one end of the bars without looking up from where he was placing his feet. 'Elizabeth. Brian. This is my wife, Diana.'

'Hello.' The girl spoke so quietly that Diana could hardly hear her.

'So you're Brian and Elizabeth. I've heard all about you.' Diana smiled. 'What have you got there?'

'Pete made it for us,' the boy said. 'Look.' He held out his toy towards Diana. 'You have to follow the bendy wire with the loop.'

'Without touching it,' interrupted the girl. 'If you do, it does this,' and she jogged the boy's arm to make a loud buzzing sound.

'And a lamp lights up too.'

'So it does.' Diana thought how beautifully made the little toy was with its carved handle and smooth red-painted base.

'And an infernal racket they make with it too. I can't think what came over me.' Push looked at Di quickly and gave another wink before facing ahead again.

The boy made a long buzz and wriggled about on his chair giggling before suddenly starting to cough. Push carried on taking steps, slowly and carefully. Miss Hillier put a finger to her lips. 'Shh, you two. You can watch, but you're meant to be taking it gently and not getting excited,' and the children sat quietly again as Push approached the wall beside them.

'I can't believe how natural your walking is beginning to look now,' said Diana after a moment or two. 'Daddie said you had really come on and I can see what he means.'

'He's been working very hard.' Miss Hillier was clearly as proud of Push as Diana was herself. 'I don't think I've ever had such a diligent patient.'

'He can turn round now, too,' the girl called Elizabeth said.

'I'd like to see that.' Diana stood in silence as Push slowly moved towards the wall. He halted, then waited until he was completely balanced, released Miss Hillier's hand and quickly grabbed for the bar. Elizabeth and Brian clapped loudly.

'Thank you, thank you. I'd take a bow, only I might fall over and that would rather spoil the effect.'

The children laughed and Miss Hillier said, 'That's next on the list.'

'That's the trouble with being such a tall boy,' Diana said. 'Oh! You're not wearing your irons.'

Push waited until he had completed his turn in a series of short shuffles before replying. 'No. They're revolting and they don't fit.'

'He told Russ that he wouldn't wear them under any circumstances.' Miss Hillier looked delighted as she reported Push's rebellion.

'Couldn't. I said, I couldn't wear them. They hurt me dreadfully and I could see them rubbing holes in me within no time at all.'

'Russ wasn't happy. He said they'd been measured by one of the most experienced technicians they had. He came down from Roehampton especially. Hold onto my other hand, Pete. You can start walking back now, if you've caught your breath.'

Push examined his feet to check that they were in line, then he leaned forward, swung his hip and relaxed his knee. The right leg came forward and the left took his weight. 'Makes me tired, though. Not having any support. I can't work for very long before everything starts to shake and I can't stop my knees bending.'

'Good. That was a perfect step.'

Brain looked at Push and held both his thumbs in the air.

'So what did Russ do?' asked Diana.

'I told him that his technician may be one of the best they had, and the irons I had may be a perfect fit, but they must have been measured for someone else because they didn't fit me.' Push wobbled slightly and gripped the bar hard, the veins in his arm standing out like whipcords. 'Oh dear! I haven't quite mastered the art of walking and talking together.'

'Sorry, Push, darling. I'll just stand here and keep quiet until you've finished.' Diana shook out her dress and brushed her damp hair out of her eyes. She really had got horribly wet while she was waiting for the bus. What a dreadful time for the trains to go on strike, just when Caramela was waiting for repairs in the garage.

At exactly five o'clock, Miss Hillier guided Push back to his wheelchair, waited until he had dragged it close to and watched as he sat down and arranged his feet on the foot rests. He was breathing hard and his shirt was almost as damp as Diana's dress.

'Are you going to manage without the irons, then?' Diana asked.

'For the time being.'

'Is that wise?'

'Some walking without braces can be a good thing,' said Miss Hillier. 'It builds the muscle up faster but it is also very tiring so you have to reduce the time you can exercise.'

'It only works if you have some muscle to start with. And I have now,' Push said.

'Plus the messages are getting through to tell which muscles to move and when. We've managed to persuade new pathways for the nerves to grow. It's all very encouraging.' A loud buzz interrupted Miss Hillier's explanation.

'Oo, it's too difficult!' Brian scowled furiously.

'Give it here. I want a go,' Elizabeth said, and Brian handed her the toy reluctantly.

'Russ has agreed to send the technician down again before Pete leaves, but he'll have to wait for the new irons if they agree to redo them.' Miss Hillier opened a cupboard and started putting her equipment away. 'If they do redo them, it'll take at least a fortnight.'

'They'll send them direct to Thelveton but we'll have to take the crutches with us,' There was another loud buzz as Elizabeth hit the rod with the loop. 'Hop along you two,' Push said. 'Isn't it your supper time soon?'

'No.' The children caught each others' eyes and grinned.

'I think it is.'

'I don't like fish,' said Brian.

'That's no excuse. You won't get better if you don't eat all you can.'

'Come on.' Elizabeth got up. Brian gave a deep,

theatrical sigh, tucked the toy under his arm a said a rather formal goodbye to everyone before leaving in Elizabeth's wake.

'What's the matter with them,' asked Diana.

'TB, like the rest of us.'

'What a shame.' Diana walked beside Push as he wheeled back up the ward towards his bed.

'Brian's going to miss Elizabeth. They've been company for each other but she's going home soon too.'

The door swung behind the children and the movement of air stirred Diana's hair.

'It's so good to see you upright again,' she said, kissing Push and getting a strong arm around her waist in return.

'How was Thelveton?'

'Very gay. We arrived with a cocktail party going on. Then Willie took over mixing the drinks, he made them so strong that Anne said they were knock-out drops, and I got hiccoughs.'

Push laughed. 'Sounds quite a night. Who was there?'

'All sorts of people and all longing to see you. They asked me to give you their love. Phyllis's mother was there with a spread of green ostrich feathers in her hair and Pa P immediately asked her what on earth she'd done to her head. She was wonderfully tipsy and very funny. You should have been there.'

'And next week, I shall be.'

'I can't believe it. We'll have you home properly and we won't be thinking about this horrid hospital any more or having to count the days until we have to take you back.'

'People have been very good to me here, Didie. We mustn't forget that.'

'I know they have, but you know what I mean. We can put all this behind us and concentrate on getting you walking in our own way. And you can see your friends and I won't have any more travelling to do every week. And I'll have you all to myself, that's the best bit. Every day and every night.'

Push gave her another squeeze around her waist. 'Did you get a chance to see Mr Sleight?'

'Oh, Mr Sleight. I nearly forgot.' Miss Hillier must have overheard the name as she walked towards them. She made an entry in Push's file. 'I'll just get the report I've prepared for him,' then she trotted away towards the door.

'Isn't she wonderful? She thinks of everything.' Diana watched Miss Hillier's retreating back. She turned to look at Push again. 'Yes, everything's ready. The parallel bars are perfect; absolutely solid and just as you planned. In fact…' She looked towards the far end of the ward where Push had been practising. 'I would say that they might be even better than the bars you have here. And Mr Sleight will come to see you at Thelveton to begin with, to make sure that you're working properly on them. Then, he says you can see him twice a week in Quidenham.'

Diana put her red bucket bag on the bed, took out her purse and opened it. 'I saved something for you. It was on the calendar for my last day at work. Captain O-B said I could cut it off.' She passed two small cuttings to Push. 'The other's my horoscope in this week's Woman. It's rather appropriate, I think.'

Push read the cuttings out loud, the horoscope first. 'A go-ahead happy week! Originality and the necessary *push* enables you to complete a special plan for the future. Go ahead with an ambitious home scheme. A thrilling surprise will come for the girl concerning plans for the future.' He put it to one side. 'Good heavens! I hope that comes true. Now, let's see... Those who hold firmly to a belief in their ability, have already won half the battle.'

'What's that?' Miss Hillier had returned with a large brown envelope in her hand.

'It's an aphorism that Didie had on her calendar.' Push passed her the slip of paper.

Miss Hillier read it to herself and looked up. She nodded. 'It's what I've always maintained. You should keep that to remind yourself not to lose faith.'

'I will.' Push tucked the cutting carefully away into one of the pale blue tins he had on his bedside locker. 'But I don't think I'll need reminding, I've heard you say almost exactly the same thing enough times.'

Miss Hillier handed Diana the envelope. 'In there should be everything Mr Sleight might need. I've charted Pete's progress and outlined all the exercises that we're doing at the moment. But if there's anything, anything at all that he needs to know from me, you mustn't hesitate to tell him to pick up the telephone and ask. I'll be only too happy to speak with him.'

'But this won't be the last we see of you. You will come and see us in Norfolk, won't you?' said Push.

'Yes,' agreed Diana. 'You must come to Thelveton.

Ma P loves having people to stay. The more the merrier, she always says.'

'You try and keep me away!' Miss Hillier smiled at Diana, then turned to Push and held out her hand. 'Good bye, Pete. You will keep me in the picture, won't you?'

Push engulfed her hand in his and to Diana's surprise, pulled Miss Hillier down towards him. He kissed her on the cheek. 'I promise, I'll write to you with my progress regularly.' He clasped her hand tightly with both hands. 'And thank you for everything you've done for me. I couldn't have got this far without you.' Eventually he let her go.

Miss Hillier flushed a deep pink. 'God Bless, Pete.'

Present: June

The sounds of early morning at Thelveton were abundant and various but it was the cackle of pheasants that was as immutable as the house itself.

I tried to picture my father's sense of relief and joy on waking in his childhood home on the morning after his arrival in late June, 1955. It had been a long time since the false dawn of his visit the previous Christmas.

Nevertheless, my father was back in Norfolk and it was a time for rejoicing. Most people of that generation marked a point in their lives as before the war or after the war. Events in my father's life were always before he was ill, and after he was ill. One June morning, my father awoke to the familiar pheasant-chorus of self-important crowing, and must have felt that it was the beginning of a point that was to become *after*.

Thelveton: August, 1966

It's half past six in the morning and nearly the end of the school holidays. I finished at Miss Ingate's in July, and in about two weeks I start my new school. Mummie says that now I'm eight, I'm more than ready to board away from home and I'm here at Thelveton for a week by myself to get used to it. Usually I love being here with Grannie, but I can't enjoy it properly as I keep remembering what's just around the corner, and then my heart gives a lurch and I feel a bit sick.

I was born in this room. It's really big and there's a connecting door where Daddie was waiting for news with Thom, his silver tabby cat, in the bedroom next door.

I smooth the underneath of the green eiderdown back and forth on my top lip to feel the cool satiny material and I think I can smell Mummie's evening scent, Joy. This was her room as it's the only bedroom in the house with a basin. Above the basin is a looking-glass surrounded by a round frame of painted wooden fruits unlike anything else in the house. I can't make my mind up if I love this even more than the glass on Grandpa's dressing table that is held up by two mahogany swans' heads on necks curved like snakes.

Way over on the other side of my bed is a built-in cupboard with a white painted door. I hang my dressing gown and coat in here and it smells of the cloves that Grannie packs into little silk ribboned sachets to keep out the moths. In the summer, we make clove bags for our wardrobes and lavender wands for the laundry cupboards and for the church sales. We pick fresh lavender before the buds are fully open, tie them tightly just below the flowers and fold the stems back on themselves. Then we weave ribbon in and out until we've made a silky basket filled with lavender buds, and tie a bow to leave the stems free like a little handle. I have a fresh one each year for my underwear drawer and when I sniff it, I'm reminded of Grannie standing up to her knees in the Thelveton flower beds, arms full of lavender and roses.

In the room next door that was Daddie's—where Will stays when he's here—there's a fireplace too. And on that mantelpiece under a glass cover, is a model of the golden royal coronation coach pulled by eight white horses.

With my eyes still closed and without moving from my bed I listen to the waking-up noises of the house. There are clicks and rumbles from the boiler as it heats the water. I can hear birds welcome the sun and the crow of a cock pheasant and the gentle, um-um of a hen pheasant walking around the shrubberies. I always sleep with the bottom sash open and I can remember sounds of the farm horses going to work when I was very little. I'm sad that they've all gone now and we only hear tractors. My curtains—red-striped chintz that match the two little chairs that sit either side of a spindly dressing table—belly out into the room with a shushing noise.

Grannie is always up first. The kitchen window is

on the same side as my room and I can hear her throw it open to chuck scraps from last night's dinner party to the birds. In a few minutes Mrs Gardener will arrive to make a start on the grates. She's very stout and rides a black bicycle which squeaks in time with her peddling. Grannie will pull back the bolts on the back door with a loud grating sound and walk out to meet her. Then it'll go quiet as the house swallows them up. Later, Marjy will open the smoking room door, which is under my window, to cut flowers for the drawing room.

Lily peddles slowly up the front drive at seven, also on a black bicycle, only hers has a brittle plastic triangle attached to the back wheel. If the kitchen window's open, I might catch a whiff of buttery shortbread. She bakes her biscuits almost every day and if I run down in time, she lets me push the cherries into the warm sugar. And then lick my fingers before she catches me.

This is my last morning at Thelveton before boarding school. I stroke my lip with the satin, reach into the corners of my bed with my toes to find fresh cool linen and turn my face from the door as my grandmother knocks.

Chapter Seventeen

Present: June

'How's your mother?'

'Fit as a flea,' I replied. My friend Maryrose had come to help me make sense of something, but as usual we started talking about my mother.

'Is she still playing tennis?'

'Two or three times a week, now the weather's improved. And bridge.'

Maryrose nodded and smiled one of those smiles that says, I thought as much.

'Oh, and she's taken up golf this year,' I added. 'She's having lessons and any spare half-hour she has, she's at the club practising her drives.'

I knew what was coming next and I wasn't disappointed. 'Your mother's incredible.' I'd heard this response for the last two decades at least. My mother ran marathons for the first time aged fifty, and I had a lot to live up to.

'I think she's actually getting younger; she's found the elixir of life and is supping deeply,' I said and we both laughed. Maryrose had known my mother since her father moved to Suffolk to farm apples when we were both about twelve, and we weren't altogether sure that I hadn't spoken the truth.

We sat at my kitchen table sharing news of our families like gardeners exchanging cuttings. We didn't see each other often but we were best friends as teenagers and we'd maintained and nurtured our friendship to arrive at this easy unspoken familiarity now.

In our twenties, and while I was working in London as a young graphic designer, Maryrose was completing her physiotherapy exams. A little later she specialised in paediatrics and worked at the Great Ormond Street Hospital for Sick Children. She never treated children suffering from the paralytic effects of polio—the national immunisation programme had been operating effectively for a generation by then—but in her current job, fitting non-walking people of all ages with the appropriate wheelchairs, she had certainly seen what polio could do.

'Let's see this chart, then,' Maryrose said, getting to the point.

I'd found something among my father's papers that I couldn't understand, but thought Maryrose's training and experience might provide some answers.

I cleared the coffee cups away and, after taking some slips of paper from a clear plastic sleeve, I pushed the largest of the three across to Maryrose and watched as she unfolded the dirty cream sheet. It bore deep creases and faint brown marks showing where it had been folded into four. She bent over the pencilled columns of dates and data and studied them in silence.

Finally she raised her head. 'How long would this first entry have been made after he first got ill?'

'About nine months.' The first date logged was June,

1953. 'He was still resting during the early stages of TB and having what they called passive therapy.' She nodded slightly and ran her forefinger down the columns, checking them against the dates at the side. I knew the layout by heart and had already guessed in part at its meaning.

'We know it's his leg measurements. That's obvious by the title. But what do you think the three columns indicate?'

'I'm pretty sure that they're two inches, five inches and nine inches above the patella.' Maryrose rubbed the end of her nose with the palm of her hand in a gesture that went back to when we were children. 'In other words, he's measured the circumference of his leg at those precise points and charted them to see if there's any improvement over time.'

I got up and walked around to her side of the table and we looked at the figures together.

'He made good progress.' I heard the same optimistic pride in my voice that I might have used about my children's work at school.

Maryrose looked up at me sharply for a moment or two. She wasn't smiling. 'Did he?' she said. 'Did he?'

I looked at the figures again and checked that each column steadily ascended in value. Had I made some elementary mistake? I studied them again but I couldn't see where the figures did anything other than grow incrementally.

'Have you got a tape measure?' Maryrose said suddenly, standing up.

I found one. She took it from me and let it unroll with characteristic abandon.

'Put your foot here.' She indicated the chair she had just vacated. I put my foot on the seat and stood, knee bent and level with my hip. 'Now. If I measure two inches above your patella...' She used her first two fingers to ascertain the edge of the top of my kneecap through my jeans and I saw the professional clinician in her movements. She kept a finger pressed onto my leg and, with a practised flick, caught the tape around the top of my knee, slid it up exactly two inches and pulled it taut. 'What do you measure?'

I peered at the tape. 'Sixteen and-a half inches.'

'Sixteen and-a-half inches,' she repeated, letting the tape go. It snaked to the floor in a yellow coil, I snatched at it before it hit the tiles and started to roll it up again. 'And you've hardly got tree trunks for legs,' she continued. 'What's the first measurement he recorded?'

'Eleven and-three-quarters. But it goes up to fourteen and-a-half'

'Yes, but that's over a whole year, Sarah.' The last entry was 1 July, 1954. 'And he was a very big man at the peak of his strength. His legs should have been huge.'

She was absolutely right, of course. Maryrose was used to seeing measurements in terms of what was normal and what was liable to give concern. To me these figures had no starting point, no bench-mark and therefore held no relevance but, by using my own leg, my friend had brought this home to me. I released the tape measure again and made it into a circle of eleven and-three-quarter inches. I held it by the tip of figure and thumb and imagined it around my father's leg. It was tiny. It was the same diameter as my upper arm.

'Would the muscles really have wasted so much in such a short time?' I was still looking at the loop held in my right hand.

'It takes no time at all. Have you ever broken a bone?'

'Only a rib.'

'You must have seen someone whose leg has been in plaster for six or eight weeks?'

'One leg becomes much thinner than the other,' I admitted. I turned my attention to my father's chart again. Even at nine inches above the knee, probably at the widest point of his thigh, the last recorded measurement was only one and-a-quarter inches larger than the lowest point above my own knee.

'Imagine the amount of atrophy over nine months. Your father couldn't put any weight on his legs and directly after the onset of TB, he would have been allowed absolutely no exercise apart from stretching with the physio to stop his tendons shortening. He couldn't possibly have hoped to make up the loss.'

But that's exactly what he had done. He always lived in hope. However unrealistic it may have been, that insidious hope was what had kept him—had kept them both—moving on.

I put my head in my hands, and my friend put her arms around me.

Before Maryrose left, I showed her the photograph of my father on the parallel bars. She confirmed that he was carrying no weight on his legs. Finally, she took a quick look at the other sheets of paper I'd found; one, a diagram of coloured circles, apparently unconnected dots, and arrows. It had the words 'depolarised' and 'power as required' and other words too scrawled to decipher. After a short silence, she sat back. 'I seem to remember something like this in the text books we had at the very start of my training.' She thought for a moment longer. 'It had something to do with a Fara… A Faraday…' She groped for the words and made an unconscious circle with middle finger and thumb.

'Coil?' I suggested; her gesture reminded me of a new battery-free torch we'd recently bought which worked by storing energy made by shaking a Faraday coil within the torch.

'Yes! It had something to do with faradisation. We had to practice everything we learned on each other and I recall it was very painful. Not nice at all. We never used it on patients that I can remember. Far too brutal.' She looked at her watch, gathered up her bag and got up to go. 'It works by electrically stimulating the muscles. Remind me to find the book.' We gave each other another hug before she lifted the latch of the back door and walked out into the garden. I followed her out to the yard, lifting my face to the sunshine and holding my hair so it didn't blow into my eyes. It'd been a long time coming, but June had come in style. A couple of crows swooped in the warm thermals high above us and swallows crowded the telegraph wires.

'Bye, Sarah! Thanks for the coffee.' Maryrose raised a hand as she climbed into her car. 'Electro-galvanic therapy, that's it. I'll find the book somewhere,' she shouted into the wind. Then she drove off. I watched her brake lights glow red for a second before she turned into the road, listened to her engine change tone as she climbed the hill. Then she was gone.

Walking back to the house I thought of her words. I wondered how much pain any one of us in my father's position would be prepared to put ourselves through if we felt there was any hope—any hope at all—that we might be cured. Then I considered my father's decision to hide all this evidence away.

'Can you tell me what your days at Thelveton were like?' I was back in Suffolk anxious to learn more from my mother.

She rubbed her knees with both hands and closed her eyes. 'We just spent a huge amount of time exercising.'

I guessed that she meant my father spent time exercising. I was certain that she was there always helping him.

'On the parallel bars?' I asked.

'Those and with the machine at Mr Sleight's—one of those pulse things.' She passed her hand over her eyes remembering the physiotherapist who helped them both for decades, and added. 'Then we got a machine at Thelveton so Push could work on it at home.

'We had a very concentrated regime,' my mother explained. 'Push worked on the bars twice a day without callipers for several hours at a time. He went in his chair to the bars, then got up between them, practising swinging his legs and taking his weight.'

'Up and down the laundry corridor?'

'Yes, by those box rooms and then around to the back bathroom.'

'How did he get round the corner?'

'Still on the parallel bars.'

'You mean they went all the way round to the bathroom?' This was radical news to me. For as long as I'd known Thelveton the bars were in a straight line, from the window at the far end of the laundry corridor to where it ended in a sort of open T-junction at the top, and there they stopped. If the bars had continued around these two corners—past a small kitchen and on to the large, cold bathroom and separate lavatory that Will and I used when we stayed there—it would have more than doubled the distance that my father had available to work in. It would have also seriously inconvenienced other members of the household.

'The main problem was that Ma P wanted to keep her social life going and we were expected to put in an appearance, but Push was just focused on what he needed to do to get better. It was like getting ready for the Boat Race. He had every minute mapped out and was resentful of Ma P's parties.'

'What about you?' I asked my mother.

'Oh, you know me, I liked meeting everyone. But Push felt if he wasn't working, he was wasting his time.'

'It sounds as if, even though he'd left hospital, he was recreating the same structure at Thelveton.'

My mother began to nod her head. She stopped stroking her knees. 'Yes. He was recreating the structure,' she repeated, as though thinking about it for the first time.

'And did it work?' I asked her after a moment's silence.

She took her hands off her knees. 'After a while he

could do this.' She moved her knees apart and together a couple of times without touching them with her hands.

She was right, I could recall my father sitting on the sofa, feet flat on the floor, swinging one thigh left and right from the hip to ease the perennial ache that collected there like rust. But it couldn't have been worth all that effort to be able to make a single occluded movement, could it? Of course, he wasn't to know that would be the extent of his success.

There was another passage in one of Miss Hillier's long letters from February, 1956: *I was overjoyed to hear on Saturday from you and Di that you can crawl in the bathroom and can cross over your legs—this is a very great improvement and is not just one of us telling you, but you can see it for yourself.*

For nine months, my parents concentrated on improving my father's ambulation. There may have been progress—my mother was insistent that there was—but it was all painfully slow and her recollections were of work done entirely with unbraced legs between the bars.

The intense and unrelieved claustrophobia of exercising at Thelveton finally got too much, even for two people with such a fixed goal. More than anything, my father's creativity needed an outlet. With the coming of an early spring in 1956, my mother reawakened her love of tennis and made a circle of friends beyond Thelveton, while my father looked for an alternative activity that was fun, inexpensive and, above all, depended on no more than he could give from his chair.

All through their childhood and teens, Push and his

brother had enjoyed building and flying model aeroplanes. Wickie Higham, a keen aeromodeller and great family friend, became his frequent companion. The day-bed was pushed to one side as the back kitchen at Thelveton became a workshop overflowing with plans, marine ply, balsa wood, tissue paper and the volatile, peardrop-stinking varnish known as dope. They favoured the fixed-line, petrol-motor propelled aircraft so that Wickie wouldn't have to race across fields to rescue any errant aircraft, and as the days grew longer, they spent happy times in meadows around Thelveton perfecting the trim and flying patterns, before attending meetings further afield to fly their creations competitively at the weekends.

My father wrote to the Aeromodeller magazine from time to time to ask for advice and the response was inevitably swift, detailed, and carefully considered. Aeromodelling at this level was clearly a deadly serious business.

When we were children, my father made us kites, so beautiful it was an agony to fly them, but he also shared his joy of aeromodelling and taught us to make aeroplanes, flawlessly constructed to stay airborne for twenty minutes, even half-an-hour at a time, until our necks were ridged with the strain of looking skywards.

Thelveton: 1956

Despite the aeromodelling, Diana and Ma P were concerned that Push had begun to drive himself too hard. Wickie found he couldn't spend so much time at Thelveton and, in any case, the summer would soon be over; in the vacuum Push had increased his work on the bars. He needed another distraction. At the end of August, his mother suggested to Diana that he should have a cat of his own to replace his beloved Oswald. They heard of a litter of silver tabby kittens in Oxfordshire and made arrangements to collect one.

From the moment they picked Thom out and brought him back to Thelveton, Push was entranced. But his new cat caused mayhem in the rest of the household. Thom was of a deeply nervous disposition which swiftly turned to aggression. He terrorised Marjy's cats, he attacked Ma P's Shetland collie, and hunted the game birds on the estate. But Push didn't care and Diana could see that he loved Thom from the start. The cat had been an ingenious suggestion and socialising him into the Thelveton menagerie became Push's project.

It may have been Thom that provided the catalyst for change, or it might have been that the time was simply right for Push to at last find time in his punishing schedule of exercise and electro-therapy to enjoy himself. His social circle began to widen as he sought to indulge his previous interests. Back in 1949, shortly after Diana first met Push during the Henley Rowing Regatta, Push had been present when the Aston Martin driver St John Horsfall, known as Jock, had been killed at Silverston driving an ERA. It was the twentieth of August, Push's twenty-third birthday, and he never forgot the shock of being in attendance at this horrific event. Jock's brother, Geoff, lived with his family near Thelveton in a house within the grounds of Redgrave Hall and it was inevitable that Diana and Ma P would meet him sooner or later. They invited him to one of the many Thelveton parties.

Geoff was nearer to Ma P's generation than Push's own but it was no surprise to Diana that the pair found an instant connection and went on to become great friends, spending hours in the extensive workshops at The Stables. Diana knew that they would have much in common, but she hadn't realised quite what a brilliant innovative engineer Geoff was. He built hugely complicated but inspired solutions to mechanical problems, while Push's engineering skills lay in developing and refining ideas. It turned out that they spoke the same language and complimented each other's expertise beautifully.

As promised, Miss Hillier kept in touch through long and detailed letters. Anne Johnson came for visits and Push continued to see Mr Sleight for physiotherapy twice a week. Visits to Brentwood for TB checks were reduced to just twice a year.

Had they not, Dr Rusby might have noticed how thin Push was becoming, but Diana, the rest of the family and those who saw him regularly considered him to be fit and well. He had lost his hospital pallor completely, the continuous exercise over the past year had toned his upper body to a level Diana hadn't seen since he'd been in training for the Olympics. He was happier than he had been in years, and he was as determined as ever that he would one day be able to do without his wheelchair.

Everyone thought he was recovering well.

In September Diana drove him into Diss for a routine dental check-up. He'd been suffering some discomfort for a while and it was decided that he needed an impacted wisdom tooth removed. Because of the impossibility of treating him within the dentist's chair, he was referred to the General Hospital at Ipswich and his extraction was booked for mid-October.

Diana took him in and then waited while he had the simple procedure so she could see him when he woke up from the anaesthetic.

Present: July

'When he came round he was terribly, terribly cold.' My mother spoke quietly and almost to herself. She hunched her shoulders forward as though it had been she with the chill all those years ago.

The temperature had been rising and rising since the beginning of July and it was now thirty-one degrees. We'd spent the morning sweating in the local hospital having my mother's cataracts assessed, and the drops they'd used had made her vision blurry. When we were finally released after sitting for several hours in a series of windowless waiting rooms, we'd decided to come back to my house, then go for a walk around the Broad until her sight had cleared enough to drive home.

Putting one foot in front of the other in a sunny fog had suddenly seemed to unlock a desire in my mother to finish the story. 'He was shivering so hard the bed was shaking.'

'What did you do?'

'We went back to Thelveton. Push seemed to have caught a dreadful cold, but when we went to Brentwood a few weeks later for his six-month check up, they found another shadow on his lung.' She slowed and struggled to pull her sunglasses from a little cross-the-body bag she was wearing. 'The TB had broken out again.'

My mother regarded me steadily before pushing the dark glasses over her nose. We both looked away and gazed towards the water. A coot was peeping somewhere nearby and a fish plopped the surface, no doubt after a mayfly. I'd guessed what was coming, but it was distressing just the same.

'We came home for a couple of days to collect our things and then he was driven back to the Annexe.'

'Oh, God!' I put my hand over my face for a second. 'He had to have all those streptomycin jabs again.'

My mother nodded, then shook her head. She looked back at me and I felt her eyes boring holes in me behind the black lenses. 'Russ said the strep wasn't any good, and he warned that Push might have to have a huge op to take out the bit with the shadow.'

'What did he mean, the strep wasn't any good?'

'That it wasn't good enough by itself to finish the job. To cure him. Which is why the TB had broken out again. They did put him on the strep again, but he had to wait several months before he could have the surgery, to develop a canopy of cover.' She accentuated the last phrase to indicate that she was giving me the medical term.

'It'd all been a bit too good to be true.'

'I suppose so. Kathleen Hillier said it'd been a sign

from God that the hole in his lung had closed up.'

'Like a miracle.' I couldn't keep the cynicism from my voice.

'Well, she really believed it.'

After a moment, she said, 'And Push believed it too. They both had such faith; it's what kept him going.'

We'd arrived at a bench and I sat down, patting it to encourage her to join me.

'It was a shock. Such a shock. We never expected it,' my mother said suddenly. She took her sunglasses off but didn't move to sit down beside me. Then she reached into her bag and drew out another bundle of azure blue envelopes and put them into my hands. 'I found these a couple of days ago in my desk. They're all from Push.'

Chapter Eighteen

Present: August

This was the first time I'd read of my father's fears and anxieties in his own words or seen the hospital wards through his eyes. He was loving, reassuring, anxious and, almost certainly, still censoring information to protect my mother. Old habits die hard, even when promises have been requested and granted.

Unlike my mother, who filled her letters with how she occupied her days, addenda to previous conversations face-to-face in the ward and energetic encouragement, my father described his state of mind and his cautious approach to the next set of treatments, but rarely the future, except in the most general of terms. And, in every letter he recorded what he could see from the window. *I looked at the windows, but they were rather steamed up. It was very foggy out, and I worried about your journey. ...trying to write lying down and only seeing the tops of the trees from this position. It's been a glorious day, and I hope it's been the same in Norfolk.*

My father's preoccupation with the weather was easy to understand. From those first weeks lying flat in a room at Uxbridge looking at the manicured gardens, or

Hanbury Ward on the top floor of The London Hospital for nearly six months with nothing but sky to see, then on his on his back again, often all alone during the days in Mann Ward at the Annexe in Brentwood. For years on end with little to look at except through rectangles of glass, he must have seized on any change in his surroundings. For a man who'd spent so much time on the river rowing in all conditions, incarceration indoors was particularly difficult to endure. Even when the hospital days were long behind him, poor weather put a halt to most outdoor activities; he couldn't slip on a pair of Wellington boots and fling a rain-coat over his shoulders before running outside like the rest of us. So when we were children, it became routine for us all to look at the forecast before any outing, and while out, we continually monitored the sky for imminent changes. My father's lap presented a large area to the rain, his twill trousers and comfortable, suede Hush Puppies ankle boots would soon soak through, and his chair was not improved by exposure to water. Macs and umbrellas were kept in the car, just-in-case. We became adept at looking for shelter if the clouds seemed threatening. He rarely complained, but we became attuned to the risks of my father getting wet or chilled.

The London Hospital Annexe: 1956

Alexander Ward — Sunday, 9th December
My darling Didie,
Although it is a bare 24 hours since we arrived here,

it seems a great deal longer. I miss you very much indeed and think about you all a good deal. Don't think that I'm miserable, I'm not; but it takes time to make friends and settle down into a routine that makes the time pass more quickly.

I can't tell you anything about future prospects yet, and we shall have to wait for a fortnight or three weeks, I expect, until Russ can get an idea how things are shaping and make plans accordingly. Anyway, keep your chin up and let us pray that it won't be too long before we are together again.

This ward seems to have a cat of its own: a sleek black job, called "Banjo"! I must admit that I didn't get much sleep last night—inevitable I suppose, in a new place with light and noises to contend with. Added to which, my mind seemed full of thoughts, chasing each other round and round. However, the tedium was considerably relieved when the aforesaid "Banjo" cornered and killed a mouse under someone's bed! It was absolute bedlam for a few minutes and I just couldn't think what was going on.

What sort of a journey back did you have last night? I looked out of the windows once or twice to try and see if it was foggy, but they were rather steamed up and I didn't learn much. The one time I could have done with the windows open, and they decide for once, that it is too cold.

I think that we have got a decent lot of nurses on the ward—as far as I can tell in such a short time—and I don't think the other patients are living up to the unsavoury traditions that Alex. Ward used to have.

I think that I had better stop now because there

really isn't anything to say, except that I love you very, very much and miss you terribly. God Bless you all, my love to Pa, Ma, and Mrs B.

With a very special stack of love to you, honey,

Push

Home, Suffolk: 1965

I'm not good at sleeping, but I don't mind getting up in the mornings. Usually I pull on my clothes and run downstairs but if I'm too slow before Daddie goes to the bathroom, I'm stuck in my room, waiting.

Mummie checks the landing before Daddie goes for a wash. She pokes her head around our doors and warns us to stay in our bedrooms. Once I forgot and came out too early. Daddie really doesn't like to be seen doing his morning rituals.

It takes him a long time to get ready. He wakes up. I can hear his grumbles and coughs through the wall, then he switches on the wireless. He likes to listen to the Home Service. He's full of aches and pains and Mummie massages him every day to help his muscles. He wears special night-shirts that she makes for him because he doesn't like pyjama bottoms that wrinkle up under him in the night. It hurts him a lot and makes sore places. Our parents have two beds that are pushed together. They have shiny eiderdowns which are dark pink, with pretty pink, green and white flowery frilly bits round the bed. They match the curtains and the blocked-in fireplace behind their heads, which has wallpaper to look like a headboard. Daddie can't bear any weight on his legs, so his covers go over the cradle at the bottom of his bed. Thom likes to sit there, sinking between the square metal bits like a grumpy old man slumped in a hammock.

Sometimes, on his birthday or Christmas Day when Daddie has a lie-in, Will and I might go in and see him in bed and he pretends to be a mad person locked away in the attic and tells us a story which has us laughing and scared all at the same time.

On those mornings, we stand close to the bed, but not touching it. We mustn't bump his bed or chair. But most days he wakes up, Mummie rubs his legs and then he does... I don't know. Whatever it is that he does before getting into his chair while Mummie is downstairs letting James out for a run, opening all the shutters and getting in the post and the papers.

The time I saw him on the landing, he was almost bare, except a towel across his lap. He balances the Roberts there, so he doesn't miss the weather forecast. I've seen him with his back to me emptying his night bottle down the lavatory. The back of the little chair is a muddy colour, sort of like Grandpa's shooting bag, and the canvas digs into his back which is all slumped and rounded. He's sat so long in a chair that he has something called scoliosis of the spine, which just means that it's crooked like the giant capital S at the beginning of my name.

On his shoulder all the way down to his waist is a reddish-coloured scar, in a big curve. He had lots and lots of stitches. I know that it was twenty-six on the outside and thirty on the inside, which is fifty-six in all. They took a piece of lung out when his TB refused to get better. He's not told us much about being in hospital but I asked him about his scar when I saw it by accident on the beach in Cornwall. He told me what it was, but his voice made me shiver and I shouldn't have mentioned it and I know I must never, ever talk about it again.

We hardly ever see his legs, except perhaps a tiny bit peeping out above his socks if his trousers have got hooked up. They're very thin and look a bit like sticks but his skin doesn't really look like skin, it's more like silvery tissue paper.

A few days ago when we went out to lunch, we were all playing with some kittens when two ran up the flapping open bit of his trousers. I think they thought his legs were tree-trunks. One kitten went up each leg. He said it felt like having needles driven into his flesh. He had to roll up his trousers and show his legs so somebody could unhook the kittens. I think his watery eyes were as much to do with that as for the pain and the blood. When we got home he said he was really worried about getting ulcers and he asked me to stroke Germoline very gently over all the bad places because Mummie had to rush out to a meeting. I had to do it again today, but you can still see scratches and punctures, as though someone had gone a bit mad with a red biro all over his white skin.

Present: August

If my father was to be believed, practical jokes seemed to be regular occurrences in hospital. I was surprised to learn this, but Sister Anne explained that it was tough for patients seeing their treatment out (often for years), especially when they felt reasonably well six or eight weeks from beginning a long course of streptomycin. In the intervening time before their lesions were completely healed and they were able to resume their lives on the outside again, they had to do something to keep boredom at bay. An elaborate joke could occupy much of the TB patients' days, from planning to execution.

Although the father we knew hated practical jokes or surprises, the fun and pranks he told us about inured us to the reality of his life in hospital.

That is, until he told me that he'd developed a dependence on morphine.

I was in my mid-teens and we'd been discussing the damage done to the family of some nearby friends by their daughter's drug addiction.

My parents were worried about the progressive public school to which they felt they'd been forced to send me, after I failed my common entrance exam to their preferred option when it was time to move on from my sheltered preparatory school.

From the first day that they left me at my new boarding school, where we were greeted by pupils dressed in Biba tops, flowing kaftans and scarves, it was clear to my parents that the place was full of hippies. Hippies took drugs and, therefore, it must stand to reason that I was in mortal danger of the rampant drug culture that was bound to be prevalent within the school. It wasn't, or at least not within my sphere, but my father couldn't dismiss his initial impressions.

As always, his reaction was to tell me a story, a parable, and trust that, suitably informed, I'd make the correct choices.

'Because my legs didn't work, they didn't want to cut this big muscle here.' He pointed to the pectoral muscle over his heart. 'I need all the strength I can find in my arms to shove myself about, and any weakness might have caused difficulties later. So, they decided to get to my lung through my back.' Having seen his scar, I knew exactly which bit of his back he meant. 'It was pretty painful, they had to force my ribs apart. Afterwards I was stuck lying on my front with a drainage tube coming out of the wound.'

Then he gazed at me intently, which meant I had to concentrate because what I was about to be told might not be fun, but was going to be good for me. 'They gave me morphine as they do after most operations. And then they had to give me more because the pain was too bad. Eventually they gave me the highest dose they could day-after-day. And I became addicted.'

He said it in such a matter of fact way, I didn't really believe him.

'You were addicted,' I repeated. 'How did you know if they were in charge of giving it to you?'

I never did learn to watch out for his tripping points.

'Because, Sarie, I would stare at the hands inching

around the clock, desperate for it to be the time when the next injection would make the pain fade and ease enough to sleep. Morphine's made from opium which is in turn made from the seeds of the opium poppy, and you also make heroin from the same poppy. They're all opiate drugs that are highly addictive.' I knew about opium because I'd been a Sherlock Holmes fan from the age of thirteen, but I knew nothing about heroin.

My father's stories rarely ended where you expected them to. It wasn't enough to explain that he'd been an addict. He had to make a picture powerful enough for me to carry in my head for the rest of my life.

'One day, I heard the nurse who gave my injections talking outside my room. The hands crept around the clock face. Five minutes past, ten minutes past, and she was still out there talking. I couldn't stand listening to her anymore. It'd got beyond the alleviation of pain. What I wanted was the injection. The drug in my system. I needed that feeling of separateness; taking me right out of myself, the hospital and everything that had happened.' He looked over my head and stopped talking.

I waited and eventually I said in a very small voice, 'What happened then?'

My father glanced back at me, his grey eyes were unseeing as stones. Then he blinked. 'Oh. When the nurse finally came into my room, she found me on the floor. I'd fallen off my bed in order to drag myself to the door and tell her to get a bloody move on. The tubes were all wrenched out of my back and there was blood and mess everywhere.' He sat back in his chair and looked at me very kindly. 'That's what addiction does. That's how I know I was addicted.'

My mother had talked about his surgery a little after she found the first bundle of letters. She'd tumbled from one traumatic event to another, bumping up against her own emotions and squashing them down with the weight of her indignation on my father's behalf. After all that time, she was still incensed at some of the treatment he'd received.

'It was a terribly painful operation,' she told me. 'They went in through his back. They didn't cut a rib out; instead they wrenched his ribs apart with some sort of tool.'

The date of the procedure wasn't recorded, but from the gap in the letters, a cluster of Get Well Soon cards and a move to the surgical ward, I deduced that my father's lobectomy was scheduled for the twenty-fifth of February, 1957. In the two weeks before, he had more visitors than ever. At the end of one day, he listed the goodies his friends had brought with them: flowers, cigarettes, tea, sugar, peaches, eggs and homemade fudge. His mother brought him an orchid and my father mentions its longevity over many weeks and recorded that it had been borrowed for two dances! But for all the kindness and concern of his many friends, he felt guilty for sometimes wanting my mother to himself; almost the exact same phrase used by my mother several years earlier, in her letters to him. Visiting times were so limited that he was resorted to saying what he needed to tell her in his letters.

The London Hospital Annexe: 1957

21st Feb, 1957 Mercer Ward
My darling Didie,

It was lovely to see you yesterday and I hope you feel happier now that you have seen me safely installed up here—I felt that you were a little bit on edge when you first came along...

...Please try not to worry, darling. I know it is very difficult not to; but remember these two things: Firstly, I am quite sure that Russ would not have suggested this op if he wasn't certain that it would be all right. And you can be equally sure that V.T, who is one of the best surgeons in the country, wouldn't take it on if he wasn't happy about it from every aspect. Secondly, and even more important, remember that I love you more than anyone, or anything, else in the world—and I hate to see you worried about me. I know it isn't really my fault, but it seems a bit like it sometimes.

I have told you that you are a wonderful wife to me. You have proved to be a wonderful partner in all ways— agent, secretary, muse and physio! You are really my legs in some ways. I look forward to being with you again now more than I did last time I was in. I loved you very much then, but I wondered how we would get on when I came back to you. In some ways it was more like a concentration of our engagement than married life.

When I <u>did</u> come home, all my fears were gradually dispelled. I lost my embarrassment over being helped to the 'country seat', into the bath etc., and you showed me *how truly wonderful married life can be. You really are a marvellous girl, and I love you more than ever before—in a deeply satisfying and indestructible sort of way. It's a lovely feeling.*

So just help me over this last hurdle by trying not to worry. If Pa and Ma have been a little crabby—remember that they are anxious too. Help them as you have done me during these past difficult weeks. They love and admire you very much. Give my love to Pa and God Bless you, honey.

My love to you, Push.

Chapter Nineteen

Present: August

Will and I drove to my Aunt Dorothy's house in late August.

We were going through a pile of old prints when Dorothy picked up a grubby maroon board-covered notebook a little smaller than a paperback. It had clearly seen much use. The front cover had separated from the main body, and was now attached only by two strips of Sellotape, yellowing and brittle as pastry, with no title or mark of any kind on the binding.

'The Drake's recipe book!' she announced, and handed it to me.

Two postcards dropped to the floor, both from the Wellington Branch Mother's Union.

'They're recipes for...' The large jerky handwriting that spread across the card, filling all the available space, was faded and difficult to read. 'No. Receipts for Mince Meat ECP 1936, and Xmas Plum Pudding 1936 SEP.'

'That must be Ellen Cordelia,' said Aunt Dorothy. 'Married to William Walker Pulman. Your father's grandparents; your great-grandparents.'

Dorothy put on her glasses and took her turn to look at the faded black ink. She was in her eighties herself, thin but wiry, and showed no sign of mental confusion or slowing down. The last time I came to visit, I'd had to hold a ladder while she pruned the wisteria. My offer to reverse our roles was refused, politely but firmly. One didn't argue with Dorothy.

'You'd better have this, Sarah.' Dorothy handed me the recipe book.

I glanced at Will to be sure he was happy with the decision. He nodded. 'Absolutely. That's yours, Sarie.'

I flicked through the little book enjoying recipes such as Policeman's Sauce, Punctual Pudding, and Belgian Stew, which appeared to be deprived wartime fare.

There was Orange Meringue, which I at first took to be Grange Meringue until I saw the list of ingredients, and Patchul Cake with the word Holkham after it in brackets.

Recipes were entered in a totally haphazard way. Several on the pages near the beginning, followed by an unlikely loose cutting from the Daily Mail listing popular street food: pirozhki from Russia, Mexican antojitos, and Singapore noodles. Did my grandparents ever try them? It was hard to imagine. Other newspaper cuttings were glued in firmly for a few pages, then a number of late entries written, recognisably, by my grandmother in blotchy blue ballpoint. I turned through a number of empty pages and all at once the recipe for Lily biscuits lay dead-centre, bookmarked with a brown envelope postmarked 26 January 1973. I was certain it was the Lily biscuits we'd eaten every day, in spite of being headed Cherry shortcakes. Such a simple recipe! 2 oz butter (margarine had been crossed out and butter written at a later stage, perhaps after rationing had ended), 3 oz flour, 2 level tablespoonfuls sugar and a pinch of salt. No mention of cherries except in the name. Beneath, Grannie had added and then crossed out again, *Part corn flour is an improvement.*

At the end of the tatty red notebook were recipes for lemon cough syrup, furniture polish, Cambridge chutney (which had enough chillies in it to need the cough syrup as an immediate antidote), then three pages of preserves.

And there it was: *Marmalade—Drakes Place* and on the facing page, in a much older copperplate hand, faded to a raw umber, *Marmalade—Kinnersley House.* The book sat on my knee, lying perfectly flat and open at this point as though the pages were used to being pressed and examined. The paper was spotted, stained and splattered to such an extent that the ink had run and furred at the edges. Additional instructions added in pencil at ninety degrees, with suggestions of alternative quantities, were barely visible under the marks.

I lifted the book to my nose, and drew in nothing but the scent of old paper. Not a hint of citrus remained in the coffee-coloured daubs and splashes: the juice from oranges grown in a Spain under Franco; possibly even earlier, in Alphonso's reign.

A whole history of Pulman breakfast tables, my own included, lay before me over those two pages and I felt more connected with this scrappy volume than with any number of items bearing the Pulman otter or other family crests. Pulman furniture still lived on in all of our houses, but how much of what was left on Dorothy's floor was passed on with deliberate intent? My little dull-red book had been in the hands of generations of women who were not entitled to take the symbols of their birth families with them when they married. They took the recipes—or receipts—of their kitchens, and unbeknown by the men in their families, they carried forward a legacy of quite a different nature. A legacy that was off-the-record, undisclosed and uniquely personal. Few of those other, so-called, valuable heirlooms could excite in me a desire so urgent, so needy or able to instill such a sense of belonging. More than anything, I wanted to cook from the book and see if I could discover other tastes and scents from my early childhood, and make them live again.

The three of us sat together in the gathering dusk, picking over books and photographs, recognising younger faces of old friends and family members, and others whose identity had gone forever.

'Who's this?' I recognised the face, but not the name, from my parents' wedding album.

Dorothy looked over my shoulder at the portrait of a woman with carefully waved white hair, circular horn-rimmed glasses and a fox fur stole slipping off one shoulder. She gazed out at me with a small half-smile and mischievous eyes. 'Oh, that's Aunt Dolly. She stayed at Thelveton and drank like a fish. By six o'clock she always had to have a glass in her hand. She found Thelveton very cold and could always be found smoking and drinking G & T in the greenhouse.'

Instantly I could see Aunt Dolly, pink with tropical heat and gin, lifting her crystal tumbler, ice chips clinking against the glass, face all-but-obscured by dangling fronds of salmon-pink bougainvillaea, and laughing, while gulping a heady mix of gin, tobacco and the fragrances of rose-scented geraniums and brugmansia trumpets. I wasn't surprised Dolly had liked the Thelveton glasshouses so much. So had I. They were one of my own favourite hiding places, an inside-outside building so potent with colour and fragrance that I almost swooned with the intoxication of humidity and exotic vegetation that engulfed me.

'There's a photo album here.' I pulled a wide book with a bootlace tying its black board covers together onto my lap and sat back into the little green tub chair that used to be in the morning room at Thelveton. I opened the cover and saw a photograph of thirty-seven aircraft making the letters GR VI in a sky scattered with thin cloud.

'Look at that!' said Will, when I turned it round to show him. 'George the Sixth.'

I turned to the next page, which was scattered with tiny pictures of cars, motorcycles and light aircraft.

'There's the Aston,' Will said. It was parked on the drive outside the drawing room windows at Thelveton, the limbs of bare beech trees spread out behind and, to the right, a neat round flower bed full of spring bulbs and as big as a swimming pool.

I turned more pages to find my father's youthful self, standing in the sea wearing shorts and a knitted tank-top, kneeling in the cut hay trimming model aeroplanes, in a field, sitting along a wall with friends in the sunshine.

And then there was Drakes Place. Four pictures showed different sides of the house. Surrounded by foreboding cedar trees in the parkland, it rose heavily from a leaf-strewn drive and unkempt gardens. In the foreground, my grandparents have paused in a field disconnected by some way from the house and lawns by a wire fence, and from each other by a double arm's length. They look at the photographer solemnly and unsmiling. Grandpa, slimmer then and upright as a ramrod yet carrying a walking stick, has his other hand tucked into a trouser pocket, his ever-present gold watch chain clearly visible. Far behind them, a ladder stands against a grimy, stained and unpainted wall of the house. I guessed these pictures were taken after the war and just prior to the sale.

I turned a page and my parents looked out at me, my mother young and very pretty, my father formally dressed in jacket and tie, both, inexplicably, holding enormous mushrooms. The height difference was always striking; my father towering over my mother, who was small and dainty by comparison. On the next page, they lean against a wall with Sir Jack Mann, and on another they're enjoying a holiday on the Norfolk Broads.

The last picture in the book, out of sequence, was of my father dressed in RAF uniform and cap, leaning his arm on the roof of a black VW beetle bearing the words BAFO Gatow, with the flat, concrete plains of the German airfield used in the Berlin Airlift spread out for miles, blank and empty behind him.

I flipped back a page or two. 'Who's this?'

Dorothy looked carefully at the young woman, appearing to appraise her dark wool suit, her tiny waist enhanced by a thin leather belt, her small hat with a large bow at the back, her bag and gloves held loosely in her hand, and one foot raised on a short flight of steps out-side the door to a town house. 'That's me.' She turned the album round to face me again and got up. 'That wasn't long before Willie and I were married.' Then over her shoulder, as she walked out of the room to check on our supper, she added, 'We were married the day before your father came out of the TB hospital for good.'

The final letter in the bundle of letters that my father wrote from The Annexe at Brentwood was dated 30 May, 1957. On the envelope my mother had written, *Just before Will's & Dodo's wedding—Push came home next day*. My grand-parents must have been overjoyed for the future of both their sons. My father was coming home, and my parents were to be together again. For everyone, the relief must have been immense because this time they knew that the TB was finally beaten. It'd been four years almost to the day since his second diagnosis.

At once, my parents threw themselves into a busy routine of rehabilitation and recuperation. The summer flew by in much the same way as the previous one.

My mother had mentioned that she'd sometimes felt under an almost claustrophobic scrutiny by a never ending parade of visitors to Thelveton, and became exhausted by a constant need to be on best behaviour.

'By the autumn, I was feeling very tired and sort of low,' she'd told me. 'Pa P had some sort of spinster cousin who lived in Bruges and he very generously arranged a little holiday for me, but I was dreadfully sick on the boat and felt terrible when I arrived.'

'You're always ill when you travel.' I admired my mother's determination to keep travelling, despite this uncomfortable affliction.

'But this was different. When I arrived at Cousin Olive's beautiful little flat, I still felt horrible and she put me straight to bed. She'd arranged all sorts of lovely things for us to do and see; the problem was, I couldn't stop being sick. I thought I must have caught a bug.'

We'd been wandering around her garden, my mother deadheading roses as we talked. 'I think Cousin Olive might not have been quite as spinsterish as I'd been led to believe. I remember her coming into my room, sitting on my bed and saying that she didn't think I had a tummy bug. She told me that she thought I was probably expecting a baby.'

'It all made sense. The tiredness, the bloaty feeling, my sickness. Of course, I was pregnant.'

'That must have been wonderful,' I said. 'All those years with Grandpa fearing that his son and heir might not have children of his own to carry on the family name, and now, here you were, able to say that you'd be having a family after all. After everything, what a joyful moment!'

Thelveton: October, 1957

Diana paid the taxi driver and watched him get back into the car and drive away. She stood beside her suitcase in the gateway of the drive looking up at the house. A single 'Albertine' rose was still in bloom amongst the dying leaves and stems against the wall. Thelveton appeared deep in post-prandial silence. The weather was more autumnal than it had been in Bruges early that morning and Diana rubbed her arms briskly. Push would be resting on his day-bed in the back kitchen while the rest of the family were, no doubt, having coffee in the drawing room. Lily would be washing up and looking out over the side lawn, and Pa P might be in the smoking room, but that was a risk she had to take. She wanted to see Push before anyone else, so she followed the track ahead of her, avoiding the front of the house, and walked up the back drive, turning right through the avenue of beech trees to arrive at the back door.

She clicked the latch and opened the door a crack. She felt queasy again and stood for a moment leaning against the wall in the semi-dark, listening to Push's wireless mumbling quietly through the thick wooden door. Every now and then, she heard the rumble of his voice. He was saying something to Thom, who unfailingly appeared at rest-times.

Diana left her case in the passage, lifted the latch and shoved the heavy door with her shoulder. It caught on the floor with a sharp grating noise and Push raised his head from the newspaper he'd been reading. Bushy, one of the Thelveton cats, ran inside ahead of her and leaped onto a windowsill to peer through a web of greenery into the kitchen garden.

'Didie! We weren't expecting you until this evening.'

'I know. I caught an earlier train.'

'You should've rung ahead. Mother would have collected you from the station. Did you have a lovely time?

Are you feeling better?'

Diana walked towards Push, caught his hand and leaned forward to hug him, but she didn't sit down. 'A little,' she said. 'I got a taxi. I didn't want to bother anyone. In any case, I've got some important news.' She smiled as she spoke.

'News? What sort of news?'

Push still had Diana's hand in his and she put her other hand over his to press it tightly. She paused, looking into his grey eyes trying to calculate his reaction. She was silent so long that he started to look confused, so she just went ahead and told him. 'The reason I felt so lousy...' She took a deep breath. 'Is because we're almost certainly going to have a baby.'

Push pulled his hand away so quickly that Diana nearly fell over. She stumbled to regain her balance and her heart started to bang about inside her ribs. She stepped backwards until she felt the edge of a chair against her legs. As she sat down, a wave of nausea rose in her throat. She swallowed and breathed steadily until it subsided.

In the slightly unreal, subterranean light from the vegetation-obscured windows, Push's face took on an almost greenish tinge. His forehead was deeply furrowed.

'But, how...?'

'How do you think?' Diana spoke rather more sharply than she'd intended. She shrugged her shoulders, but didn't apologise.

'Are you certain?'

'As certain as I can be.' From the moment Cousin Olive had convinced her that all the signs pointed towards her being pregnant, Diana wouldn't allow herself to think about how she felt about this baby. She'd tried to convince herself that Push would be utterly delighted at the news. But, if she was honest, she wasn't surprised at his reaction. After all, a baby had not been part of the plan.

Present: August

I thought about the way my mother had narrowed her eyes, which had nothing to do with the brilliant sunshine, and then looked at me carefully. She'd folded one hand over the other and gripped her secateurs.

'Not joy, no,' she'd said slowly, never for one moment looking away from my face, although she wouldn't have been able to see my eyes behind my sunglasses. 'It was horror. He was going to have to give up his dream of walking.'

Chapter Twenty

My parents had also been enjoying a warm September in 1958 when I was just four months old. It might be supposed that after my father's last visit to the Annexe for the surgery that finally put an end to his TB, there would be no more long stays in hospital, but the letters I'd been handed when we'd been walking by the Broad weren't all the result of more unexpected TB treatment. Some were addressed to Ward 3X at Stoke Mandeville Hospital in Buckinghamshire.

When my father returned to Thelveton from Brentwood after his lung operation, the tuberculosis had been beaten and he was a healthy man. However, he lacked the one thing he craved above all others; he still couldn't walk.

Becoming a father appeared to have concentrated his mind and galvanised him to abandon the round of exercises and painful sessions using the muscle toning machine; reluctantly, he came to believe that the years of effort had been largely futile. He realised that in order to resume living a normal life, he needed three things: employment, a family home and to be employable. The first two were a given; remarkably after so many years, he still had a job waiting for him at Alan Muntz, so Burnage in Iver was the obvious choice for a family home but, despite reassurance to the contrary, my father was convinced that he would never be able to reach his earning potential unless he learned to do away with his chair, at least for some of the time. Even FDR, though stricken by paralysis, had felt the need to conduct his presidential business standing up and it became clear to me that my father refused to believe that he couldn't do the same. He felt that if he only made enough effort, he would walk again.

There was a stark difference to my father's stay at Stoke Mandeville: there, in the specialist spinal injuries hospital under the supervision of the renowned Dr Ludwig Guttmann, he was to be a patient as a result of his own free will. For once, my father had been able to exercise choice and some control over his own future. This was one last effort to learn to walk again for the sake of my mother and me.

Ward 3X, Stoke Mandeville: September, 1958

Thelveton 25 September, 1958
My darling, darling Push,

Things seem very bleak here as always when you are away, but I pray & hope that this really will be the last of our separations & that after you come home we will really be able to start a proper married life together plus wee Sarie and any future babies!

I do hope my darling, that the place is <u>not</u> as bad as you fear. There are always some nice people in any

establishment & you being who you are, will find that peo-
ple will want to help & love you—you are always such a
wonderful companion & such fun to be with that you are
bound to find somebody who will be falling over to help
you, or perhaps I'm prejudiced, but I don't think so!

...I pray for you that you won't be worked too hard
& that you will be worked in the <u>right</u> way...

Present: September

My father was worked hard, as were all the men who went
to Stoke Mandeville then; the routines were well docu-
mented. From the moment they arrived, they had to hand
over all medication that had been sent with them. They
were allowed no sleeping tablets and precious little pain
relief. The regime was a tough round of exercise and benign
neglect aimed at building endurance, strength and establish-
ing independent skills, so that every patient would be able
to look after himself and eventually find paid employment.
In the fourteen years since the unit had been set up to treat
profoundly damaged airmen from the war, the profile of
patients had changed very little. Few of the other patients
had experienced the illness that my father had. Almost all
were young, fit, unlucky men who had broken their backs
or had other spinal problems through accident and injury.
They were not there to learn to walk again but to be rehabilitated back into their communities and lead useful lives
once again.

My father found the routines and the care totally

different from the sensitive treatment that he'd been used to. Dr Ludwig Guttman ran his hospital on the same lines as the German hospitals that had trained him so effectively before the war. His staff, for the most part, consisted of white-coated male orderlies, often fellow German-Jewish refugees, who were under strict instructions not to molly-coddle patients. They obeyed to the letter. The focus was on achievement. A patient's duty is to cheer-up his visitors, Guttman was fond of saying.

Without reading the letters, I already knew more of Stoke Mandeville than I did of any hospital in which my father was a patient. He had once, uncharacteristically, opened up and talked to me in detail about some of the events that happened to him there. I wasn't sure why. Perhaps because to go there had been his choice, perhaps because, although I was only four months old at the time, Stoke Mandeville was also a part of my life—he had to leave me as well as my mother to go there—or perhaps it was because the place just made him so damned angry.

It would have been about 1976 when I was probably eighteen or nineteen, and I remember it was at the end of one of my parents' numerous tennis parties. We sat together as the shadows were growing long. Lying on the ground between us was a newspaper. He stared at it for a moment or two, then picked it up and read in silence.

'That's Guttman,' he said, passing the paper to me. A square-faced man wearing moustache and spectacles gazed out of the photograph under a piece about the Paralympics. 'I knew him once.' He tapped the page. 'At

Stoke Mandeville, where I was for a time. It was Guttmann's vision.

'It started as the Wheelchair Games, you know,' he began, always swift to see the opportunity to educate.

'He liked you to call him Poppa, but I never would.' He paused. 'I can honestly say, Sarie, that I have never been so angry in my entire life. They were brutal there. He insisted we were all the same,' he paused. 'But we weren't, of course. We weren't the same at all. They were all spinal injuries. I was the only polio patient and I don't think they really understood what it was like for me. I wasn't numb for a start.

'I had pulled muscles all over the place and my ribs, where I'd had my op, were agony when the edge of the chair jammed into my back. Each time I fell out I hit the footplates and tipped the chair forwards into my kidneys. In fact, I told him: Dr Guttmann, I said. I have spent three years learning how to take a leak by myself at a time of my own choosing and if I find that this inhumane treatment has done irreparable damage to my kidneys, I shall never forgive you. Do you know? He just looked at me with that half smile of his. Get up, he said and walked away.

'Get up and do it yourself, was all they'd say... If you fell on the floor, you had to get yourself up. Do it your-self, do it yourself, do it yourself.' He repeated Guttmann's mantra with barely suppressed fury. 'We could be bruised black and blue, and still they wouldn't help.

'I had a friend from the workshop... Jim, he was called. He was a very nice man, mild as milk, and para-lysed due to a bad parachuting accident. Unaccountably good-humoured... Anyway, he'd not been feeling so hot for a couple of days, I forget why. He fell forward and tipped his chair over and was finding it a real struggle to get it upright again. I called for one of the orderlies to come and help him. You do it, he told me. Me? I said. How? I haven't any balance. Nor does he, he said right back. That's why he's on the floor...

'It was all about wheelchair skills, you see? We didn't learn how not to have accidents. We learned that accidents were inevitable and they could be dealt with. But I still think there was no need to be so cruel.

'That first day I was there...' He shut his eyes and breathed deeply with the pain of remembering. 'It was pretty frightening. They shoved me down corridors without saying where we were going... Then all at once we were in this hut with a swimming pool and they just tipped me in. They made me swim... sort of swim, until I was completely done in.

'That sort of thing went on all the time.'

We sat in the pinking light of a setting sun and I started, very quietly and slowly, to collect the last of the glasses onto a tray. Then I sat back in my chair; I knew he wasn't ready to go back to the house yet.

'Do you remember that I was interested in archery at one time? We practised in a field quite a way from the clapboard huts where the wards were. They'd cut the barley and we had the butts out in the air... It was bliss. Blue sky, scudding white clouds way up high and swallows all over the place. Made me very homesick...

'Guttmann came and watched for a time, then he

said I might not have made it to the Olympic Games in a boat but he could see me getting to the Stoke Mandeville Games in a chair. For some reason he seemed to think this was funny.

'It was anything but funny, but it made me think, and I felt I had another goal of a sort. When it was time to pack up I was disappointed because I felt I needed another half hour to just get on top of a new technique I was trying out. I told them that I'd shoot the last of the arrows and then I'd follow on.

'They'd only been gone a minute or two when I dropped the bow, but something happened and I hit the deck. The chair went over as well. There was nothing to brace it against in the field, and there I was, stuck.

'Someone turned to come back for me, but... I could not believe it, Sarie. Guttman told him to leave me alone and I'm sure the bastard said, let him do it.'

'What did you do then?' I had to ask. 'I suppose they came for you eventually.'

'Did they, buggery? No. I had to drag myself, arm over arm across the field.' He tightened his lips. 'When I got back, it was getting dark, I'd missed supper and my arms and chest were raw and bleeding from the stubble. I'd had to abandon the chair and I was incandescent with rage and do you know what he said to me?'

'You did it yourself?'

'Have you got the arrows?' He laughed out loud. 'I had to hand it to him. Guttman got results. He would shrug and say, in that German accent of his, ven you are back home you vill have to vork. You vill haff independence.'

He sighed and began to reach for his chair. I held it steady, and he swung himself into the seat and we adjusted his cushions until he felt comfortable. 'The other men there were wonderfully good to me,' he added, as he tucked his cap and the paper down the side of the chair.

I had some Stoke Mandeville ghosts of my own to lay. My father's anger had made me partisan, but it also made me curious. I needed to see the places of his past for myself.

The day before, I'd driven south from Norfolk with my husband to look for the isolation hospital at Uxbridge. Nothing was left but the listed ornate Victorian mortuary chimney remains, rising incongruously like a finger pointed skywards within a smart estate of executive homes.

As we turned into the site of Stoke Mandeville Hospital, I discovered that the building at the end of that dramatic past had been replaced by a spanking new, state-of-the-art general hospital with a specialist spinal-injuries unit alongside. The wooden huts of Ward X were still there, lying to one side, desolate, abandoned and rotting. Unbelievably, I discovered they were in use until the early eighties when a flood caused some of the ceilings to collapse, and then in 1983 the National Spinal Injuries Centre was moved into a new purpose-built unit next door. We'd arrived just in time, the remaining buildings had planning permission to demolish and soon the site would be cleared.

We drove past the new hospital, down a concrete road, cracked and weedy like an abandoned airfield, and parked beside a sprawling collection of wooden huts connected by numerous covered corridors. It was a beautiful September English day; blue sky, crisp, white clouds high in the sky and a stiff breeze against our faces. Similar to the weather that had made my father feel homesick fifty years before.

We walked around the buildings, ignoring the Danger signs, peering in through flyblown windows, crunching broken glass beneath our feet, the waft of creosote still in the air. In one hut, the ward appeared almost intact, a few iron bedsteads still in place, an x-ray clip and lamp still hanging on the wall. I imagined my father here: lying in bed, too exhausted to need sleeping tablets, watching wheelchair 'puckball' being played in the courtyards between the huts—my father's legs were too painful for him to join in—mingling with others worse off than himself in the common rooms, immersing himself in the familiar oily surroundings of the engineering workshops or the photography dark-rooms and hearing the shouts and yells typical of young men making their own entertainment. The swimming pool was nowhere to be found, but I saw it clearly in my mind's eye; shapes moving slowly under ripples of reflected windows but with the grace that water always bestows, and white-coated orderlies insisting on more, always more.

I couldn't help but be horrified at the claustrophobically low ceilings, the paper-thin walls, the tiny staff rooms at the end of each ward. These buildings, like those at the Brentwood TB Annexe, were erected as part of a temporary wartime emergency and yet they were in use with little change for nearly forty more years. In these humble wooden huts Dr Ludwig Guttmann had a vision and started a lasting legacy in the way disability is treated in this country and the way people with disabilities think of themselves. During the First World War over eighty percent of spinal cord injured patients died within the first year. Guttmann turned that statistic on its head; in 1966 over eighty percent of spinal cord injured patients were out of hospital and employed within the first year. 'They come to me to learn to walk, but I teach them to love their wheelchairs,' he said, more than once. I doubted my father ever actually loved his chair, maybe he fought too long to be free of it, but he might have grudgingly admitted that his increased upper body strength and the new skills he learned at Stoke Mandeville liberated him from believing he needed to stand in order to have a useful future.

Before we left I wanted to see the new Spinal Injuries unit. Under the attractive triangular roofs in a peaceful atrium, I turned a full circle to look around me and smiled. This was a building truly made for wheelchair users. Of course it was, how could it be otherwise? Wide corridors with room for wheelchairs to pass each other with ease. The furniture was placed considerately and everywhere there was space to manoeuvre a chair without risk of bumping into anything. The reception desk was low. Too low for comfort for a walking person, but exactly right if you are chair-bound. We shared a pot of tea in the café. There were more people using chairs than I had ever seen together. I found I'd inherited wheelchair manners: instinctively, I allowed space for foot plates and back wheels, when being addressed I moved to the front before replying so that the person before me didn't have to contort their neck and I tucked my own dining chair and legs out of the way from getting clobbered by passing wheels. I hadn't had to do this since my father's death and all at once, I longed to see him bowling down the corridor, letting the sliding doors take the strain, visiting the gents without having to struggle. This new Stoke Mandeville was an inspiring building and would not be here without the insight and drive of its first director. I couldn't resent Dr Ludwig Guttmann anymore, for he gave me a gift: a father who was finally able to leave behind a hope he could never realise, with faith that he had a future using a wheelchair.

Outside in the paved courtyard area, we encountered a man smoking a cigarette in the sunshine; David had been here six weeks this time (it was his second visit to the Centre) with another two still to go. We talked about the huts, Dr Guttmann, the Paralympics, archery and a little of my father's history. David finished his cigarette, stubbed it out on the edge of one of the planters and pushed the butt deep into the soil. He then swung his elbow under the handle at the back of his chair and looked at me carefully.

'You should make a visit to the Guttmann Sports and Leisure Centre before you go. There are loads of photographs on the walls,' he said. 'You can walk it from here easily.' He pointed the way along a metalled path before placing his hands, thumbs upwards, on the rim of his wheels, swinging his chair around in a tight arc—a manoeuvre that was as familiar to me as the face of my own father—and rolling back into the building.

We walked down Guttmann Way. The Centre had

been built on the old archery field. Inside photographs lined the corridors, some very old, but none that I could see included my father. There was no record of him on the trophy boards either, but I didn't expect there to be, he was there in the years before records were kept. I have pictures of him shooting arrows at Stoke Mandeville. Jim, his fellow inmate and an RAF casualty, sent my father a letter from Headley Court, where he was 'getting his walking sorted out', and included photographs of them both with their bows in the old Stoke Mandeville gymnasium. Together they devised a method to capture an image at the point when an arrow leaves the bow. It seemed that my mother was right all along and, despite his fears, my father did indeed find people with interests in common and made friends while he was there.

Chapter Twenty-One

Home: March, 2002

'I wonder if you could look something up on your Google for me.' My father's lost none of his curiosity in older age and this is becoming a regular request.

Conveniently, I'd picked up his call in our chilly dining room in front of the only computer in the house with an internet connection.

'What is it you'd like to know?'

'I want you to research something called PPS.'

'OK,' I say, slowly, typing the letters into the subject bar as I speak. 'PPS. What's it mean?'

'PPS.' My father repeats the acronym, playing for time. I hear him sigh. 'It's something I've been reading about in the Spinal Injuries News. It stands for Post Polio Syndrome, only there isn't much because the Spinal Injuries Association is all about trauma and very little about disease.'

'Right.' It's been years since we talked about polio. We just never mention it. Ever. It's hard to know how to react to this and I can tell by the sound of his voice that the request hasn't been easy for him either. I decide to address another subject that's been on my mind.

'How're the shingles?'

'Painful.'

'I'm sorry to hear that.' The blisters appeared over his coccyx, which is particularly cruel for a man who can only sit or lie down. 'I guess you can't take too many painkillers.'

'No.' He sighs again. 'All analgesics seem to bung me up.' He pauses. 'That's not the only problem now. In fact, that's why I want to find out more about PPS.'

'All right. I've got a screen full of stuff now, mostly from the US, but there's a site from the UK that heads it up. Lincolnshire Post Polio Network. Hang on a minute, I'll have a look.' I click the link and we both fall silent while I scan the site. 'Looks interesting. There's a helpline on voice mail, a library, a networking facility. Oh, and here's a whole section with the title, What is PPS?'

'You might want to read that later.'

I click again and page after page of close text fills my screen. A couple of paragraphs spring out at me.

...symptoms often include NEW weakness, pain, breathing and/or swallowing difficulties, a variety of sleep disorders, muscle twitching (known as "fasiculations"), gastrointestinal problems, muscle fatigue and/or "central" fatigue. And these symptoms can occur in previously-affected muscles and/or in what were previously thought to be muscles that were not affected at onset.

Complications often include neuropathies, nerve entrapments, arthritis, scoliosis, osteoporosis and, sometimes, additional atrophy—known as Post-Polio Muscular Atrophy (PPMA).

I try to keep my voice level and calm as I read some

of the points out to him. 'Are you saying this is what's happening to you?'

'I think it may be. It's hard to tell. It might be that I'm just getting older.'

I move the handset to the other ear. My father was born in 1926. In August he'll turn seventy-six. It might be reasonable to consider that muscle weakness, fatigue and joint pains are to do with the ageing process and nothing to do with this PPS, a condition that I've never heard of and, as is clear from the website, may have its sceptics. Seventy-six! My father never thought he'd live so long. He saw a graph somewhere giving the life expectancy for paraplegics with certain conditions, did the maths and decided his time was up at sixty-five. My mother decided differently, and here they are, more than ten years on and making preparations to celebrate their golden wedding anniversary in September.

'What's more serious,' he continues, and I concentrate on listening carefully. '...is something that's happened recently to do with the shingles, and I suspect is being aggravated by PPS. But I'd like to know more and the GP can't help me.'

'Why don't you tell me what it is that you want to find out? I'll do the research and come back to you.'

'Sounds like a plan,' he says brightly, but then falls silent again.

I wait and I can hear him fidgeting about. I picture him sitting at his desk in the workshop, leaning on an elbow to support himself, and switching the phone from one ear to the other when his arm begins to ache. I've not

317

been into the workshop much in recent years, but when I do, his office looks exactly the same as it did when I was a child. The piles of magazines have grown a little higher, the spiders' webs are a little thicker, the green linoleum is dryer and more cracked than before and the tunes from the radio have been replaced by voices from BBC Radio 4, but essentially it evokes the same twin emotions of thrill and dread. I imagine him sitting by himself in his private world, looking out of the dirty window at the bare rose bushes, the copper beech branches swinging in a cold March wind and the gently swaying backs of the Friesian cattle walking in the field beyond the ha-ha.

'Daddie? What is it you want me to find out exactly?' I ask in a softer tone, but still trying to keep my voice business-like. I feel we're less father and daughter today, perhaps more professor and assistant.

'It's this shingles,' he says, eventually. 'It's affecting my plumbing. The thing is,' he says in a rush, 'It's got so I can't take a leak. I haven't been able to have a pee on my own for the last two weeks. There's a very nice nurse who has to come in four times a day to catheterise me. But I can't travel anywhere, I can't really do anything.' He pauses. 'It's no joke.'

'No joke at all.' It's a pathetic response, but I can't find the words to say anything more useful.

'It was always a bit of an act of faith anyway. There shouldn't really be any muscles that work around there, but somehow, I've always been able to sort of think myself into it. It's been my saving grace. There are plenty of others who aren't so fortunate.'

I think about this for a moment and reflect that most of us take all our bodily functions for granted and never give them a moment's consideration. Now, because of the worry that he'll precipitate another unpleasant condition, he can't take painkillers for one of the most distressing of common viral infections. Finally, he has to contend with this further indignity. I close my eyes and wonder what else he'll meet on the journey through old age. I open my eyes again and take a deep breath. I'm glad he can't see me, he hates excessive sympathy. 'And you think it's too much of a coincidence that this... this act of faith, has failed you now.'

'That's about the size of it. The GP's never heard of anyone getting this side-effect from shingles and I'm perfectly certain, positive, in fact, that it is PPS.'

'I'll get back to you as soon as I can.'

'Thank you, Sarie. I know you're busy and I'm very grateful.' He sounds almost humble, and this unfamiliar tone disturbs me.

'No. Thank you, Daddie, for asking me. I'm glad to help.' I wait on the line until he says goodbye and for the click that tells me he's put the receiver down.

I scroll through pages of information on the Lincolnshire Post Polio site, no longer noticing the icy chill in the room until I go to reach for the keyboard and find my hands can barely type. I send an e-mail to the LPP contact and within minutes I receive a reply. Dr. Richard Bruno in America is the world expert on PPS, and he might be able to answer my questions.

I call my father the next afternoon. 'I've had an

e-mail conversation with Dr Bruno in the US. He's just about the top man on PPS.' My father is silent. I think he's surprised, and perhaps a little impressed. 'He's very interested, but hasn't really got an answer.'

I hear him breath out with a little groan. It's what he expected.

'However, it might be significant that shingles is a reactivated chicken-pox virus and there's a school of thought that thinks PPS might be a reactivated polio virus.'

'Is there a connection?'

'Who knows? Dr Bruno thinks not, but he's right at the cutting edge of this research and it could lead anywhere. He thinks there may be more of a link with ME. You know, chronic fatigue syndrome?'

'Yes, I know what you mean,' he says at last. He falls silent yet again and I can hear him clicking the top of a ball-point pen.

'The other contact I've heard from thinks it may be to do with the limited nerve run that you managed to rebuild way back at the beginning of your rehabilitation. It may all be a bit fragile and too near the area affected by the shingles.'

'I see.'

'But Bruno thinks there is every chance you might get the use of the muscles back spontaneously,' I add.

'I hope he's right.' He pauses again. 'It's a real bind, this, Sarie.'

'It must be, Daddie. I can't imagine how you're coping.'

'People are very good. Now I can't get out, they visit

me instead.'

I know this. My mother has told me how she's been keeping an unofficial appointment book, just like in the old hospital days but, despite her efforts, he still gets very tired. 'We'll come down at the weekend.'

'That would be lovely. But, Sarie?'

'Yes, Dad?'

'Just you, hey.'

Present: September

Only a few years later, Post Polio Syndrome featured on the NHS website, and more was becoming known, but it still comprised a collection of symptoms for which it was difficult to make a definitive diagnosis. It was thought that around 120,000 people who had polio when they were younger were living in the UK, and there was a suggestion that perhaps 15%—or as many as 80%—may go on to develop PPS. Nobody really knew. But the theory that it may be a dormant virus that had been reactivated, had been disproven.

What was becoming clear was that the effort polio survivors like my father had put into their rehabilitation and learning to walk again may have been the very thing that aggravated the potential to develop PPS. Nerve pathways were destroyed during the initial onset of disease but exercise and perseverance could encourage the growth of new pathways for the communication between brain and limb, occasionally even good enough to regain mobility.

Over-use of these secondary pathways may have caused the nerve terminals to eventually malfunction and, progressively, permanent weakness and eventual atrophy occur.

My father's shingles and his struggle to relieve himself may have been unconnected; he recovered from his painful condition and bladder function spontaneously returned.

In the September of 2002, my parents celebrated their golden wedding anniversary. We had a quiet and joyous get-together with all the family present, but it was obvious to everyone who knew him that from that point onwards my father became steadily weaker, more fatigued and increasingly depressed about his future. In a few months, it got to the point that he was unable to heave himself from his chair to his car and, once again, he became unable to travel away from home. Being shut in the house was not how any of us wanted to see his last years playing out.

However, I was excited to hear that this restriction of his liberty and control had re-ignited his old drive and determination. The following spring, he bought a purpose-built vehicle in which he could travel, sitting in his own chair with no need to get out of it first. He called it his Pope-mobile and in the week before its delivery, he was the happiest he had been for months.

On the morning of its impending arrival, I received a telephone call.

Suffolk: 28 May, 2003

I drive surprisingly calmly, given the circumstances. The journey from my house to my old family home takes just over half an hour. The roads are mostly narrow with poor visibility; I drive quickly but it makes no sense to hurry unduly and there is little traffic.

The house looks particularly striking when I arrive on this late May morning, sitting in its shingle drive and tidy lawns, wooden half-tun barrels flanking the front door filled with blue and yellow pansies, white paint bright against a pale sky of high cloud. The curtains are open, the windows clean and shining in the morning light.

Jen, a nurse and the daughter of my father's late business partner and great friend, Geoff Horsfall, is already here. Her car is parked in the backyard.

The old door-pull has too much slack in the wire, and requires a powerful heave before I can hear the brass bell pealing deep within the house.

I wait and nobody comes. I ring harder and longer. For the first time since the telephone call, I feel a crawl of panic begin, like something clammy and unmanageable.

Nobody's going to answer. I run round to the front of the house, leap up the porch steps and stand with my finger on the doorbell and keep it there. It rings loudly, uninterrupted.

Still nobody comes. I run further, to the south side of the house, and stare up at my parents' bedroom window. I shout, then bend down, scoop a handful of gravel and hurl it upwards. I've seen this done in films.

My father is dying and no one will let me into the house.

They've got me here, but locked me out.

I stand on the edge of the lawn under my parents' window and press buttons on my mobile.

My mother answers; there's a telephone in the bedroom. She says something but I'm not listening. 'It's me,' I howl, staring at the window. 'I'm outside. You've locked all the doors.' Above me, Jen's face appears for an instant, my mother must have said something, then vanishes.

I race back to the front door and hear the key in the lock and the bolts being drawn. 'I think he's just gone.'

In my parents' bedroom it is light and very still. My mother has pushed her bed apart from Daddie's and is sitting on the edge, feet invisible between the two, reaching out and holding his hand.

My mother, dry-eyed, looks at me and gives a faint smile of welcome, I go to sit beside her and grip her free hand. 'I think that was his last breath,' she says.

Finally, I look at Daddie. He's lying on his back, head back on a pile of pillows, quilt laid loosely over his chest. He's wearing an old, soft cotton nightshirt, washed so often that there's nothing left in the colour. With his eyes closed and his face still pink, only his mouth gives away that he's no longer asleep. Slack and unmoving, it has fallen open, a thin line of saliva glistening in one corner.

'Take his hand,' my mother says, making room for me on her bed and passing his left hand into mine. It's warm and relaxed. I feel the calloused fingers, the skin on his palm thickened from so many years propelling his wheels around. I push my fingers into his, holding tight, just as I did whenever I wanted him to comfort me. My hands are wide and strong, just like his, but his engulf mine. I breathe deeply, forcing the tears back.

'Good-bye, Daddie.'

Jen kneels down and grips his right hand, our eyes meeting over his chest. She's known my father since she was a child. She's crying, too. Only my mother sits dry-eyed still, her hand linked into my arm, our legs pressed close.

'He knows you're here,' she says.

We sit, talking quietly together. The day is bright, we hear traffic go down the hill into the valley, the rooks complaining to each other as they crouch on their untidy platforms, the occasional lowing of cattle in the fields beyond the lawns, but none of it intrudes into the room where we sit still. Looking at Daddie. Until there's a scratch at the door and a mournful meow.

'It's Pip,' says my mother. 'How did he get in?'

Jen opens the door. My father's silver tabby curls past her legs, walks over to his bed and jumps, so lightly he could have been floating. We watch, transfixed, as the cat stops and stares at my father, then he walks the full length of the bed, puts his face half-an-inch away from Daddie's nose and finally rests his huge body across my father's chest, lays his head down and begins to purr.

My mother reaches out to stroke the cat, then touches Daddie's face, her blue eyes abnormally bright. The cat lifts his head, opens his yellow eyes to look at her and stretches his paws out as if to embrace the man beneath him.

'I think we could leave them together.'

He'll be safe here with the last of his silver tabby cats, each one loved and indulged. We get up to leave the room, but my mother pauses for a moment to lay the backs of her fingers against his cheek again.

'Push, my darling Push. God gave you a rotten life, but he's given you a wonderful death.'

I look at her through a haze. 'He didn't have a rotten life.' I say, gently. I need to make this clear because I do truly believe it. And it really is all that matters. 'He had us.'

She pauses, still looking at her Push. 'No, you're right. It wasn't rotten. But it was very, very hard.

Epilogue

Norfolk: October, 2003

The start of every run was always the same: a brisk walk to the farm, left at the horse pond where, however quiet I was, water hens scuttled across the surface. In a few minutes I was up and out of the valley to the highest point at the start of the hogsback ridge.

In the earliest weeks, I began to puff and gasp almost within the first minute. My legs felt leaden, my feet slapped the ground and my hands would fill with blood and throb until I learned to hold them high, relax my shoulders.

From the top of the ridge, the landscape rolls away to the south into undulated folds of glacial moraine like a giant bed with the eiderdown askew. At a wide opening into the field at the top, I'd stop and do some stretches and then, after gazing around me for a time, I would surprise myself, tip forward beyond the point of balance and start to run, eyes almost immediately beginning to water from the light or the chill on my face.

The track passed through a medley of fields, and as I ran, a Mexican wave of bird life—crows, pigeons, starlings, partridges—rose from feasting on fallen grain, turned on the wing to check that I posed no threat, only to sink back into obscurity amongst the standing stalks and weeds.

That day there was winter in the air and I had to force myself to run with more determination than usual. The sky was buzzard-grey with clouds barely higher than the surrounding hills. As I skirted the corner of the house, a spattering of rain made my face smart and I had to bend my head and set my shoulders against the wind, but I was determined to run my first full mile.

At the field opening, I stretched and clapped my hands together, took off my sweatshirt, gasping as the wind clutched at my bare arms, tied it around my waist and leaned into the wind.

There are two large, granite gate posts either side of the lane conveniently set at the half-mile point where the track takes a slight downwards shift. When I reached these ancient markers, I dropped my shoulders, allowing the effect of lifting my consciousness from my chest and out into my surroundings. The weather ensured there were no birds to be seen, no hares zigzagging across the barley stalks or brown rats dashing across my path, and no sound other than the rush of the wind and the rain. As always, I ran alone but, on that chill, grey morning, I felt another runner swing in beside me. I concentrated on placing my feet to avoid the worst of the puddles and as I did so, I lengthened my stride to bring it more in keeping with the ease of the runner tucked into my left-hand side. I never glanced round but somehow I knew who it was, and I smiled until my gums hurt in the wind.

It was my father, but never as I'd known him. I'd never seen my father stand upright, never seen him walk, but here he was, running beside me, matching his long stride to mine and shielding me from the wind. My muscles warmed with the effort, became languid, my breathing deepened and I felt exuberant; I heard the beat of two sets of feet hit the ground and, at the point where I might have struggled, I increased my pace again. Through slitted eyes, I watched for the bend in the lane and the welcome lee of a cowshed. I didn't dare to turn my head in case he disappeared, but in my mind's eye I saw my father clearly. Tall, upright, young, with fair hair sweeping back from a face that was browned from months spent training on the river, bare-legged and running in thin white pumps. I sensed his eyes on me, felt him urge me to sprint the last hundred yards, to pass the marker at my top speed, to not consider for a moment that I might begin to slow now that the end was in sight. I lifted my face into the rain, decided the path I would take and ran as if my life depended on it. As I sped around the road sign, I felt his legs pound past me, lighten and vanish just as the sky brightened and the rain reduced to a drizzle.

Author's Note

If we lay aside the family name, property or valuables, what is it we have to pass to the next generation? All my life, I lived within a family who thought about legacy to the point of obsession. The choice was not to make a choice; it was enough to ensure the continued protection of our past, be that physical or cultural, but the story-line—the very thing that defines the next generation—was broken.

I learned that when I was born, my father had to give up his dream of getting back to the beginning again. However, with informed hindsight, I don't believe he was giving up his dream of walking once and for all when he made me a present for my eighth birthday, a present to walk as tall as he had been, balanced on my glorious yell of red.

I believed he'd made a different choice. He chose to draw a line under a time of sorrow and make something beautiful, playful, deeply personal and ultimately highly symbolic. From his past, and my future, he made me a legacy that I still treasure.

After my first daughter was born, what I looked forward to with all my heart was dusting off the cobwebs and passing on to another eight year old a hidden history of loss and joy co-existing within a transformative pair of red stilts.

At the start I wrote to connect with other families like mine that had disability at the centre. I wanted to give people like me a parallel with which to identify emotions, losses and possibly a bridge to explain the strangeness that a childhood within our sort of households can bring. I hope some of you have felt this helpful. However, the world has changed in the fifteen years it's taken me to get this book to publication. The rise of social media and invisible information, fake and real, is having an influence far beyond anything anyone could have imagined, so today I have an additional objective. One group in particular has concerned me almost more than any other and, fuelled by non-evidential, unsubstantiated, misleading and incorrect information, a meteoric rise in the fear of vaccination has meant that people are choosing not to immunise their children. I've said it before and I'll repeat it now. *We are just one sugar lump away from the horrors of polio as described in this book.* Vaccination is safe and effective, but we all have to take part for it to work properly. Do we want to expose our children to the risk of death or living a life of disability and pain as my father did? Because what is contained in this book is the reality of a non-immunised generation.

I would like to thank Prof George Lomonossoff and the JIC research laboratories for continuing to work on immunisation research to develop improved TB vaccines and a new generation of even better products than the Salk and Sabine vaccines that have kept us all safe for the last fifty years and have almost, but not yet, eradicated polio from the globe. We are all indebted to their skills and perseverance.

Links:
World Health Organisation - www.who.int
British Polio Fellowship - www.britishpolio.org.uk
Polio Survivors Network - www.poliosurvivorsnetwork.org.uk
Post Polio Health International - www.post-polio.org
Polio Survivors Association - polioassociation.org
TB Alert - www.tbalert.org

Afterword

Though the introduction of the Salk inactivated polio vaccine (IPV) and the Sabin oral polio vaccine (OPV) in the 1950s and 60s has effectively eliminated the scourge of poliomyelitis in most parts of the world, the virus has not been eradicated. This is because, although they greatly reduce the incidence of the disease, existing vaccines rely on the propagation of the infectious virus and, in the case of OPV, the spread of attenuated virus in the population. Thus, continued control of polio relies on continuing effective vaccination programmes.

This is not always possible in conflict or disaster zones.

To finally eradicate polio, WHO have initiated programmes to develop next-generation vaccines that will not require the propagation or deployment of infectious virus. These will be based on synthetic poliovirus particles that do not contain the viral genome and hence are completely non-infectious. These can be produced by synthesising just the protein that forms the outer shell of the virus and allowing it to assemble, an approach successfully used for the production of vaccines against human papillomavirus (HPV). However, with poliovirus there is an additional complication: protein shells are not very stable in the absence of the genome. It has therefore been necessary to find means of stabilising the synthetic particles. This has now been achieved and the synthetic stabilised particles resemble infectious virus sufficiently closely that they can stimulate protective immunity in experimental animals.

The next challenge is to find a system to produce the synthetic particles in sufficient quantity and a low enough cost for them to be deployed worldwide. A number of systems are currently being investigated including yeast, insect cells (both of which are used to produce HPV vaccines), mammalian cells and plants. Once the majority of the world's population is vaccinated with these next-generation vaccines, the virus should cease to circulate, as was the case with smallpox which was eradicated in the 1970s.

This is one of the areas of my research and I hope my efforts and those of my colleagues will finally see the end of this terrible disease.

Professor George Lomonossoff
John Innes Centre, Norwich.

Acknowledgements

To the memories of Tim Mason
and Sister Anne Johnson

Help and guidance has been sought and freely given from so many friends, colleagues and professionals during the course of the writing of *Push* that I wish to acknowledge and thank every one of you. Particular thanks should go to my editors and mentors, Sam Ruddock, Julia Webb, Anna De Vaul and Dr Anna Reckin as well as my beta-readers, husband Dennis and his brother Barry, Chris Yeomans and Tim Mason.

Thank you also to: Prof Anne Osbourn FRS, Sister Anne Johnson, the Lincolnshire Post Polio Network now known as the Polio Survivors Network, Sarah Cushion, Eva van Eeghen, Mary Rose Lillingston, Sally Anne Lomas, Mary Mustoe, Laure Powell, Pat Boyd, Wendy Shaw and the Burning Bush Barn Breakfasteers, as well as all the members of Julia's Friday Class. And almost certainly others that I've shamefully forgotten to mention.

Push was written and published with the assistance of Arts Council England. The workshop excerpt from *Push* appeared first in the American online journal, *Six Hens*, under the title 'Signet Rings'

Finally I must acknowledge my family for supporting this project and for nurturing me in so many ways. Dennis for your endless encouragement and skilled copy editing; you have never complained. Lizzie and Maria, thank you both for always being there for me with advice and tissues. Thank you also to my aunt, Dorothy Pulman for giving me family photograph albums and remembering all the names. However, the greatest thanks of all must go to my brother Will and especially my mother Diana Pulman. Thank you both for hours of your time, for painful memory-mining of your own and for allowing me to use what are your stories too. I know it's been hard, but I am profoundly grateful.